David Miller

Arbroath and it's Abbey

David Miller

Arbroath and it's Abbey

ISBN/EAN: 9783744725538

Printed in Europe, USA, Canada, Australia, Japan

Cover: Foto ©ninafisch / pixelio.de

More available books at **www.hansebooks.com**

ARBROATH AND ITS ABBEY

OR

THE EARLY HISTORY OF THE TOWN AND ABBEY

OF

ABERBROTHOCK

INCLUDING

NOTICES OF ECCLESIASTICAL AND OTHER ANTIQUITIES

IN THE SURROUNDING DISTRICT

BY

DAVID MILLER

EDINBURGH
THOMAS G. STEVENSON, 22 FREDERICK STREET
LONDON : HAMILTON, ADAMS & Co
GLASGOW : MURRAY & SON

MDCCCLX

PREFACE.

THE following pages have been published chiefly for those who take an interest in the locality of the ancient and now flourishing town of Arbroath, and also with the view of removing the obscurity which has hitherto involved the history of its once magnificent monastery. Among other sources of information the Chartulary of the Abbey is entitled to stand first in rank. The most interesting portions of these monastic writings have been digested and arranged in this volume. An endeavour has thus been made to bring out the points in which they, along with other authentic documents, tend to illustrate the history of the district.

In alluding to the history of past times, our ancestors have been allowed as far as possible to appear in their own dress, and speak in their own words. This will account for the number of quotations in the antique style, which may probably render the perusal of some portions of the book a little difficult to readers otherwise well educated. But if months or years are spent in the endeavour to acquire a knowledge of dead languages two or three thousand years old, some trouble ought to be taken with the view of being able to read with facility our own living mother tongue, in the garb which it wore two or three centuries ago, so that it may not be unintelligible unless expressed according to our present conventional orthography. Many details, which to general readers not acquainted with the locality may appear sufficiently minute, are inserted in the text, instead of being placed in foot-notes, as it was considered desirable to avoid that distraction of attention which numerous notes invariably occasion. For the same reason references to the pages of the Arbroath Chartulary have not been made, as these, if introduced, would have become innumerable and cumbersome. They would, at the same time, have been of no use to those who do not possess that collection of writings; and those, on the other hand, who may wish to verify any statement founded on it, will be at once able to do so, by the names and dates referred to, with the help of the tables of contents and indices of the published Chartulary.

It was omitted to be stated in the tenth chapter that the lands of Aldbar have been ranked among the possessions of the Abbey on the authority of an entry in the "Charge of the Temporalitie," 1592, which is not altogether conclusive in the absence of corroborative evidence; and that although Cotside and others near Barry have been generally ranked among the Abbey lands, the authority for placing these lands in the catalogue is not very satisfactory, as they do not appear in the proper monastic writings under their modern names.

While these sheets were in course of preparation the Author made every effort to procure definite information on the subject of the alleged pillage and conflagration of the Abbey Church about the time of the Reformation. He has not, however, succeeded in being able to fix the exact manner in which that building was unroofed and laid desolate. But a careful study of every contemporary record within his reach has tended to confirm him as to the correctness of the statements made in the text, that whatever might have been threatened or attempted, no general pillage or burning of this majestic edifice had taken place at the period in question; and that its state of ruin can be easily accounted for on other grounds, by a simple reference to the churches of the Abbeys of St Andrews, Lindores, Coupar-Angus, and others, where the demolition is much more complete than at the Church of Arbroath, and where the agency of fire has never been stated to have been applied.

It need scarcely be explained that the notices of the town of Arbroath have been in general limited to the period when the monastic establishment existed in its neighbourhood. The history of Arbroath during the last hundred and fifty years, including the extension of its population, buildings, manufactures, and commerce, within that period, could not have been added without swelling the volume far beyond the limits originally contemplated; and is a subject which, along with the traditionary history of the burgh and its vicinity, yet remains to be taken up by one who can devote to it the necessary amount of time and research.

The Author does not flatter himself that what is now given to the public can escape what every book of the kind is peculiarly liable to, namely, the detection of errors and omissions. He has endeavoured, however, to make no definite statement, unless upon good authority: without being deterred from offering this contribution to the history of the district by that over-scrupulous dread of mistake which has prevented many persons well read in the affairs of Scotland from giving to the world the benefit of their researches. There could not be found a more striking instance of this than in the case of the late Reverend Principal Lee, who has allowed much of his vast stores of information to die with him; and who, under the influence of this sensitiveness, most kindly dissuaded the author several years ago from engaging in an undertaking of a nature somewhat antiquarian, by referring to another friend who had devoted much time and labour to the early history of a northern county, which, when published, "after all contained some mistakes, and there were several things omitted."

In the preface of a book devoted to the detail of facts regarding Arbroath, an allusion to a work of fiction supposed to bear reference to the same place may be allowed. An attentive reader of Scott's inimitable novel, "The Antiquary," acquainted with the vicinity of Arbroath, will have little doubt that it contains the scenery of that story. The allusions to the battery, the common, the Grecian porch of the new Council-house, the great interest taken in merchandise and linen manufactures, and the doings of the postmistress, are, among other marks, quite sufficient to identify the town of Arbroath forty or fifty years ago with the *Fairport* of the novel. Auchmithie and Ethie-haven are described with Scott's usual power in his pictures of the fishing hamlets, and contain fisherwomen who might sit any day as the originals of Maggie Mucklebackit. Ethie House is the only mansion in the neighbourhood that suits the description of Knockwinnock. But the claims of identity with Monkbarns are divided betwixt Seaton and Anniston, while the description does not exactly suit either. The high rocky coast between Arbroath

Ness and Redhead will supply Halketheads and Ballyburgh Ness Points in abundance. A poet's license is taken in placing "the root o' an aik tree" among the cliffs, and in making the sun set over the waves of the German Ocean during the storm ; and also in removing the ruins of St Ruth (described as Arbroath and Melrose Abbeys intermixed) from the bustling vicinity of a large town into one of the dells of the district, such as the den of Arbirlot. These liberties were obviously used for greater effect, and probably to involve the narrative in some degree of disguise. The veil becomes, however, very transparent when the writer makes Edie Ochiltree meditate on his appearance in the eyes of the villagers while he was "coming down the edge of Kinblythemont"—a phrase which will suggest to every inhabitant of the neighbourhood the bluegown's return toward Arbroath, along the old Brechin road leading by Chapelton and the policies of Kinblethmont.

The Author takes this opportunity of returning his thanks to those gentlemen whose subscriptions have led to the present publication ; and also to those who have facilitated his researches by affording information or access to original documents.

The frontispiece, engraved by Mr J. Adam, Edinburgh, a native of Arbroath, is from a drawing which the author made in order to shew the front of the Abbey Church as it now exists, and would appear to passengers were the view not obstructed by modern buildings which have been erected within a yard or two of its walls.

ARBROATH, 1st *November* 1859.

CONTENTS.

GENERAL INTRODUCTION.

Page.

The Monastic Writings of Arbroath : Historical subjects on which they supply information: Introduction of surnames: Topographical names, and variations, changes and translations of same: Anglo-Norman and other settlers in Angus : Royal residences from 1178 to 1249 : Introduction of Shires and Sheriffs : Formation of Parishes : Adoption of Tutelar Saints : Nature of Abthaneries : The Culdees and their Abbes : Culdees of Abernethy and Brechin : Causes of the fall of their order : Indications of Culdees at Monifieth and Arbirlot.   1-38

CHAPTER I.

THE TOWN OF ARBROATH AND ITS DEPENDENCIES.—1. Origin and Condition till the foundation of the Abbey. 2. The Harbour. 3. Formation of Older portion of the Burgh. 4. Formation of Newer portion of the Burgh in the Almory. 5. Local Terms in the Town and neighbourhood.   39-66

CHAPTER II.

CONSTITUTION AND RANK OF THE BURGH.—Arbroath at first a Burgh of Barony and Regality : Made a Free Burgh by special grants: Temporarily represented in Parliament A.D. 1579 : Made a proper Royal Burgh in 1599.   67-72

CHAPTER III.

SOCIAL STATE OF ANGUS IN THE TWELFTH CENTURY.—Condition of Rural and Urban Population at the time of the foundation of Arbroath Abbey : Slavery of the Rural Population : Power of the Barons : Burghs as Fountains of Liberty and Progress : Emblems of Burghal Freedom in Arbroath and other Burghs : Early state of Urban Inhabitants.   73-84

CHAPTER IV.

ARBROATH FROM 1440 TO 1640.—Depression of Scotland in the Fifteenth Century : Civil broils : Chamberlain Aires : Subjects of Investigation : Condition of Craftsmen : Arbroath at the Reformation, and after its Erection into a Royal Burgh.   85-95

CONTENTS.

CHAPTER V.

ERECTION AND STYLE OF THE ABBEY BUILDINGS.—Date of commencement: Mixture of Norman and Early English Architecture: Stages in the progress of building: Succeeding styles of Architecture shewn in the buildings.   96–101

CHAPTER VI.

HISTORY OF THE ABBEY BUILDINGS.—Accidents to Great Church during the Romish Period: Contract for roofing the Choir: Damage done at the Reformation: Greater destruction since that Period: Other Conventual Buildings, Ecclesiastical, and Civil: Precinct walls and towers: Ruin of the Buildings.   102–116

CHAPTER VII.

SUBSIDIARY ALTARS IN ABBEY CHURCH.—1. Altar of St Catherine. 2. Altar of St Peter. 3. Altar of St Lawrence. 4. Altar of St Nicholas. 5. Altar of St Mary the Virgin. 6. Altar of St James. Appearance of Church on Festivals.   117–121

CHAPTER VIII.

DISTRICT CHAPELS IN ARBROATH AND NEIGHBOURHOOD.—1. Chapel of St Vigian at Conon. 2. Chapel of St John Baptist at Hospitalfield. 3. Chapel of St Michael in the Almory. 4. Chapel of St Ninian at Seaton Den. 5. Lady Chapel of Arbroath, with the Altars of St Nicholas and St Dupthacus. 6. Chapel of St Lawrence at Kinblethmont. 7. Chapel at Whitefield of Boysack. 8. Chapel at Boath, Panbride Parish. 9. Chapel at Panmure Castle. 10. Chapel at Kelly Castle. 11. Chapel of St Lawrence at Backboath. 12. Chapel of St Mary at Carmylie.   122–143

CHAPTER IX.

CHURCH OF ST. VIGEANS.—1. Fabric of Church and Old Monuments. 2. Altars of St Vigian and St Sebastian. 3. Priests and Ministers of St Vigeans since A.D. 1200.   144–155

CHAPTER X.

POSSESSIONS OF THE ABBEY.—1. Lands, Baronies, Villages, &c.—In Angus, Mearns, Perthshire, Fifeshire, Lanarkshire, Aberdeenshire, Banffshire, Inverness-shire. 2. Tenements in Burghs. 3. Fishings. 4. Ferryboats. 5. Woods and Forests. 6. Saltworks. 7. Churches, Tithes, &c. 8. Original Annual Rents. 9. Burghs. 10. Rents at Dissolution of the Abbey.   156–170

CHAPTER XI.

SUBORDINATE OFFICERS OF THE ABBEY.—1. Sub-Prior. 2. Steward. 3. Chamberlain. 4. Terrarius or Land-Steward. 5. Sacristan. 6. Granitor. 7. Cellarer. 8. Master of Works. 9. Judge or Deemster. 10. Justiciar or Bailie. 11. Mair and Coroner. 171-181

CHAPTER XII.

THE ABBOTS OF ARBROATH.—1. Influence and incidental Advantages of Monasteries in early times. 2. Scottish Ecclesiastics at and previous to the foundation of the Abbey. 3. Biographical Sketch of the Abbots of Arbroath, from 1178 to 1606. 4. Causes of the Dissolution of the Abbey. 182-234

CHAPTER XIII.

DESCRIPTION OF THE CONVENTUAL BUILDINGS.—Form of the Church, Towers, Divisions, Columns, Roofs, Doors, Windows: Dimensions of Buildings: External and Internal Appearance of Church: Remaining Statues: Conventual Seals: Bell Rock. 235-244

APPENDIX.

No. I.—NOTE on the Decay of Feudal Power and Emancipation of the Rural Inhabitants of Scotland. 245-252

No. II.—SKETCH of the Life and Times of JAMES MELVILLE, Minister St Vigeans, during the period from 1560 to 1600, being a supplement to the Sketch of the Abbots of Arbroath. 253-273

No. III.—SELECTIONS from the Records of the Magistrates and Council of Arbroath, illustrative of the Manners and Customs of the Inhabitants about the time of the Reformation. 274-294

ERRATA.

Page 15, lines 12 13, after Invercoyth delete "(?)," and insert *(Inverquiech Castle, in parish of Alyth).*

" 27, line 11, for *Abbaciae* read *Abbacie.*

" 58, " 30, for *position* read *portion.*

" 121, ". 5, for *Frances* read *Francis.*

" 266, " 15, for *St Andrew* read *St Andrews.*

" 269, " 8, for *article* read *paragraph.*

ARBROATH AND ITS ABBEY.

GENERAL INTRODUCTION.

THE MONASTIC WRITINGS OF ARBROATH: HISTORICAL SUBJECTS ON WHICH THEY SUPPLY INFORMATION: INTRODUCTION OF SURNAMES: TOPOGRAPHICAL NAMES, AND VARIATIONS, CHANGES AND TRANSLATIONS OF SAME: ANGLO-NORMAN AND OTHER SETTLERS IN ANGUS: ROYAL RESIDENCES FROM 1178 TO 1249: INTRODUCTION OF SHIRES AND SHERIFFS: FORMATION OF PARISHES: ADOPTION OF TUTELAR SAINTS: NATURE OF ABTHANERIES: THE CULDEES AND THEIR ABBES: CULDEES OF ABERNETHY AND BRECHIN: CAUSES OF THE FALL OF THEIR ORDER: INDICATIONS OF CULDEES AT MONIFIETH AND ARBIRLOT.

THERE are perhaps few towns in Scotland, in regard to the formation and early history of which more information may now be gleaned than in the case of Arbroath. This is owing to the fortunate preservation of the Chartulary, or collection of monastic writings framed at its Abbey, in all their integrity and fulness. The publication of these writings for the Bannatyne club, commenced under the joint editorship of two learned and indefatigable antiquaries, Mr P. Chalmers of Aldbar, and Mr Cosmo Innes, Advocate, and since Mr Chalmers' lamented death, recently completed by Mr Innes, with the interesting prefaces written by them, and the full and correct indices prepared under their superintendence, have greatly enhanced the value of the monastic writings of Arbroath, and have not only shed a flood of light on the Abbey, town, and neighbourhood, but entitle the collection to take its place among those authentic and valuable, although (perhaps to popular taste) *dry* documents by which our true national history in early times can be fixed and illustrated; and in which "there is to be found, although in a shape very barbarous and repulsive to the general reader, the most fresh and living pictures of the manners of the times." (Tytler's Hist. ii., 357.)

The Chartulary of Aberbrothock is perhaps the completest specimen of records of one of the most complete monastic establishments in the kingdom. It exhibits, during a period of three centuries and a half, a full register of charters from kings and nobles, down to private burgesses, papal bulls, grants and concessions of every description in favour of the convent; with feuing charters, and charters by progress, dispositions and infeftments, leases of teinds, lands, fishings, and houses, presentations to churches and chapels, records of perambulations of marches, decrees and settlements of disputes of all sorts, appointments to offices, and other writs, granted by the convent solely, or in conjunction with others, with deeds of mortification of houses, gardens, and annual rents, to altarages for the benefit of the relations of the founders; and various writs of other kinds too numerous to be here specified, generally in Latin, but sometimes in quaint old doric Scotch; and all more or less interesting, not only to those who are styled antiquaries, but to every one who wishes to obtain an accurate and intimate knowledge of the history of his country in former times, including its monastic and parochial economy, its agriculture, its currency, its system of education, jurisprudence, and internal government.

The writings *in favour* of the Abbey alone include and describe pieces of land ranging from a small garden to baronies and parishes (formerly styled shires), muirs, woods and fishings, saltworks, ferry boats, hostelries or lodges in various towns; the custody of ancient banners, parish churches and district chapels, with the lands and teinds attached to them; rights to levy large and small customs, privileges of barony and regality, with power to erect burghs in Angus and Mearns; power to wear mitre and pontifical robes, and confer minor church orders.

The chartulary forms an excellent subject for the student of philology. It commences at a period when few or no super or surnames existed in the district. It shews the introduction of surnames first among the foreign settlers in the coast towns, with their gradual progress among the more rural population; and it exhibits the process of their adoption, such as from paternity (*Mac*ormac, Ander*son*, Duncan*son*), from blood (Scot or English, Inglis), from a superior (Gilchrist, Gilcom—servant of Christ, servant of the Earl), from complexion (Black, Brown, White), from professional employment (Baxter, Barber, Smith, Wright, &c.), from office (Dempster, Dorward, Mair, &c.), from lands and possessions (Guthrie, Carnegie, Kilgour), while other surnames appear to defy all attempts to ascertain their true origin.

The first volume contains few or no surnames in the simple form in which they are now used by us, and scarcely any such surnames as those with which we are familiar. The additions of the names of lands, residences, or parents, in the manner used for distinction in those early times, can scarcely be called surnames. It is not till about the end of the fourteenth century, when Arbroath harbour was built, that surnames began to be commonly used without the intervening *de* (of) or *filius* (son of); but the habit rapidly prevailed after that date, so that by the end of the following century, the practice seems to have been as universal as it is now, to use at least two words as Christian name and surname, without any preposition. The following appear to have been the most common surnames occurring in the Abbey writs during the last hundred and fifty years in which they have been published, and it will easily be seen that, with some exceptions, they are surnames very prevalent about Arbroath and its vicinity at the present time—viz., Anderson, Bois, Bridie, Brown, Douglas, Dorward, Gray, Graham, Guthrie, Hay, Jameson, Keith, Lamb, Leighton, Lyall, Lyndsay, Lyn, Lyon, Meldrum, Mill, Ochterlony,

Ogilvy, Ramsay, Reid, Rany (Rennie), Scot, Scrymgeour, Stewart, Seton, Simson, Sinclair, Smart, Smith, Sturrock, Strachan, Thomson, Thornton, Tyrie, Watson, Wishart, Wood, Young. It will be observed that then, as now, the initial letter S takes the first rank among surnames in this district. The name *Brown* seems to have been as common about Arbroath four hundred years ago as it is still. The name of Ogilvie occurs more frequently than any other in the latter portion of the chartulary, not because of its prevalence in this part of the county, whatever may have been the case in the district about Kingoldrum, but in consequence of the many grants and leases made to persons of that name through the influence of the Airlie family, who for a long period held the important office of the Bailiery.

The writings in question are also interesting, as shewing how little material changes in pronunciation the names of towns, farms, streams, muirs, &c., have in general undergone during the last seven centuries. Such transformations or changes when they *do* occur, are not less curious. Thus, soon after the foundation of the Abbey, two places at several miles distance from one another are mentioned under the name of "Gutheryne." One of these names, by losing the central letter "e" and the last consonant, has in course of time become *Guthry* or *Guthrie*. The other name, by a very different process, lost its middle syllable, and had its last consonant hardened by the letter "d," and appears in the following consecutive forms—*Gutheryne, Guthyn, Guyn, Gund, Guynd*. Ballysak (Town of Isaac) is afterwards Bysak, and now Boysack. Ballindoch is corrupted into Bawndowff, and now called Pandoch. Vuirinchoke is also shortened to Inchok.

The names of places exhibit many curious orthographical variations, even while it is probable that little change took place as to their pronunciation.

Thus the name of the stream Vinny is written by the Monks in such forms as Ouany, Ovyngny, Ovynnie, Ovynny, Ovyny, Owyny, Owynyn, Vuaney, Vuany, Vueny. From want of local knowledge the learned Editor of the second volume is evidently puzzled by the name of the farm of Windyedge, which he prints in italics, according to the Monkish spelling of *le vynde age* and *le vynde eigge*. Aberbrothock being a long word, and recurring more frequently than any other name, affords an almost endless variety in spelling. It appears as Aberbrud, Aberbruthoc, Abbirbroht, Abbirbroth, Abberbrothoc, Abbyrbrothoc, Abberbroth, Abbirbroith, Abbirbrothoc, Abbirbrothoch, Abirbroth, Abirbrothoc, Abirbrothok, Abyrbroth, Abyrbrothoc, Abyrbrothok, Aberbrothoc, Abirbrethot, Abirbrothak, Aberbrothot, Aberbrotoht, Abirbroyth, Abirbrutoh, Abbyrbrothoch, Abyrbroyth, Arbroith, Arbroth, Arbrothe, Arbroyth, Ardbroith. The name of a neighbouring parish appears in such forms as Abereloth, Abireloth, Aberheloth, Aberhelot, Abrellot, Aberellot, Abberellot, Abbirlot, Abbirellot, Abirloth, Arbirloth, Abyrelloth, Arbirlot. Another neighbouring parish possesses an equal diversity in its names. Thus, Inverkeleder, Inverkelethir, Inuerkeleder, Inverkeler, Innerkelar, Innerkeldour, Innerkelor, Ennerkelor, Innerkelour. Ethie appears as Hathin, Athin, Athyn, Athe, Athy. The names of the two places Braco and Brax being somewhat similar, have been gathered under one head in the index, but ought to have been separated into two clusters thus—(1) Brekko, Brekky, Breco, Brakie; (2) Brakkys, Brekkis, Brex, Brax, the most ancient form being Brakhous.

Instances of the change or translation of the names of places from an early to a later language are sometimes given, and are not without interest. Thus, in a writ of the date of 1256, a place in the parish of Kingoldrum bearing the Gaelic name of *Hachethunethouer*, is said to be called in *English* Midefeld; and a certain marsh is referred to as called according to the Scotch ("*Scotice*"), *Moynebuche*. At an earlier period, King William, in his great charter, says that the Church Lands of Old Montrose were called in Scotch *Abthen*. Although this word may not be in itself a very old Gaelic term, these indications afford further proofs of the fact that the Gaelic was formerly called the Scotch language, to distinguish it from the Saxon or English language; and that it was afterwards called the *Old Scotch* as contradistinguished from the modern or Lowland Scotch.* In a description of the marches of Kingoldrum in 1458, the *Gaelic* name of Midfield disappears, but a considerable number of other Gaelic names are translated into English by Abbot Malcolm Brydy, in these terms:—" *Myllaschangly*, that is to say Scottismyll—the burn of *Athyncroith*, that is to say the Gallow Burne — *Tybyrnoquhyg*, that is to say the Blyndwell—*Carnofotyr*, that is to say the Pwndiris Carne—*Claischnamoyll*, that is to say the Mekylhyll—the pwll of *Monboy* [*Moynebuche*], that is to say the Yallow Pwll—the *Claische*, that is to say the Reyske—the burne of *Haldyrischanna*, that is to say the Gled Burne."

The number of old Gaelic names in the vicinity of Arbroath given in the Chartulary, and not still in use, are very few. They consist of *Athenglas, Hathuerbelath, Sythnekerdun*, and perhaps *Glauflat*, all in the neighbourhood of Kinblethmont. Indeed the whole number of British or Gaelic topographical terms in the tract of ground round Arbroath, between the waters of Elliot and Lunan, is small, when compared with those which can be more or less traced to the Gothic or Saxon languages. This fact, coupled with the state of the district

---

* The dialect of the lowlands seems to have obtained its now common name of Scotch ("Scottis") when Douglas translated Virgil in 1513; and there is no reason to believe that the Statute of 1542 allowing the Bible to be read "in the vulgar toung, in Inglis *or* Scottis, of *ane* gude and trew transla-"tioun," had any reference to the Gaelic, notwithstanding Pinkerton's opinion to the contrary.

within the recollection of its older inhabitants, shews that its Celtic population must have been very limited before the introduction of the Gothic races. And if it could be definitely proved that such a name as Pitmuies or *Petmuis* had its origin from the grave of Muis, and that he was interred there so lately as at the defeat of Camus, it would tend to establish the view of Chalmers and others, that the use of the Gaelic tongue was retained in this part of Scotland till the eleventh century, namely, the century preceding that in which the Abbey was founded.* The oldest names in the district referred to are those of the streams, and the hamlets situated near their mouths, such as Aber-Elliot, Aber-Brothock, Inver-Keillor, and Inver-Lunan. The other principal seats of the Celtic people, the names of which have no apparent affinity to the Saxon tongue,—were obviously Auchmithie, Ethie, Inchok, Kinnaldy, Rhind, Gilchorn, Balmullie, Boysack, Kinblethmont, Conon, Peebles, Letham, Crudie, Cuthlie, and one or two besides; and it may be observed that these names denote places favourably situated, and such as would naturally be early selected for cultivation and residence among the muirs and marshes with which the country formerly abounded.

There is little information as to the introduction of Saxon topographical terms; but we may notice that in 1219 the marches of Kinblethmont are given entirely in Gaelic, as are likewise those of Tarves, Aberdeenshire, in 1251 (although this will not prove that the Saxon tongue was not by that time introduced); while the familiar Saxon terms of *Fishergate* and *Greystone* appear among the marches of Dunnichen at the probable date of 1300; and these names of later origin continue to increase rapidly during the subsequent records. On this point it may be also stated, as an indication of previous Saxon

---

* The name *Baledgar*, given to the royal castle which King Edgar had begun to build 1101-7, would lead to the belief that the Gaelic had remained in the district of Gowrie till that time. (Hollinshed's *Chronicle*.)

colonisation that the first appearance in the Chartulary, about 1200, of the name of St Bridestown is almost in its present form of Panbride, it having thus early degenerated from Ballinbride to Banbride and Panbryd, or Pannebryd; and that the Saxon name of Muirhouse, then appears under the already corrupted form of Muraus.

Like the records of the other great Scottish monasteries those of Arbroath suggest, but do not afford an answer to the enquiry, how the Scottish kings, from Malcolm III. to Alexander II., came to be possessed of, and to confer on them, and on numerous foreign immigrants, so many large tracts of valuable land, without any other reference to the occupiers than the indications given in the earlier grants that they were given along with the lands. The subject is involved in considerable obscurity; but there is reason to believe that these Scottish kings of Anglo-Norman tastes and feelings had at this period copied the example set by the Norman kings of England, so far as different circumstances would allow, and held themselves to be the absolute proprietors of the whole *lands* within the kingdom, except those in the hands of the more powerful chiefs, with liberty to dispose of the same at their pleasure, without respect to the ancient rights of the actual occupants, who do not appear at that time to have possessed any written titles. The lands were probably in many instances resumed as fallen to the king when the possessors died without leaving full-grown male heirs. We suspect that the pious David I., instead of being, as one of his successors styled him, " a sair sanct to the crown," was in reality only a *sair sanct* to his poor Celtic subjects in the lowlands. The practical effect of this Norman system seems to have been the reduction of these occupants to the condition of serfs or slaves to their new landlords (as will be afterwards more fully alluded to), or at best to the position of tenants-at-will, liable to be ejected at the fiat of their Anglo-Norman lords, like the cottars and small farmers of the highlands at the present time. The unceremonious manner of treating the poorer occupants of land in the twelfth century may be inferred from the laws which it was found necessary to pass for their protection in the fifteenth century, until which time they continued liable to be summarily removed by the new proprietor at any period of the year without respect to the leases which might have been granted to them.

Next to the kings themselves the new Saxon or Norman settlers, to whom they gave lands, were the most munificent donors of the monasteries of royal foundation like Arbroath, as if it had been expected that they must give back to the king's favourite religious house a part of those possessions which they had received from his hands. On this account the records of Arbroath Abbey are peculiarly full of the names of proprietors of French, Flemish, Saxon, and Norman extraction, especially of those who settled in Angus and Mearns about the time of King William and those of his predecessors, David I. and Malcolm IV. Of these we may name the families of Arbuthnott or de Blundo, Baliol, Berkeley or Barclay, Bosvill or Boswell, Cheen or Cheyne, Cumin, Durward, Fitz-Bernard, Fitz-Thancard, Frivill, Hay, Hastings, Leslie, Lindsay, Lundyn or Lundie, Malherbe, Malvill or Melville, Meldrum, Moncur, Montalto, Montfort, Mohaut or Mowat, Moray, Morham, Mortuomari or Mortimer, Mubray or Mowbray, Ramsay, Rewell, Rossyn or Rossie, St Michael, Sibbald, Strachan, Valoins, Vaus or Vallibus, Wischard or Wishart. Many of these will again appear in the list of the Abbey lands and possessions as donors; and the names of others often occur as officers of State and landed proprietors, attesting deeds, in conjunction with the older and uncouth names of those barons of Celtic lineage who had still retained their possessions.

The Angus and Mearns families of Baldowy, Boyce, Burnet, Carnegie, Dempster, Douglas, Gardyne, Guthrie, Irvine, Ochterlony, Ogilvie, Scrimgeour and others appear largely among the Abbey writs at a later period.

Leaving the history of these numerous families to the "Peerages" and other genealogical works, we can only here refer to three or four of the Anglo-Norman settlers who erected towers or fortalices in the immediate neighbourhood of our Abbey.

Walter de Berkeley was Chamberlain of Scotland, and proprietor of the estate of Inverkeillor, when he granted the Church of that parish to the Abbey, soon after its foundation. He was succeeded by Ingelram de Baliol, who married his daughter or heiress during the reign of King William. This Ingelram is termed in the Chartulary the lord of Redcastle, and was the builder of that fortalice, if it was not erected by his predecessor, as Chalmers asserts. (Caledonia i. 529.)

During King William's reign Richard de Mallevill obtained the lands of Kinblethmont, and granted the chapel of Kinblethmont to the Abbey. He was one of the magnates of the district, and was a witness to the Charter of John Abbot of Kelso, at the dedication of the Abbey in 1178. Twelve years afterwards, his name is found associated with those of the bishop of St Andrews and others in a letter of safe conduct granted by King John of England. Before the year 1227 the lands of Kinblethmont seem to have come into the hands of one named Gwarynus de Cupa; and in 1283 Welandus de Seynclau was lord of "Kynblatmund."

Philip de Mubray, one of the settlers of that name, obtained from King William certain lands in Fife, and gave to the monks of Arbroath a toft in the burgh of Inverkeithing. He witnessed many of the king's charters, and was often employed in State affairs. It is probable that he was the first builder of a tower or castle on the south bank of the Elliot water; as in 1208 the Abbot and

Convent of Arbroath granted to Philip de Mubray liberty to have an Oratory or Chapel for his private family within the court of his house of " Kellyn," without prejudice to the rights of the Parish Church which belonged to them. This house could have been no other than a castle at Kelly, of which the large existing building may be a successor. It must, however, be stated that for a considerable time, both previous and subsequent to that date, the lands of Balcathie, in the immediate vicinity of Kelly, seem to have been in the possession of one " Roger de Balkathin," who appears as a witness to many of the Abbey writs. The antiquary, Commissary Maule, states that the Mubrays possessed the estate of Kelly till the Black Parliament in the reign of Robert I. (MS. account of the family of Panmure, in Panmure House); after which it seems to have come into possession of the Ochterlonys.

Philip de Valoins obtained from King William the lands of Panmure and Benvie, and held the office of Chamberlain. He was succeeded in his lands and office by his son William, who died about 1219, and left an only daughter, named Christian. She became the wife of Lord Petrus de Maule, of the family of Malville or Melville in Lothian, and who was afterwards styled proprietor or lord of Panmure, the name of which was by that time corrupted from Ballinmuir to Pannemor. From that union the family of Maule and Panmure has descended, and the erection or enlargement of the castle of Panmure may be ascribed to one of these barons during the reigns of William or Alexander II.: although Commissary Maule thinks that it had previously been one of the king's castles, like Glammiss, occupied by a thane or bailiff, who dispensed justice and drew the king's rents in the district: and he supposes that a knoll on the lands of Scryne got its name of *Lawbothen* from it being the place where justice was administered by the thane. (Ibid.) He derives Panmure from *Pan*, a chief; and

More, a lord; "as who would say the overlord or chief lord."

The Morhams possessed the lands of Panbride in the reign of King William; and after his death John de Morham, who had been his clerk or chaplain, confirmed the royal grant of the church of Panbride to the Abbey; and Adam, the brother and successor of John, confirmed the same grant. This family does not again appear. But a castle or fortalice stood at Panbride which is traditionally stated to have been seized by the English when they took the castle of Panmure during the wars of the fourteenth century. In the next century the family to whom Hector Boyce the historian belonged, appears in the Chartulary as proprietors of Panbride under the name of Boys; and William Ramsay of Panbride was one of a jury which met at Forfar on 3rd October 1495 for determining the marches of Balnamoon Mire.

But a building much older than any of these castles had stood within the parish of St Vigeans, on the hill called Cairnconon. The traditions of the district bear that it was called Castle Gory or Gregory; and that Gregory, one of its proprietors, was slain in battle in the parish of Monifieth, where his grave is still pointed out at a cairn called Cairn-Greg, near Linlathen. To pass from tradition to written documents, we learn from the Chartulary that at or previous to the foundation of Arbroath Abbey the estate of Conon, consisting of this hill and its declivities, belonged to a chief bearing the Gaelic name of Dufsyth. His son Matthew was witness to Ingelram de Baliol's confirmation of the church of Inverkeillor in 1180; and "Matthew, son of Matthew the son of Dufsyth of Conon," was one of the perambulators of the marches of Kinblethmont on 23rd September 1219. The lands of Conon at this time did not belong to the Abbey, but were most probably held as fallen into the king's hands. They were granted four years afterwards, on 6th December 1223, to the Convent, by King

Alexander II., along with the lands of Dumbarrow, in forestry. The residence of these Celtic barons of Conon is traditionally indicated as having been situated a little southwards from the top of the hill, near the northern boundary of the lands now forming the farm of West Grange. At this spot a primitive stone vault has recently been discovered by accident. It is nearly in the shape of a common beehive, with the stones overlapping each other, so as to form a rude conical roof. It seems to have been constructed in a hollow or excavation of the ground, which is principally formed of freestone rock; and was entered by a passage which has not yet been explored. It is difficult to assign a reason for the construction of such a singular vault, except that it was intended as a place of concealment on occasion of sudden assaults from warlike Scottish barons, or still more merciless invaders from Denmark and Norway, to whom the east of Angus was then much exposed. After the lands of Conon were acquired by the Convent, they regularly held regality courts at Cairnconon, to which they took their vassals bound to appear three times every year. This was done in the Abbot's charters so late as 1580. As some of these courts were held at the cold season, it is evident that a building had existed at Cairnconon for the accommodation of the Abbot's officials and retainers. But it is impossible to ascertain whether this was identical with, or the successor of, the residence of Dufsyth. It is believed in the district, that the last remains of this castle of Conon were removed by the feuars of Colliston after its alienation from the Abbey by Cardinal Beaton, and the materials employed in the construction of the present mansion house of Colliston.

The places of residence of William I. and Alexander II. who reigned over Scotland during the brightest and liveliest period of its early history, may be a point of interest to some; and the numerous grants by them to the Abbey supply considerable information on this point, as the place of granting is invariably stated in the royal charters of that period; although not in charters granted by subjects, so that these records give no hint of the usual residence of the great earls of Angus in former times. King William's charters sometimes contain a notice of the day and month, but no notice of the year of grant. Many of them bear to be granted at the places where his predecessors David I. and Malcolm IV. usually lived, except that by his time their seat of Scone was granted to a religious house, and their seat of Kinross was granted to a settler named Henry of Kinross. Of sixty-one charters by this monarch, recorded in the Chartulary, nineteen were granted at Forfar, several of them apparently on the same day. The original royal seat at Forfar was situated on the knoll to the east of Castle Street. King William seems to have left this old tower for a newer and more commodious residence on the west side of the street; for he bestowed the "place of the old castle of Forfar" on Robert de Quincy, who feued the same to Sir Roger de Argenten for a pound of pepper payable yearly at Pasch. (Reg. St Andrews, p. 354.) Hector Boyce says that Forfar was once "strengthened with two royal castles, as the ruins do yet declare." Notwithstanding this grant it is quite possible that the English had afterwards garrisoned the older fortalice, being the strongest in situation, until it was surprised and taken by the Forester of Platen in the war of independence. Five of King William's charters were granted at Perth, nine at Montrose, five at Alyth, four at Stirling, two at Selkirk, two at Kinghorn, two at Aberdeen, two at Elgin, and one at each of the following places, namely, Roxburgh, Haddington, Traquair, Linlithgow, Lanark, Clackmannan, Dunfermline, Arbroath, Kincardine, Kintore, and Klonin (Clony). He sometimes resided also at Crail and Jedburgh, and granted charters at these places. At the most of these towns the kings at that time possessed castles or occasional lodgings.

King Alexander's charters at first bear no date, but afterwards they contain the day and month and year of reign, and in one instance the year of the Christian era. He granted twenty-seven charters to the Abbey, seven of which bear to be executed at Forfar, four at Perth, two at Edinburgh, two at Coupar-Angus Abbey, two at Kintore, one at Lifton, one at Haddington, one at Newbottle, one at St Andrews, one at Kincardine, one at Fyvie (on 22nd February 1221), and one at Invercoyth (?). He had resided at Barry during the spring of 1229, as he there granted two charters on 4th March and 24th April of that year; and he granted a charter at Arbroath on 7th March 1244-5. This monarch's gifts to the Abbey, his father's favourite religious house, were very liberal; but his son Alexander III. had probably thought it was sufficiently endowed, as he does not appear to have made a single grant in its favour.

The Abbey records contribute information regarding the introduction into this part of Scotland of our modern divisions of shires and parishes. They also afford traces of the existence of more early divisions which have now fallen entirely into disuse. The records of St Andrews allude to the Thanes of Falkland and Dairsie with strange Gaelic names. In the writings of Arbroath reference is made to the Thanes of Inverkeillor, Monros (Montrose), and Edwy (Idvies). Their possessions seem to have borne the title of Thanedoms. The thaneries or thanedoms of Aberluthnot (Marykirk), Glammiss, Tannadice, Fettercairn, Boyne, Aberdeen, Aberkerdor, and others, are mentioned in the titles of these lands, and elsewhere. Some of these districts were at a later period called lordships or "territories," which among the once Celtic population of Fife and Angus may have been similar to the divisions still called "countries" by the present Celtic population of our highlands. Among others the *territories* of Abernethy, Lindores, Glammiss, Inverkeillor, and Kirriemuir are referred to in the Abbey writs; and these districts were probably larger than the modern parishes now bearing their names.

It is believed by several writers of research that shires or sheriffdoms were gradually introduced as the Scoto-Saxon people gained on the Celtic or Keltic inhabitants, and were part of the innovations made on their older institutions. (Chalmers' Caledonia i, p. 715.) But it is probably more correct to say that the titles of *Comes* (or ancient earl) and *Thane* were the Anglo-Saxon designations of the nobility and their law officers or bailiffs during the intermediate period betwixt the disuse of the earlier Gaelic titles of *Maormor, Toscheoderach,* and *Derach,* and the introduction of the later Anglo-Norman titles of baron and sheriff. Arbroath Abbey was founded at the close of this intermediate period, and the only trace of the old Gaelic titles found in its writs is in the name of *Derethy* given to the officership of the barony of Tarves, Aberdeenshire, in 1463. The chartularies of the religious houses shew that shires were introduced into a large part of the lowlands during the twelfth century, from the reign of Alexander I. to William the Lion. The first sheriff on record is mentioned in Earl David's charter to the Abbey of Selkirk in 1120. Several grants by David I. to the Priory of St Andrews mention the shire of Haddington in the period from 1124 to 1153. In the foundation charter of the Priory of St Andrews, dated in 1144, and in the writs of that house for some years afterwards, there is no allusion to the title of shire as applied to districts lying to the north of Forth, even in reference to districts which came to be termed shires or "schyres" immediately afterwards, in the days of Bishop Richard from 1163 to 1173; and in whose writings the names of parishes as well as shires first appear in the eastern district of Fifeshire. In a charter to the same Priory by Malcolm IV., who reigned from 1153 to 1165, Gillemore is named as sheriff of Clackmannan. And in Bishop Arnold's time, about 1160, Hiweno was sheriff of Scone; and at the same period Macungal and Malcolm were *Judges* of Fife. In Bishop Richard's grants the district round St Andrews came to be called Kilrimund-schyre; part of Forgan parish is called Forgrund-schyre, and the lands about Blebo in Kemback parish were called Blathbolg-schyre; while the first *parish* named in the Priory writings is that of the Holy Trinity of Kilrimund, now St Andrews. After this, the peninsular tract between Forth and Tay, formerly known as Fife and Fothriffe, contained a great number of these small *schyres*. Besides those already named the ecclesiastics of St Andrews possessed lands known as Bischop-schyre (Portmoak Parish),* and Muckhart-schyre (Muckart Parish). The Abbey of Dunfermline possessed large tracts of land in Dunfermelin-schyre and Kinghorn-schyre. It also possessed the whole of Gaitmilk-schyre or Kinglassin-schyre (Kinglassie Parish), Dolor-schyre (Dollar Parish), and Nethbren-schyre (Newburn Parish). Besides these church lands the same district contained the schyres of Karel (Crail), Rires (in Kilconquhar Parish), Kennochyn (in Kennoway Parish), Weymiss (Wemyss Parish), Kyngorn (Kinghorn and Burntisland Parishes), Loquhor (Auchterderran and Ballingry Parishes), and Kynros (Kinross and Orwell Parishes); all of which remained solely or principally in the hands of the king or great barons; and contained old castles such as those of Crail, Rires, Wemyss, Kinghorn, Lochore, and Lochleven; to which the shires or estates were attached. The whole of these shires, except the last, have become extinct; and the shire of Kinross would have shared the same fate before this time, had it

---

* This parish was till very recently, if it be not still, familiarly styled Bishopshire by the people of the district.

not been for the annexation to it by Act of Parliament in 1685 of three neighbouring parishes and some other lands; notwithstanding which it is still the smallest county in Scotland.

Tracing the formation of shires from north to south we find a district on the Tay, called the shire of Dunde (Dundee), in a Papal Bull in favor of the Priory of St Andrews, dated about 1183; and about the same time King William granted various tracts of land in Forfarshire, which were then his property, to the Abbey of Arbroath, under the names of the schyres of Aberbrothoc, Athyn, Dunnechtyn, and Kyngoldrum, although the smallest of these tracts (Ethie) is not so often dignified by that title as the others. We have not observed in the writings of Arbroath, Brechin, or elsewhere, any other allusions to *small schyres* in Angus, nor indeed in any part lying to the north of Lunan Water. The great districts of *Anegus* and *Moernes* (Angus and Mearns) are mentioned together as well known divisions in a writing about the year 1210, but are not formally styled shires.

Makbeth, Sheriff of Scone, the Thane of Strathearn; Constantine, Judge of Strathearn; and Bricius, Judge (or "Judex"), are among the witnesses to Laurence of Abernethy's grant of that church about 1190—and afterwards, during the reigns of William and Alexander II., this Bricius is often witness to charters granted at Forfar and elsewhere under the title of the King's Judge; although during the same period King William alludes to "William Cumyn, my Sheriff of Forfar," as a donor of land to Arbroath Abbey. The shire of Forfar was probably at that time only the king's estate of Forfar. John Wischard was Sheriff of Mearns about 1210, and Galfridus was Sheriff of Fife in 1212. John de Moray was Sheriff of Perth in 1214; and in 1219 Hugo de Cambrun was Sheriff of Forfar, and Adam was Judge of the Court of the Earls of Angus, and afterwards (probably on the death of Bricius) he became Judge of the King's

Court, and his brother Kerald succeeded to his office in the Earls' Court. In the recognition of the perambulation of the marches of Kinblethmont, held in the King's Court at Forfar, on 27th January 1227-8, the judicial powers of the Court seem to have been exercised by John de Hay, Sheriff of Perth, Thomas Malherbe, Sheriff of Forfar, and others; while Kerald, Judge of Angus, and Adam, Judge of the King, are ranked among the inferior functionaries as jurymen. Soon after this period (viz., about 1229) William de Blundo is styled Sheriff of Perth and Scone. In 1248 Thomas Wyseman was Sheriff of Elgin; and a writ dated in 1299 refers to Lord J. Earl of Athol, then Sheriff of Aberdeen. There were no Sheriffs beyond Inverness till the reign of James IV., about 1503. In further illustration of the introduction of sheriffships at this time, it may be here remarked that King William's earliest grants to the Abbey are addressed simply to all good men, clerks and laics; but afterwards they are addressed to Bishops, Abbots, Earls, Barons, Justiciars, *Sheriffs*, and all good men, clerks and laics.

From the above it may be fairly concluded that in the twelfth and thirteenth centuries the new territorial divisions termed shires were introduced into the whole lowlands of Scotland; that the kings of the family of Malcolm Canmore, among their other importations from England, applied the new name to various tracts of their own lands, and styled their judicial officers Sheriffs; and that it accordingly became fashionable for the great lords and barons, and even some of the Abbots to follow their example, and apply the term to their estates. It is to be presumed that in many instances, especially in the larger shires, the Sheriff exercised the functions which had been previously exercised by the old Judges or their deputes, and that the office of Judge became a sinecure like the more modern judicial office of High Sheriff. It appears that in the legal as well as the ecclesiastical department the old Gaelic and Saxon titles and offices may have remained for some time after the introduction of the newer functionaries. In various districts the Judge and the Sheriff, as we have seen, are both mentioned at the same time; but it may be observed from the names already specified that the Judges' names were usually Gaelic, while the names of the Sheriffs, especially toward the east coast, were in English. There is little reason to doubt that along with the change in the title of the administrator, there was also at that period a considerable change in the mode of administering the law, if not in the law itself; and that the old Celtic system of commuting every crime by a fixed money payment was then abolished. The Norman Judges seem to have gone to the opposite extreme of punishing minor crimes, such as theft, with death; an abuse which lasted till the present century was commenced. Some of our historians have been unable to discover any presiding Judge enjoying the title of Sheriff over these minute divisions called shires. It was not to be expected that Sheriffs would be continued in the schyres which were entirely given to Arbroath and other Abbeys, after the date of the gift—their officers were termed Stewarts and Baillies. But two of the largest "schyres" in Fife undoubtedly possessed Sheriffs; as "Gillebride, Sheriff of Dunfermelin," is a witness to King William's general Confirmation to the Priory of St Andrews; and William and Galfrid, both termed Sheriffs of Crail (Karel), are successively witnesses to other grants about the same period to that religious house. For some time also the great barons seemed to have styled their judicial officers Sheriffs before they were styled Bailies. With the exception, however, of the shires which have been retained till the present time, the most of these small shires were lost to public notice, or were merged into the newer divisions of Constabularies, Regalities, Stewartries or Baronies, by the time of King Robert Bruce. Where the royal castles existed at Kinghorn, Crail, and Dundee, these shires came to be termed Constabularies. But in many instances the names of the small schyres were retained in the *feudal descriptions* of lands, till the last remains of them were included in the sweep of the Act 1748 abolishing the heritable jurisdictions.

The introduction of parishes into this part of Scotland, and more particularly the causes of the particular boundaries and formations of parishes, are subjects on which considerable light is thrown by the Abbey records. No reference to parishes in Scotland has been found earlier than A.D. 843. They are, however, mentioned in the grants of Alexander I. and David I. to the monasteries of Dunfermline and Scone, and, as has been already noticed, the parish of Kilrimund is mentioned about the year 1170. Monikie (Muniekkin) is the first parish alluded to under that title in the Chartulary of Arbroath, toward the latter end of the reign of King William; and about the same time the parish of Ecclesgreig in Kincardineshire is mentioned in the register of St Andrews. But from the death of Malcolm Canmore till a considerable time after the foundation of Arbroath Abbey, the districts now termed parishes were, as already mentioned, generally termed *schyres;* as in King William's great charter he grants not four parishes but four schyres, with their churches and pertinents. After King William's death the references to parishes become more numerous, but are far from being frequently mentioned in descriptions of lands during several succeeding centuries. The situation of lands was for a long period much more commonly indicated by the name of the secular division of " schyre," regality, barony or lordship in which they lay, at least in writings executed for secular purposes. Indeed the modern and less systematic custom of describing lands by reference to the ecclesiastical divisions of parishes and the secular divisions of counties is of a late origin, and only came into general use after the date of the Act of 1748, already referred to.

It is very apparent that at the formation of a great number of the parishes in Scotland they were simply estates, or tracts of land, the proprietors of which built the church and provided for its endowment by tithes payable from their own surrounding grounds. As already stated, these districts were at an early period termed shires, territories, and lordships in the writings of the religious houses; and were afterwards formed into baronies and portions of regalities. Thus the four parishes in Forfarshire given to the Abbey were termed shires in King William's days,—were afterwards incorporated into the regality,—and are spoken of in the reign of King James VI. (1592) as baronies. With the exception of a few small parishes, the changes of property during several centuries have led to the division of most parishes among several proprietors; but it will still be generally found that the boundary line of two parishes is at the same time the boundary line of two estates, or at least of lands acquired by one family at different periods.

It is, however, to be kept in view, that several of the older parishes of great extent are found to have been in the hands of various proprietors at a very early date, so as to lead to the conclusion that the proprietors had either from their own motive, or by the authority of some civil or ecclesiastical ruler, acted together in the erection and support of one church, which became the Parish Church of their several lands.

The strange shapes of parishes, and the origin of their detached portions, are subjects that are capable of explanations by an attentive perusal of these old monastic records. There is no evidence that the detached barony of Inverpeffer and the detached estate of Dumbarrow formed parts of the shires (parishes) of Aberbrothock and Dunnichen when these were granted in property by

King William at the foundation of the Abbey; but the Chartulary bears that the same king afterwards granted the lands of Inverpeffer in property not to the Abbey but to Walkelinus, one of his officers, to be held of the Monks of Arbroath as superiors; and the lands of Dumbarrow were not granted to the Abbey till the reign of Alexander II., and could not have previously formed part of the shire or parish of Dunnichen, which his father bestowed more than thirty years previously. The conclusion then is evident, that after the Monks acquired these tracts of land they disjoined them from the parishes to which they had originally and naturally belonged (viz., Inverpeffer from Arbirlot, and Dumbarrow from Idvies or Kirkden) and annexed them to the nearest of the other parishes, which consisted of Abbey lands in their own possession.

The annexation of the lands of Kirkbuddo to the parish of Guthrie, from which it is several miles distant, took place at a period comparatively recent, namely, after the Reformation. Previous to that era the proprietor of Guthrie had become patron of the parsonage of Kirkbuddo, with right to the glebe or church lands and pasturage for six cows; and after being supplied with a reader for some years the church of this small parish was suppressed, and its tithes given as an addition to the income of the also small parish of Guthrie.

There is no indication that at the time of the foundation of Arbroath Abbey any of the churches bestowed on it had been distinguished by the names of Patron Saints. This is shown by the confirmatory bull of Pope Lucius, granted on 6th April 1182; and although in King William's general charter, dated between 1211 and 1214, no less than twenty-five churches are included — the church of Old Montrose (Maryton) is the only one mentioned in connection with the name of a Saint, who in that instance was St Mary the Virgin. This seems to have been the first church thus dedicated by the Monks; and they very soon affixed the names of various Saints to other churches obtained by them, and got the titles recognised in confirmatory grants. Thus Roger, Bishop of St Andrews between 1188 and 1202, confirmed the grant of Aberbrothock church under the name of the church of "Saint Vigian of Aberbrothoc;" and in the title of the document given in the Chartulary the Monks have styled him St Vigian the *Confessor*,—that is, one who has suffered for the truth, but not to death. The name of *St Murdochus* or *Murdacus* is not found mentioned in connection with the church of Ethic till between 1219 and 1226, when Henry, Prior of St Andrews, confirmed it to the Abbey under that title. Walter de Berkeley granted simply the "church of Inverkeillor" to the Abbey, and King William confirmed the grant without reference to a Patron Saint. But in grants soon afterwards made by the same persons relative to hunting and pasturage in the territory of Inverkeillor, the title given to the church is that of "*Saint Macconoc* of Inuivkeleder," a Saint not mentioned in the Scottish calendar under that name, but who, it has been suggested to the Editors of the Chartulary, may probably have been St Canech or Kenny, the contemporary of St Columba, who visited him at Hy or Iona, and who gives name to Kilkenny. Among others, the church of Banchory was afterwards dedicated by the Monks to St Ternan, and the church of Aberchirdir to St Marnan or Marnoch. Other monasteries adopted the same practice; as, for example, the Monks of Restennet consecrated their church of Dunninald to the memory of St Skaoch or St Skay, the church of Craig was dedicated to St Braoch, and the Monks of St Andrews dedicated the church of Ecclesgreig to St Cyrus; so that during succeeding centuries every church belonging to a religious house, if not every lay parsonage, was consecrated to one Saint at least, and sometimes to two or more; while the more eminent

Saints, such as St Mary, St Andrew, St Ninian, St Nicholas and others, had churches, chapels, and altars bearing their names in various parts of the country.

It may be remarked that, as one effect of the prevalence of Saint Worship during this period, it became fashionable to distinguish places solely by the names of these tutelar demigods rather than by the more ancient terms. Thus Kilrymont was superseded by St Andrews, Inveerie by St Monance, Aberluthnot by (St) Marykirk, and Conveth by (St) Laurencekirk. In other cases such as Perth, the ancient term (a contraction of Aberthay) has been fully recovered, while the Papal name of St Johnstown has again become obsolete. This reverse process was taking effect in the case of St Vigeans, when it was arrested by the erection of the new church in the town of Arbroath, which, for distinction's sake, led in course of time, to a restriction of the ancient British term Aberbrothock to the modern church, and of the newer tutelar title St Vigeans to the ancient church. But on this account, during more than half a century after the Reformation, it is sometimes difficult to discover to which of these churches the title of "Minister at Aberbrothock" is to be applied.

The obscure subject of Abthanes and Abthaneries is one on which a remark or two may be made in connection with the Abbey records. Some have held the Abthane to be a superior or Archthane; while others, such as Chalmers, consider it clear that the term *Abthane* denoted the Abbot's thane in contradistinction to the king's thane; and that he was an *ecclesiastical* bailiff or steward. But if the term ever denoted an office it was at a period earlier than the date of any existing records, and must, we think, have had references to Abbes or Abbots of the Culdees, or other ecclesiastics, before the introduction of *Papal* Abbeys into Scotland; for wherever we have found the word in the original charters granted to Papal monasteries and otherwise, it has been applied as descriptive of *land* and not of office; and the relative term Abbe fell into disuse on the suppression of the Culdees. Thus King William granted to his Chancellor the lands of the "Abbacie of Munros" (Montrose) to be held of the Monks of Arbroath; and as the Editors of the Chartulary state, this "Abbacie" cannot be identified with any possession except the land of the church of "St Mary of Old Munros," which in Scotch is called "Abthen," as explained in King William's great charter, where the grant of these church lands is confirmed to the Monks. Between 1201 and 1204 Gilchrist, Earl of Angus, granted the church of Monifod (Monifieth) with its chapels, lands, teinds, and pasture to the Monks of Arbroath, who held the same for centuries. But seventeen years afterwards (about 1220), Malcolm, Earl of Angus, granted the whole lands of the Abthein of Monifod, with mills, waters, fields, pastures, muirs, marshes, fishings, &c. to Nicholas, son of Bricius, priest of Kirriemuir (one of the old married clergy); and the grant was confirmed by his daughter Maud or Matilda, Countess of Angus, about 1242; one of whose charters granted to the Abbey about this time was witnessed by the same Bricius, styled parson of Kirriemuir; as also by *Nicholas, Abbe of Monifod* (apparently he who obtained the Abthein); and by one bearing the newer name and title of William, vicar of Monifod, the acting priest under the Monks. In the succeeding charter of the Countess Maud she granted to the Monks of Arbroath " the whole lands to the *south* of the church of Monifod, which the Keledei held in the lifetime of my father, with the toft and croft on the *east* side of that church;" and seventy years afterwards (in 1310) Michael of Monifieth, the "proprietor of the Abbathanie thereof," bound himself to pay to the Convent of Arbroath six shillings and eight pence of sterlings, with half a boll of mustard seed, for the toft and croft which he held of them in the territory of the Abbathanie. Now although we can scarcely agree in the opinion of the Editors of the Chartulary that "this toft was without doubt" the land to the *south* of Monifieth church which the Culdees had held—(it may have been the toft and croft to the *east* of that church),—yet these notices serve to show that in this case lands called Abthein, and the name or title of Abbe were used in connection with a church where the Culdees had lived, or at least had held lands, for about thirty years after the foundation of Arbroath Abbey.

The Monkish term Abbacine and the Scotch terms Abthane, Abthein, Abthen or Abden were names given to lands in the neighbourhood of various ancient churches situated in favoured or striking localities, where the earlier Christians or Culdees may be supposed to have settled. Thus King William gave the lands of the "*Abbacie* of Eglisgreig" (St Cyrus) according to its ancient boundaries, with the church of the parish and the chapel of St Regulus to the Priory of St Andrews. The same Priory also obtained the church of Dull in Perthshire from Hugh, Bishop of Dunkeld, including among its pertinents the "Abthanie of Dull." The ecclesiastics of St Andrews also acquired the Abden of Kinghorn, lying contiguous to the church. There were also lands called Abden beside the churches of Ratho, Kettins, and Blairgowrie, and probably at the old church of Lindores, now called Abdie, situated on the banks of its picturesque lake. But we are unable to state the history or circumstances connected with the last-mentioned cases. From what is here given (and the sources of information are very limited), it may, however, we think, be safely concluded, in the words of the preface to Arbroath Chartulary that the *Abthein* "was land, the property of or connected with an Abbot or Abbacy—perhaps of a Columbite or Culdee house;" and that it also very probably formed the church lands of a Culdee establishment under the possession and management of its Abbe or superior (as *Ab* in Gaelic is said to mean Abbot), for behoof of himself and the other incumbents.

The ancient order of churchmen called Culdees is a subject which has long engaged the attention and interest of historians and antiquaries; and it is gratifying to find such an amount of authentic information on this favourite topic of enquiry as is given by the early monastic writings of Arbroath. The histories of the Abbey of Scone and of the two great monasteries in Fifeshire take up the subject at an earlier date. Alexander I. displaced the Culdees of Scone for Augustinian Monks about 1115. The Dunfermline Chartulary shows that in the reign of David I. the Culdees of that place were superseded by English Monks, who soon got possession of Kirkaldy, which is generally believed to have been another Culdee seat; and about the same time that they and the Monks of St Andrews contended for and were allowed to divide betwixt them the lands of *Balchristie* (Town of the Christians) in Newburn parish, a Culdee establishment of ancient date. The register of St Andrews very clearly exhibits the suppression of the Culdees or Hermits of Lochleven, who had received the patronage of King Makbeth, his Queen, Lady Makbeth, (whose true Gaelic name was *Gruoch*), Malcolm III., and other Scottish monarchs. It contains King David's grant of the Island of Lochleven to the Canons of St Andrews that they might there set up canonical order, with the declaration that if the Culdees found on the island would live regularly (that is, according to the new Canons) with the Monks they might remain, but that if they resisted they should be "ejected from the island." That they were soon ejected there can be no doubt, for the king's favourite Bishop Robert of St Andrews, about the same time, granted to the Canons of St Andrews the Abbey of Lochleven with all its lands, churches, and rents, even "the church vestments which the Chelede had," and the books of their library, of which a catalogue is given, concluding with what was evidently a Culdee controversial book of the time, titled "Exceptions or Objections to Ecclesiastical Rules," or the Regulations of the new Canons or Monks. A small Culdee house at Portmoak, in the same parish, also came into possession of the Monks of St Andrews, who afterwards maintained for some time an hospital of St Thomas for the sustentation of the poor at or near that spot. It is also well known that in King David's reign the Culdees were displaced at St Andrews itself, to make room for Augustine Monks; and that the Culdees of Monymusk were placed under the power of the Bishop of St Andrews, who, in the face of solemn engagements, afterwards suppressed their order at that place in favour of regular Canons.

Half a century subsequent to King David's *reformation* of the more southern Culdees, the Chartulary of Arbroath introduces us to further acquaintance with the two great Culdee colleges of Strathearn and Angus, Abernethy and Brechin, where they have left memorials of their peculiar architecture in the round towers, of which the square towers of St Andrews, Dunblane, and others, are the successors. Soon after the foundation of Arbroath Abbey, Lawrence, son of Orm of Abernethy, granted to it all his claims to the patronage of the church of Abernethy, with its chapels of Dron, Dunbog, and Errol, the lands of Belach and Petinlouer (Pitlour), one-half of the tithes of the property of himself and his heirs (the other half of which he stated belonged to the "Keledei of Abirnythy"), and the whole tithes of the territory of Abernethy, except those of the churches of Flisk and Cultrum (perhaps Coultray, in or near Balmerino parish), and excepting the tithes of his lordship of Abernethy, which the Culdees have always possessed, namely, those of Mugdrum, Carpow, and others. This encroachment on the Culdees of Abernethy was confirmed by King William on the same day, in a Charter wherein he speaks of himself as the donor of the church of Abernethy, with its chapels. As was to be expected under such a grant, the Culdees of Abernethy and the Monks of Arbroath were soon engaged in disputes as to their respective rights, and in which both parties vigorously contested for a long period, as fully detailed by Keith, Jamieson, and others, but in which, as in all other similar cases, the poor and now antiquated Culdees were ultimately vanquished. The sentence of the Bishop of Dunblane pronounced in 1214 against the claims of the " Prior and Kelledei of Abirnethy" in the course of this litigation is recorded among the Abbey writs, which give no further notices of this ancient religious house.

The Monks of Arbroath did not obtain any of the endowments which were in the actual possession of the Culdees of Brechin in the time of King William; although it is very probable that the lands and other privileges granted to them by the Abbes or Abbots of Brechin had formerly belonged to the Culdees. This may also have been the case with some of the churches and other gifts bestowed by the bishops of Brechin; as that see was founded by David I., and he always dealt very unceremoniously with the Keledei who came in his way. The Culdees of Brechin, who were established by King Kenneth III. about 994, however, survived the fall of many Culdee houses, and continued (in a manner, perhaps, modernised) to form entirely or chiefly the bishop's chapter during nearly a century after their suppression at St Andrews. By an early charter of King William he confirmed King David's grant of a market in favour of the " Bishop and Keldeis of the church of Brechine." (Brechin Chartulary, No. 1.) Their first appearance in the Arbroath Chartulary is as witnesses to Bishop Turpin's grant of a toft and croft at Stricathro before 1198. Their Gaelic names are " Bricius, Prior of Brechin; Gillefali, *Kelde;* Bricius, chaplain: Mathalan, *Kelde;* Makbeth, Maywen." Gillefali and Mathalan were probably simple

Culdees. The bishops of Brechin afterwards speak of them familiarly as " our Keledei." Their Priors, named Bricius and Malbryde, are successively witnesses to many of the grants by which the bishops of Brechin granted to the Abbey of Arbroath their churches of Old Montrose, Dunnichen, Kingoldrum, Panbride, Monikie, Guthrie, Katterine, with teind-fish on the Northesk, and others. A Dean of Brechin, as well as the Prior of the Culdees, appears before 1198 ; and about the end of the reign of King William the chapter of Brechin is found to be composed of " Malbryde the Prior, the Keledei, and *other clerks ;*" and in 1248, shortly before the death of King Alexander II., the Culdees disappear from the Bishops' chapter altogether, at least under that name ; as it is said to consist simply of " William, Dean, and Chapter of Brechin ;" so that by the middle of the thirteenth century we may conclude that the Culdees of Brechin, perhaps the last survivors of their order, had fallen before their more powerful rivals ; although some writers have believed that a few remnants may have survived during the next fifty years.

The Editors of the Chartularies of Arbroath and Brechin have noticed the existence of a singular class of secular Culdee Abbots about the time of the commencement of these records. Lawrence, son of Orm of Abernethy, who, as has been already stated, speaks of the lands and property of himself and his *heirs,* is, at the same time, styled by King William the " Abbot of Abernethy ;" and, without doubt, lived as a baron at Carpow (Kerpul), the old mansion or castle of the lords of Abernethy, while the real functions of the Abbot were practically performed by one of the Culdees who bore the title of Prior. So, in like manner, as early as about the time of the foundation of the see of Brechin by David I., the nominal head of the Culdee college of that place, the Abbot of Brechin had become a secular baron, styled sometimes Leod of Brechin and at other times Leod the Abbot, ranked among lay, but not clerical, dignitaries, and possessing, without doubt, the castle of Brechin and the most of the lands which had originally been given to the Culdee community. It also appears that the Abbots of Brechin were married, and transmitted their Culdee estates and their title of Abbot to their families. Donald, who styles himself Abbe or Abbot of Brechin, and who was grandson of Leod, granted certain lands to the Monks of Arbroath for the safety of the souls of his father Samson, and of himself and his heirs after him; and the Prior of the Culdees is among the witnesses. While in other charters of this period the Prior, as a clerk, takes precedence of this Donald as a laic among the witnesses. In 1219 John Abbe, the son of Malise, made a grant to Arbroath of firewood from his woods of Edzell, for the salvation of himself, his ancestors, and heirs; which is witnessed by Morgrund and John his sons, and Malcolm his brother. "John Abb de Brechin and Morgrund his son" were present at the perambulation of the marches of Kinblethmont on 23rd September 1219; and about the same time, or shortly afterwards, this Morgrund confirmed his father's grant, by a Deed which is witnessed by John Abbe and others. There were thus, from the time of David I. to William I., five persons successively bearing this title, which ultimately became the surname of the family, namely, Leod, Samson, Donald, John son of Malise, and Morgrund, with whom the race and family of the Abbes of Brechin disappear. Henry de Brechin, son of David Earl of Huntingdon, is the next person on record who soon afterwards takes his style from Brechin; and his descendants held it till the reign of Robert Bruce, along with the lordship or estate of Brechin, which may be supposed to be identical with the Abbacy or lands originally granted for the support of the Culdees.

Besides these lay Abbes of Abernethy and Brechin, there existed, as already noticed, an Abbe of Monifieth, and there was an Abbe of Arbirlot. The writs of Coldingham and other church registers afford similar instances of persons bearing this name or title at or subsequent to the fall of the Culdees.

From these and other notices, we learn that where large landed grants had been made to the Culdees, as at Dunkeld, Abernethy, and Brechin, the Abbot was allowed, as later Abbots and Bishops have since been usually allowed, to appropriate to himself the greater part (the lion's share) of their possessions, and to perform his church functions by deputy, while he gave his personal attention to the more stirring matters of state and military exercise. But the peculiarity in the case of Culdee Abbots was their marriage, and the transmission of their official lands along with the name of their office to their heirs; who having neither the desire nor ability to perform the religious duties in consideration of which the endowments had been made, were no more servants of the Church than were the lay commendators who obtained possession of church lands and tithes at the Reformation, four hundred years afterwards; and thus the gifts of the founders became alienated from their original pious purposes, and served only to enrich and maintain private families. There is no reason to doubt that the evil example thus proved to have been shewn by the heads of the Culdee houses was followed to a greater or less extent by their inferiors; and that in the latter years of their history there was too much ground for the charge made against them by their successors, the Papal Monks, that, "after the death of the Culdees their wives or children, or relations appropriated their estates, and even the offerings made at those altars whose service they neglected; a sacrilege which we should have been ashamed to mention, had not they not been ashamed to do it." The more narrowly the circumstances attending the extinction of the Culdees are examined, there appears the greater reason to form a very low estimate of their purity and efficiency for some time previously, and to suspect that it is distance which lends enchantment to the view which some writers have formed of them, as at that time self-denied confessors struggling for Christian truth amidst overwhelming foes. Although there is little doubt that piety and sincerity existed among the poorer members of the order (just as at a later period sincerity was found lingering among the poorer Papal Monks), the secularisation, both of the heads of the Culdee houses and of the inferior members of the order, help to explain the little sympathy which they received from King Alexander I. and his successors, who, we believe, were sincerely desirous to reform their National Church by the introduction of ecclesiastics then bearing in Scotland a character much superior in activity, zeal, learning, and perhaps even in purity of manners; although they afterwards sunk far below the Culdees in extortion, pride, secularity, error, idolatry, and profligacy. The monastic writings clearly show, for example, that the idolatrous deification of saints and angels did not exist among the Culdees. Their condition at this time also explains the helplessness of the acting Culdees when their possessions were attacked, and the want of assistance received from other parties throughout the kingdom in their struggles for retention of their ancient rights. It is also to be recollected that the custom, which appears so strange to us, of the children of the Culdees succeeding to their sacred offices and benefices by heirship, was part of an ancient system in Scotland, by which all offices, civil as well as sacred, became hereditary, and consequently sinecures, the incompetent heir sticking fast to the possession of the lands or benefice, but leaving the duties of the office to a stipendiary deputy, or oftener to a new official appointed and paid by the State. The last remains of this system in the civil department is scarcely yet abolished. The evils of such a system were seen in the state of the Culdees; but the idea of hereditary succession to office seems to have been then so strong, that the only effectual remedy for it was believed to be the application of a rule equally strange, namely, that the clergy should live and die bachelors, so that they could have no legal heirs to claim their benefices and official titles. The celibacy of the clergy had, as is well known, other plausible recommendations at that time; but a consideration of the corruption which had flowed from the hereditary succession of the early married clergy is necessary to explain how a law so unnatural and fraught with so many evils, as enforced celibacy, came to be submitted to and established over the whole of Christendom during several succeeding ages, until the wiser plan was devised of conferring office and benefice, not by heritage, but according to personal qualification.

These remarks on the Culdees may be fitly concluded, in a work on Arbroath Abbey, by an endeavour to give some answer to the question whether there were to any extent Culdee establishments at the neighbouring churches of Monifieth and Arbirlot.

With regard to the first of these churches it has been shewn, in the notice of the Abthaneries, that there existed at Monifieth a tract of land called *Abthein*, and also a person holding the title of Abbe for some considerable time after that church was bestowed on the Monks of Arbroath; and further, that the Culdees held land near the church in the time of Earl Malcolm, about 1220. These Culdees are styled by the Countess Maud simply as "the Keledei," without any indication that they belonged to another establishment; and it may on this account be naturally supposed that they lived and ministered at Monifieth church, which would in that case be, on a small scale, the church of a college like the early churches of Abernethy and Brechin. That Monifieth was a seat of the Culdees is the opinion of the writer of the Statistical Account in 1842, who adds that "when the old church was pulled down in 1812, and the foundations of the present house excavated, some remains of the Culdee edifice were discovered." This ancient collegiate establishment at Monifieth was very probably the origin and occasion of the choir which stood at the east end of the old church before its demolition, as mentioned in the Statistical Account of 1794; such a choir being a necessary and characteristic portion of a collegiate church. From these concurrent circumstances we are inclined to conclude, although not very confidently, that Monifieth is entitled to be ranked among the Culdee houses of Scotland.

The question as regards Arbirlot is involved in still greater obscurity. The church of that parish was from an early period ranked as within the diocese of St Andrews; and the bishops of that see claimed right to its revenues, or, at least, to its patronage. It was also situated within lands belonging to them, as the bishops possessed the lands of the parish which lay to the east of the Elliot water (on which the church stands) at an early period. Roger, who was bishop from 1188 to 1202, granted Arbirlot church along with others to the Abbey of Arbroath, but reserved to himself and his successors as bishops, "the lands of the church of Aberheloth." His successor, William Malvoisine, made a fresh grant of the church with its chapels, teinds, and oblations under a like reservation to him and his successors of the lands. The Arbroath Monks retained the patronage of the church till the Reformation; and the bishops of St Andrews continued to retain the lands in question during at least two hundred and fifty years after the foundation of the Abbey, as in the time of Abbot Panter they are styled "the bischoppis land of Sanctandros." They were part of the great regality of St Andrews; and after their subinfeudation were termed the barony of Arbirlot or of Cuthlie. But it appears from the Abbey records that, similar to Monifieth and Brechin, Arbirlot possessed its "Abbe" for several years after the church came into the hands of the Monks of Arbroath. Between the years 1201 and 1207 "Mauricius, Abbe of Abereloth," was a witness to four charters of Gilchrist Earl of Angus, by which he granted to the Abbey the churches of Monifieth, Murroes, Strathdichty, and Kirriemuir, and to a fifth charter in which he included the whole. Four of these deeds are at the same time witnessed by another Mauricius, who is styled "Chaplain of Abereloth," and who takes immediate precedence of the "Abbe;" their position being below the other clerical witnesses, and above the names of Adam Albo and Hugo de Benne, the two remaining lay witnesses. There is no further appearance of the Abbe of Arbirlot, unless he be the "Mauricius Abba," who is named among the lay witnesses to John de Montfort's grant of Katerlyn about 1212. The last "chaplain of Abereloth" on record is one "Galfridus," who is so designed, and is ranked under Nicholas of Inverpeffer, Roger of Balcathie, and other neighbouring landed proprietors, as a witness to Adam de Morham's grant of the church of Panbride in 1214.

Alongside of these obscure indications we may allude to the tradition that a religious house once existed at an old hamlet still known by the peculiar name of "the College" on the top of the north bank of the Rottenrow Burn, about a mile to the north-west of the present church of Arbirlot. The late Rev. Richard Watson, Minister of Arbirlot, alluded to this tradition in his Statistical Account of 1792, in the following terms:—
"A few years ago the remains of a religious house in the parish, whose ruins had been revered for ages, were removed. And although we cannot say at what time, or by what person it was built, yet from the accounts given of it we have reason to believe that it had been a Druidical temple." From the confusion in the minds of the illiterate as to Druids and Culdees, it is not

surprising, although in this instance, the one should be thought and spoken of in place of the other, by those from whom the minister may have derived his information. It is much more probable, however, that the religious house alluded to had belonged to the Culdees rather than the earlier Druids. The question, as already stated, is very obscure. But when the old Culdee title of "Abbe of Arbirlot" is taken in connection with the tradition and the name of the hamlet, all these circumstances concur to make it a point worth the further investigation of some antiquary as to whether it can be yet definitely proved that one of the many colleges of the Culdees formerly existed in this retired and secluded spot, or in the more immediate neighbourhood of the Kirktown of Arbirlot.

CHAPTER I.

THE TOWN OF ARBROATH AND ITS DEPENDENCIES.—1. ORIGIN AND CONDITION TILL THE FOUNDATION OF THE ABBEY. 2. THE HARBOUR. 3. FORMATION OF OLDER PORTION OF THE BURGH. 4. FORMATION OF NEWER PORTION OF THE BURGH IN THE ALMORY. 5. LOCAL TERMS IN THE TOWN AND NEIGHBOURHOOD.

I.—ORIGIN AND CONDITION TILL THE FOUNDATION OF THE ABBEY.

PREVIOUS to the erection of its Abbey, the history of Arbroath, if not fabulous, must be, to a great extent, matter of inference. We have seen no reference to its existence as a town or village earlier than the reign of King William the Lion, although its church (St Vigeans) is mentioned as existing nearly two centuries prior to the foundation of the Abbey. The high antiquity of Arbroath as a village or small seat of population, is proved by the form of its proper name "Aberbrothoc," which is said to be derived from "Aber," a very old British (but not modern Gaelic) word, signifying *mouth* or *opening*, coupled with the name of the small stream which here enters the sea. The word Brothock (formerly Brothac) has been stated to signify a red muddy stream. It has been written by Spottiswood, in his list of Religious Houses, and by others, in the form of *Brothe;* and it may be a point of inquiry for philologists whether our culinary word *broth* is not derived from the same original term. The word "Abrinca," given as one of the names of Aberbrothock in several Latin and English versions of Buchanan's description of Scotland, is obviously a misprint for its modern shortened form, Arbroath, as "Abrinca" was never known to have been used elsewhere as a genuine name. In certain old writings two singular terms have been applied to Arbroath *Abbey*, namely, *Monasterium Bujocense*, and *Aberbredock-kuidel*. These names seem to stand in need of explanation.

Coupled with its name, the natural situation of Arbroath indicates its existence as a settlement at a period long anterior, probably, to the introduction of Christianity into this part of the island. The natural fertility of the neighbouring fields, the salubrity of its air, the shelter afforded by its small creek on an otherwise iron-bound and exposed coast, and its convenience for fishing, would determine the selection of this spot as a residence for the settlement of some of the earliest inhabitants of Angus. But at this period, and for ages afterwards, it could only have been a collection of scattered huts or cabins, formed of wood or turf, set down without the slightest respect to order or arrangement; and possessing nothing approaching to the regularity of design which now characterises some parts of the neighbouring fishing villages. The inspection of any genuine highland villages at the present day shows that the idea of forming streets or continuous rows of houses did not enter into the architectural plans of our Celtic ancestors; and it has been truthfully remarked that although the names of numerous old towns and villages are derived from the Celtic languages, there is scarcely a street in one of them the name of which is not derived from the Gothic or Saxon tongues; thus showing that streets owed their origin to these later settlers on the east coast of Britain, who gradually pushed back the Celtic race, or at least the Celtic tongue, within the mountains in the northern and western parts of the island.

Like the neighbouring ancient churches of Inverkeillor, Arbirlot, and Panbride, the church of Arbroath was, long prior to the construction of the Abbey, erected about a mile distant from the shore, most probably for protection from enemies by sea and land through the privacy of its position. There is no reason to doubt that, previous to the time of the Keledei (the Culdees), a parish church stood where its modern representative stands, on a curious knoll, in the centre of a romantic and beautiful concavity, intersected by the Brothock and its two tributary streams, which meet at this point.

As was the case with almost all our more ancient churches, the first church of Aberbrothock (for the name of the Confessor Vigianus was not connected with it till after its patronage was acquired by the Abbey), would undoubtedly be constructed of wood, covered with heath or thatch. This structure would in process of time be replaced by one with stone walls and a straw-thatched roof—a long barn-like edifice, similar to the generality of our churches down till the end of the last century. During the existence of this fabric it is probable that St Vigianus, the hermit of Grange of Conon, was interred in the cemetery, at the beginning of the eleventh century; and that the monument mentioned by some of our annalists was erected to his memory. The carved figures found in the walls of the present church also obviously belong to this period. As for the original portions of the existing church, namely, a nave and side aisles with clerestorey or windows above the aisles, and short square tower—so rarely seen among Scottish parish churches—they have evidently been erected about two centuries subsequently to the foundation of the Abbey, and after the church had risen in importance from its contiguity to the great and opulent monastery in its vicinity.

The most important event in the early history of Arbroath is certainly its choice by King William as the site of the magnificent monastery which he determined to erect, nominally in honour of Thomas the murdered Archbishop of Canterbury, but in reality, in accordance with the spirit and fashion of his day, as a monument of his own beneficence to the great Papal Church of Europe, which by that time had almost absorbed the small and ancient Scottish Culdee Church, after a long struggle to maintain its independence. This institution was evidently begun and carried on by him as the great work of his reign, and as that which chiefly was to hand down his memory to succeeding ages. The selection of the site and commencement of the work, as will be afterwards explained, must have occurred a year or two previous to 1178. It is impossible to contemplate the natural situation of the monastery of Arbroath as it once stood, guarded with embattled walls, in all its grandeur—not dismantled, and surrounded, as now, with rival buildings—without admiring the wisdom and taste which directed the choice of such a site for this kingly establishment. It was planted on a dry and level plot of rich ground, having a never-failing stream of fine water running across it, within full view of the ever-varying ocean, and within a short walk of its shores, yet protected from the fierce eastern marine blasts by a range of gentle eminences, and enjoying a prospect which for extent and beauty could not be surpassed on the east coast of Britain—extending from the Grampians in the north, round by Craig Oul among the Sidlaws, Norman's Law among the Ochils, the Lomonds in Fife and Kinross-shires, the Lammermuirs in East Lothian and Berwickshire, to Holy Island on the coast of England. In the year 1742, when the ground within the precinct or sacred enclosure retained more of its original appearance, and was not covered with buildings as it now is, the Town Clerk of Arbroath thus refers to it: "There are many fine springs of water on the east side of the Inclosure, one of which was brought in lead pipes (part of them have been lately discovered on digging), for the service of the House; and the rest formed a canal which ran through the garden or close, as the whole does now. The soil is a brown clay of great depth, covered in most places with a black mixed earth, which drys immediately after rains, so that it affords pleasant walking in almost all seasons."

In tracing the progress of the town of Arbroath it is only necessary at this stage to state that at or previous to 1178, King William bestowed on the monastery, as the beginning of its large endowments, the village of "Aberbrothock, with all the shire thereof, and the church of the village, viz., Aberbrothock with its teinds and pertinents." The Shire of Aberbrothock seems to have been conterminous with the modern parishes of Arbroath and St Vigeans, not including the barony of Inverpeffer, nor perhaps the high land betwixt Parkhill and Kinnaldy, apparently afterwards bestowed by the name of Athenglass, and more recently termed the great muir of Aberbrothock. The King also conferred on the Convent the liberty to form a burgh on these lands, with a port, and a weekly market each Saturday; and provided that the burgesses of such burgh should enjoy all liberties and privileges of merchandise and otherwise equal to those possessed by other burgesses in the kingdom.

The Convent without delay proceeded to the erection of a Burgh of Barony under the Abbot, as its overlord or feudal superior. About 1180, or two years after the establishment of the monastery, Everard and Martin de Lundin, *burgesses of Arbroath*, are introduced as witnesses of grants to the Abbey. Toward the end of King William's reign, about 1214, two witnesses of a grant are described as Roger of Balcathie, and Nicholas of Wartria, *Provosts* of Arbroath. This term appears to have been applied at that early period to such magistrates as are now ordinarily termed bailies, without necessarily denoting *chief* magistrates. No "Provost" of Arbroath is again alluded to from 1214 down at least to 1646, although the two bailies of the burgh, with a large number of its burgesses, are from time to time named in the pages of the Chartulary. In the year 1394, when the harbour was beginning to be formed, the burgh possessed a common seal separate from the convent seal; and the names of its bailies were William Scott and Robert Eme, the latter of whom may probably have given a name to the piece of ground called Emeslaw. During the fifteenth century the burgh possessed two officials termed Sergeants, who are frequently introduced as witnesses to writings. These were probably the executors or officers of the law within the burgh, and servants of the magistrates.

After its formation into a burgh, Arbroath would to a limited extent follow the example set by other places in more southern counties, which had been formed into streets and regular towns by the settlement of enterprising and trading immigrants from England and the Continent. Thus the town of St Andrews shows that the plans of its streets were laid out with reference to the monastery,—towards which the three principal streets converge. And in a charter granted by King William's immediate predecessor, Malcolm IV., relating to the Trinity Church of Kilrimund, now the town church of St Andrews, he describes the inhabitants of that town as the Scotch, French, Flemings, and English, within the burgh. In further illustration of the mixed population of the lowlands of Scotland at that time, it may be added that the king addresses the same charter to all his lieges, whether French, English, Scotch, or Galwegians, in the country; that is, to the Normans, Saxons, Celts, and inhabitants of Galloway.

It is still a debatable point whether in the districts north of Tay the Gaelic or old Scotch was supplanted by the new or lowland Scottish dialect, previous to or about the Christian era, or not till so lately as the reign of Malcolm Canmore. There is reason to believe that lowland Scotch was the usual speech in the southern part of Angus, at least for some time prior to the foundation of

Arbroath Abbey. But it is apparent that during the reigns of David I., Malcolm IV., William, and Alexander II., from 1124 to 1250, many of the lands of Fife, Angus, and Mearns, still remained in the possession of barons, whose names indicate that they were of pure Celtic blood. Thus we have Angus MacDuncan, Malbryd Mallod, Duffscollock of Fetheressau (Fetteresso), Malmur MacGillemichael, Gilchrist MacFadwerth, Donald Abbe of Brechin, Gilbryd of Angus, Gilpatrick MacEwen, Dunachy, son of Gilpatrick, Gilys Thane of Edevy (Idvies), Malcolm, his brother, Dufsyth of Conon, Gilander Macleod, Gilescop Maccamby, Mauricius Macgeil, Phenich McPhenich, Donald son of Makbeth MacYwar, Duncan of Fernevel (Farnell), Madechin-MacMathusalem, Gille-colmi-Mach-imbethi-hywano, and Macmallothem Thane of Derucsin (Dairsie, near Cupar). It would not be safe, however, to conclude from this circumstance that these remaining lowland Gaels conversed in the Gaelic tongue; just as we know that the indisputable Gaelic names of many descendants of highland Gaels living among us are no evidence that the Gaelic is their vernacular language.

The strange and uncouth names of our Celtic ancestors, as given above, form a singular contrast to the names of the contemporaneous burgesses of Dundee, St Andrews, Aberdeen, and other burghs often found in the same documents; shewing clearly that the latter were not of Celtic, but of Gothic blood, and of Saxon and Norman extraction. After the application of Gaelic names had been abandoned by the royal descendants of Malcolm Canmore and Queen Margaret, they seem to have rapidly fallen into disuse among the barons of the lowlands. Other causes also tended to facilitate their extinction. Any one who observes how, even at this time, the landed estates throughout Scotland are purchased up by the successful and wealthy citizens of our large commercial towns, as these estates successively come into the market, will not have much difficulty in understanding how a great part of the lowlands came at an earlier period, as many of the estates are coming at the present day, into the hands of the latter class, to the exclusion of the former proprietors.

No direct evidence is obtainable from the Chartulary as to the foundation or existence of any particular part of the town earlier than the year 1303, a little before the accession of King Robert Bruce. Although it is probable that for a long period previous to that date the lower part of the present High Street existed under the name of the "Cowgate." And as the precinct walls could not have been finished till a considerable time after the erection of the Abbey Church, there are indications, arising from the line of the south-western part of these walls and otherwise, which lead to the conclusion that before their completion houses had stretched upwards along both sides of the High Street, perhaps as far as the head of Applegate.

But before noticing further the progress of the town as appearing in the monastic writings, it will be proper, in the first portion of the next section, to allude to and dispose of an interesting point, namely, the origin and formation of the *Harbour*.

II.—THE HARBOUR.

Considering the early erection of the village of Aberbrothock into a burgh of barony or regality, and the wealth and energy of the convent, it is surprising that no means were taken towards the formation of a harbour till the elapse of two centuries after the establishment of the Abbey, although King John of England, as is well known, had, so far back as 1204, granted to the Abbots, monks, and citizens of Arbroath, the privilege of trading to all the ports of his kingdom, except London, free of custom. Even in the time of the able and patriotic Abbot Bernard, in the beginning of the fourteenth century, Arbroath seems to have been almost without any trade. It is not till about the end of that century, when Scotland was slowly and feebly recovering from the disasters of the wars with England, that the interesting contract betwixt Abbot John Gedy and the burgesses, for the building of a harbour, appears on the pages of the Chartulary.

This document is titled a "Convention between the Monastery and the Burgh of Aberbrothoc of the making of a port," and bears the date of 2nd April 1394. According to Mr Innes' summary of its contents, it sets forth the innumerable losses and vexations, long and still suffered, for want of a port where traders, with their ships and merchandise, might land. On the one part it is agreed that the Abbot and Convent shall, with all possible haste, at their expense, make and maintain, in the best situation, according to the judgment of men of skill, a safe harbour *(portum salutarem)* for the burgh, to which, and in which ships may come and lie, and have quiet and safe mooring, notwithstanding the ebb and flow of tides. The burgesses, on the other hand, are to clear the space fixed on from sand and stones, and all other impediments, to fill with stones, and place the coffers required for the harbour, under the direction of the masters of the work; to find certain tools necessary for that purpose, namely, spades, iron pinches, and *tribulos* (perhaps hammers) at their own expense; the other instruments to be found by the Abbey. And because in the foundation of the harbour much labour and expense are required, more than the burgesses could bear, the burgesses shall pay to the Abbot yearly, three pennies of sterlings from each rood of land within the burgh, in addition to the three pennies now paid,—the additonal rent beginning the first year that one ship can safely take the harbour, and there have safe berth, notwithstanding the ebb and flow of the sea. And if it should happen, as God forbid, that the harbour in process of time fail, by negligence of the Abbot and Convent, or any accident, the payment of the three pennies shall cease till the harbour be repaired.

Like other contracts of that period, it is stated that this important writing was cut into two parts by a waved or indented line (which practice gave rise to the term *indenture*), and that the common seal of the burgh was appended to the portion retained by the Abbot and Convent, while the common seal of the Convent was appended to the portion retained by the burgh. The witnesses to the execution of the deed were—Lord David de Lindesay Lord of Glenesk, John de Lindesay Lord of Wauchope, knights; Master John Gray, Rector of the Church of Fearn; Sir or Dominie William de Conan, Perpetual Vicar of the Church of Aberbrothock (St Vigeans); Dominie John de Infirmary, Perpetual Vicar of the Church of Inverkeillor; Alexander Scrymgeour, Justiciar of the Regality of Aberbrothock; Phillip de Lindesay, John de Conan Lord of Cononsyth, Andrew de Melville, John de Setoun, Esquires; William Scot, and Robert Eme, Bailies of the Burgh; "and many others."

It is well known that the harbour formed by Abbot John Gedy lay to the eastward of the present harbour, and in front of the Old Shorehead, while the pier extended in a south-west direction from the foot of the High Street at Danger Point. It is understood to have been a wooden pier fixed in an embankment of large boulders, many of which remained in the line of the old pier till the formation of the new harbour in 1840. And it is probable that it was partly protected by the rocks to the eastward before the sea wore them down to their present level.

This harbour is again very specially alluded to in a charter granted by King James V., on 10th January 1529-30, renewing in favour of the Abbey the ancient grants of koket and customs made by his royal predecessors. From this writing it appears that the customs of Arbroath harbour had been collected by the Crown officers, in order to form part of the redemption money agreed to be paid for the deliverance of King David II. from his captivity in England about the year 1357, and that this alienation of the customs had been continued until the harbour, from want of repair, was in danger of destruction, to the impoverishment of the burgh.

About the year 1609 the community began to make extensive repairs on this old harbour, and which seem to have been carried on during the four following years. The town was divided into quarters, and supplied labourers by turns. The stones were conveyed in sledges, wheeled carts not being as yet used. The accounts of the Arbroath Treasurer, prefixed to a Court book of the burgh in Panmure House, contain a minute account of every item of expense connected with these repairs, including all the allowances for drink and music to encourage the workmen. Among many others the following entries have been selected:—" To the warkmen for drink at the setting up the first pannell xviij sh. (1610), Item, for tua gret yards to be ane slaid, and for carieng of stanes doun to the schoir, xx sh vjd ; Item, for making of ane slaid, and fitting up three slaids, xij sh ; Item, for garan naills to three slaids feet, v sh ; Item to the wrychtis that day that the pannell was sett, for thair denner, and the pypar and fidler for thair playing, at the baillies command, xiij sh iiij d ; Item, at the onputting of the barkettis on the morne, vj sh viij d. (1611) Item, for the warkmenis denner, menstrelleris, and officiaris, at the upsetting of the first pannell, xx sh ; At the upsetting of the secund, for drink to the thrid pairt of the toune, xxij sh ; Item, at that same pannell, for the warkmen, menstrelleris, and officiaris denneris, xx sh. ; Item, to the thrid pannel for drink to the quarter of the toune, xx sh ; and for the menstrelleris, warkmen, and officiaris denneris, xxx sh ; Item, for naills, schethis, ane deall, and warkmanship to sex barrowis, xiiij sh ; Item, the agricance with the warkmen to work the cors pannell ix sh ; Item, for drink to the warkmen the first day they began to work the pannell, vi sh; Item, at the lintling of every cupill of the said pannell, ane quart of aill, xxxii sh. * * * Item, to the menstrelleris for their wages, viij lib; Item, for foure gallonis aill to the haill toun, xxxij sh; Item, ten faldoum towis to the skaffoldis, xx sh; Item for mending of the sand-glass, ii sh; to the menstrelleris for St Thomas day and fyft day of August, xiij sh iiij d; for ane Lettre to the Conventioun of the burrowis, vi sh viij d; to ane stranger that convoyit the drume at St Thomas day, vi sh; To ane man that cam from the checker, vi sh viij d; For the timber hous, xl sh; For sugar quhen my Lord of Montros was maid burges, xvj sh; To Andro Chrystie for timber to ane new slaid, vii sh; For tua biustis of comfettis to Alexander Peter that nycht the Ladie Marshall was in David Ouchterlonies, xxvj sh viij d." In this manner the entries for barrows, nails, and sledges, appear during several years, mixed up with disbursements for candles to the kirk, repairs on the kirk, the North Port, the tolbooth, a wooden bridge at Horner's Wynd, and other incidental outlays as they occurred.

It is very probable that, as was the case at St Andrews, the trade of Arbroath had diminished about the time of the Reformation, in consequence of the desolation of the Convent, and that its subsequent revival was very slow. This is shown by the length of time and effort made in repairing the rude pier sixty years after that event, and by the circumstance that, while the Town Treasurer records his payments for the repair of the harbour, he does not enter the receipt of any harbour dues, although, he records at this period a source of revenue which does not now exist, namely, the "tak of the salmond fische at the watter mouth, xxiiij sh." About 1621 and downwards the "anchorage" was let, along with the town's customs, for a rent of £80 Scots, or thereby. The first "Schoirmaister" (Alexander Spink, elder) was appointed at Michaelmas 1624. Mr David Mudie, the Town-Clerk, states, in his account of Arbroath (written in 1742), that "this town had very little foreign trade till the year 1725, when they began to build a new harbour to the westward of the old, in which there was no safety for any vessels in winter storms. This work had been carrying on ever since at a vast charge for so small a town; and although it is not accessible for large ships, yet there are now belonging to the town about a dozen [vessels] of from 120 to 50 tons burden employed in trading to the northern colonies in America, to the Baltic, France, Holland, and Norway, besides smaller vessels employed in the coal trade and coasting." He adds, that in his time "the slate quarries, which ly within four miles of the town, afford outward cargoes to the coal barques, who find greater consumpt for coals (as they are free of duty), than they are able to answer, so that a great part of that commodity is brought here by strangers." This harbour—begun to be formed in 1725—was dug out of the dry land beside the ground which had been occupied by the Lady Chapel and its cemetery.

The history of the extension of harbour accommodation at Arbroath, and of its gradual increase of trade during the last and present centuries, does not lie within our immediate province.

III.—FORMATION OF OLDER PORTION OF THE BURGH.

As already stated, the first notice of any of the streets of Arbroath is in 1303, when Abbot John granted to Galfrid (Geoffry) Runeuld, son of Robert Runculd, burgess of Aberbrothoc, a parcel of land which belonged to the "office of our community, by the gift of the late Adam the Chancellor," lying in the street of *Covgate* (Cowgate) between the sun-dial which was made by Adam, the son of Martin, on the one part, and the lands of Lawrence Cryn on the other, for the yearly payment of twelve pennies, at Whitsunday and Martinmas, by equal portions. From the solemn specification here made of this solarium or sun-dial, it is likely that in these simple times it had served the burgesses as a public clock or time-keeper.

The next building charter recorded in the Chartulary refers to the same street; and by which Abbot Bernard, in 1318, granted a parcel of land in *Cobgat* to Galfrid Clulbydheued, burgess of Aberbrothoc, for twelve pennies of sterlings, as before. The name Cowgate, as applied to this street, has been lost for ages in common discourse, but its representative is still retained in the writings of the proprietors on the lower part of the High Street, under the altered form of Copegate. The Chartulary shows how the old name Cougate, (our fathers wrote their single *u* as we now write *v*, Covgate), successively appears as Cobgate, Copgait, and Copegate. Abbot Bernard inserted a clause in his charter, which is significant of his active character. He bound the feuar to build a house upon the land granted to him, with a front *according to the usage of the burgh*, within the first three years.

These writs seem to indicate a considerable degree of progress made by the small town at this period, both in regard to size and prosperity; it being kept in view that the largest Scottish towns in those days did not exceed in population what is now contained in an ordinary village. Several circumstances combined to give importance to Arbroath in the days of Bruce. From its northerly situation, its distance from the English border, and the intervention of the Firths of Forth and Tay, which would protect it from inflictions to which the more southern districts were exposed, it enjoyed comparative peace during the war of independence, although occasionally annoyed by the shipping of the enemy. A century had elapsed since the foundation of the Abbey, and all its principal and subsidiary buildings would by this time be erected. The monastic establishment would at that time be in the full vigour of manhood, in possession of all its great endowments, before they began to be alienated, and before the decrepitude of old age and misgovernment had overtaken it. But more than all, the Abbey of Arbroath was the stated residence of the patriot statesman, Abbot Bernard de Linton, who for a period of fully twenty years held the office of Lord Chancellor, under Scotland's greatest monarch, Bruce ; and he, on that account favoured Arbroath with frequent visits, and conferred on it many gifts. From writings still extant it is evident that Bruce was residing at the Abbey in February 1318, May 1319, March 1323, November 1325, and September 1328. There is no doubt that on these occasions he resided in what was then styled the Abbot's Hall, now known as the Abbey House ; and that there, in those trying and arduous times, he and his faithful and large-hearted Chancellor held many an earnest and anxious consultation regarding the means of securing Scotland's kingly independence in defiance of all her foes, whether English, Papal, or Scottish.

For the same reason we believe that the Abbey was chosen as the place of meeting of the great Scottish Council or Parliament in April 1320, which passed the famed declaration of national independence, framed most probably by the Abbot, and addressed to the Pope, and in which they stated their resolution to maintain Scotland free from foreign domination so long as a hundred of their number should remain alive, let his Holiness, or Edward of England, or even their King, Bruce himself, say or do what they might. Few, if any such documents have ever proceeded from the National Council of this or any other country, and the recollection of it ought to hallow the name of Arbroath Abbey and its noble Chancellor Abbot in the breast of every true Scotsman.

Immediately after the death of Bruce, in 1331, we find the Abbot and Convent granting feus of land in the street called Marketgate, which from the description given of it as running north and south, is the street now known by that name. It was still in process of feuing for a century afterwards, down at least till 1438, as appears from the descriptions in feuing charters of that date. But in the fifteenth century the records of the Abbey refer to a street running east and west, under the name of Aldmercatgate (Old Marketgate). This is not the street previously mentioned, which in reference to it seems to have afterwards acquired its formal written name of *New* Marketgate, still retained as its proper title in feudal writings. In the year 1483, a piece of land is described as lying on the *south* side of the Old Marketgate, which precludes the idea of its having been the Old Shore Head. A few years earlier, in 1474, a charter was granted by the Abbot and Convent to Nicholas Hornar, burgess of Aberbrothock, for his services, of five parcels of land in Aldmercatgate (Antiquum Fori). This Nicholas Hornar was a man of consequence in those days, as we find him a Bailie of Aberbrothock, presiding at a Brieve of Inquest, on 20th October 1483. He would, without doubt, erect houses on the land conveyed to him in the Auldmarketgate. And as the title of Marketgate had already been bestowed on the newer and more spacious street, which still bears that name, we may venture to assume that, from the inconvenience of applying nearly similar names to different streets, the older street or lane came to be ultimately spoken of as Hornar's Wynd, in commemoration of Bailie Hornar, the builder of part of its houses. Arbroath affords several more modern instances of this mode of applying names to streets.

In the fifteenth century the following old streets—including those already mentioned—are often referred to by the Chartulary, as in existence, and bounded partly by tenements or houses, and partly by lands or gardens, viz., Neugate or Newgate ; Seagate, called Segate, Seygat, or Vicus Maris ; Cowgate, called Covgat, Cobgait, or Copgate ; Auldmarketgate,—New Marketgate, or Novus Vicus Fori ; Ratounraw or Rattonraw ; Apilgate or Apylgate ; Lorburn, Lordburn, or Lortburngate ; Millgate, Mylgate, or Myllgayt, with the lands of "Grymsby." All these streets are described as being within the burgh at that time. The ground on the south side of Lordburn, on which the great tanwork now stands, was a garden, known by the name of the Greenyard. It was granted on 4th November 1505 as an endowment to the altar of St Nicholas in the Lady Chapel at the west bridge. A rent roll of the year 1455, to be afterwards alluded to, shews that before that time the Abbots had granted the feu-duties of many of the properties in these streets as an endowment to the Lady Chapel.

The milldam still known by the name of the "Mawkin Pool" is mentioned in 1457 as the "Water of Brothac, vulgarly called *Malkynnis Pvil*," a mode of expression which leads to the belief that the name is derived from the person who first formed the dam or pool for the service of the Burgh Mill. This may have been the father or other relative of Walter Makvnis or or Makwnys, a notary public who acted as clerk to the Abbey Chapter in the years 1494 and 1495. A John Makwnis is also named as a witness to an Abbey Charter on 25th September 1497.

The ground which lay on the south or east side of Malkin's Pool was called, four centuries ago, Cobbscroft, and was bounded on the south by the lands of Patrick Hagus, a person who also possessed houses and gardens in that upper part of the High Street, which was formerly styled the Almory ; some parts of which properties may have descended to him from William Haggus, a proprietor in that quarter about 1427, or thirty years earlier. These names seem to be the origin of the term "Haughhowssched" or "Haghousched," applied in the Abbey writs to a rood of land near the Brothock, about the years 1521, 1530, and 1534; and which term has descended to our own times in the shape of Haggis-yard, denoting a spot of ground at the point where the stream of Lordburn falls into the Brothock.

The point where Ladyloan and Millgate-loan meet at Gayfield was known in 1519, as it is still known, by the names of Touties Neuk, from its being the station where the keeper of the town cows blew on a horn, or *touted*, in order to bring them home from the Common. By a misprint in the initial letter, this locality appears in the published Chartulary as "Fowteys Nwyk." About the same period (1513) the Ladyloan is referred to under the name of "Our Lade Lyon" and "Our Ladylone," in relation to the chapel of the Virgin Mary, commonly called Our Lady. At this time a portion of ground on the north side of the Ladyloan belonged to the Priory of the Island of May in the Firth of Forth.

In the same year, 1513, "Brydokys Wynd" was the name of "the common gayt" which led westward from the Copegate. This wynd is not now known. Newgate had tenements on the west side, one of which, or a part of the road or grounds where it stood, then bore the name of "Bawtak." And at an earlier period the high bank called Boulzie Hill bore its present name, although slightly disguised under the forms of "Bowchishil" or "Bowlishil." There is, perhaps, some connection (which might be explained by those versant in the ancient game of football) between the terms Boulzie Hill and Baw-tak, the latter term denoting a point near the foot of the bank where one would be well placed for *taking the ball*.

All these localities noticed above appear to have formed part of the burgh at an early period; and to have been, with a few exceptions, feued from the Abbot and Convent before the death of King Robert Bruce. Very few original charters of building stances below Lordburn appear in the Chartulary after that date; and when once feued, the writs transferring the properties from father to son, or from seller to purchaser, do not generally appear in the Abbey records, and were probably entered in the burgh records under the charge of the burgh magistrates. In the century preceding the Reformation the principal information regarding tenements and streets in the burgh is to be obtained from those curious documents which detail the grants of tenements, or of annual rents from them, for the support of chapels or altars, such as the altars of St Nicholas and St Dupthacus in the Lady Chapel, and the altar of St Sebastian in St Vigeans' Church, of which notices will afterwards be given.

IV.—FORMATION OF NEWER PORTION OF BURGH IN THE ALMORY.

There is a considerable portion of ground, now ranked as within the royalty of Arbroath, which is nowhere described in the Chartulary as forming part of the burgh, down till 1536, or within twenty-four years of the Reformation. This is the eastern portion of the ground which had formed the Old Eleemosynary or Almory of the Abbey. The Almory grounds had originally extended alongside of the western part of the proper burgh and the Abbey precinct, reaching from the neighbourhood of the Mawkin Pool, along the ground now occupied by Panmure Street, the back of Lordburn, and up the west side of the High Street, or Almory Street, which it crossed north of Hamilton Green, by Hopemount, till it terminated at the boundary of the lands of Smithy-Croft (then called the Croft of the Master Smith or Master of Works), near the North Port. This establishment was in some respects separate from the Abbey, although dependent upon it, as many feu-duties were taken payable expressly for the

Almory and its Monks. It was situated beyond or outside the precinct of the Abbey; and it contained a chapel, which was sometimes styled the Chapel of the Almory, and sometimes the Chapel of St Michael the Archangel. This chapel appears to have been situated near James Street, and not far from the Almory Hall or Great House of the Almory; and it was reached by a lane or entry leading from the High Street, which at this part was called the Street of the Almory. On the 29th March 1467, Malcolm, Abbot of Aberbrothock, granted to John Chepman, Burgess of Aberbrothock, a charter of a piece of land lying in the Almory of Aberbrothock, betwixt the lands of Jacob Wyot on the south, and the house of the Almory on the north, and the gable of [the Chapel of] St Michael of the Almory on the west, to be held in perpetual feu, for six shillings, " to be given to us, or our Monks of the Almory, at two terms in the year: saving always our right of regality."

This is a specimen of those numerous writs recorded in the Chartulary, from which we see the progress of feuing that part of the Almory ground which is now incorporated within the burgh. This process of feuing appears to have commenced about 1423 with the ground on the High Street, immediately north of Lordburn, till it reached the house and enclosed garden of the Almory, where Mr Suttie's shop, house, and garden are now situated, and which remained unfeued till about the Reformation. The Almory House had a court or *close*, in which the alms were given to the poor: so that the Almory-close became the best known position of the establishment; and the neighbouring fields acquired from it the title of the lands of *Almerieclose*, which they still bear. There are instances of the Almoner's premises bearing this identical name of Almerieclose at Winchester and elsewhere. The feuing out of the Almory grounds was resumed on the north side of the Almory House; and about 1500 and afterwards, it embraced the grounds about Hopemount, lying to the north of the Homlow Green, now Hamilton Green. It is probable that the feuing was continued previous to the downfall of the monastic establishment in the year 1560. This may account for the circumstance that one part of the Almory grounds (the feued building stances), is now included within the burgh; while the remaining part of these grounds, viz., the stance of the Almory house and close, the Almory garden, and Almory *crofts*, not feued at that time, are ranked as extra burghal. It will also help to explain the indented and zigzag nature of the burgh boundary between the foot of Lordburn and the North Port, arising from the feuing of stances near the street under the demand for houses, while the grounds behind were reserved for the Almory gardens. We have had no means of ascertaining the time when, or the manner in which these grounds were annexed to the burgh, further than that the annexation must have taken place sometime previous to 1564, as in that year the bailies of Arbroath are found deciding as to marches at Almeriecloss. (Old Burgh Court Book.)

Whether the term Homlogrene or Homlowgreyn be derived from the hemlocks (vulgarly pronounced humlocks or humlos), which may have grown on it, or from the process of humbling barley, it is, perhaps, impossible to determine. But the locality in question bore this title at the beginning of the sixteenth century, and about forty years before the great family of Hamilton had any connection with the Abbey. The name Homlowgreen, still recollected by some of the older inhabitants as in use, is the only term recognised in the Chartulary, and had evidently suggested the corrupted term of Hamilton Green, by which it is now more generally known.

The Chartulary gives no indication that gates were then erected across the streets at Guthrie Port and North Port. The street now called Guthrie Port is simply described as the way leading to the water of Brothock. In the beginning of the sixteenth century persons of the name of Guthrie acquired the lands afterwards called Guthrie's Hill and other grounds in this quarter, from which circumstance it is probable that the port and street derived its modern name. Not far from Guthrie Port lay a piece of land known under the names of Guys-dub or Guys-Puyll (goose-dub or goose-pool), apparently near the present boundary of the burgh. The street leading by the North Port, towards Smithy Croft and Barngreen (which were then unfeued), is described in the year 1523 as "the common way leading to the great cemetery," showing that the present burying-ground, to the north of the great church, had been used for purposes of interment previous to that date. The original entrance to it appears to have been from the west—probably at the north-west corner, where some remains of an entrance are said to have been recollected by persons of advanced age. It is certain that before the demolition of the church and north precinct wall, there could have been no access to the burying-ground by either of the present modes of entrance. The lesser and more ancient cemetery—the special burying-place of the Monks—appears to have been at the south-east side of the great church, in the northern end of the green, still called on that account the Convent Churchyard.

This subject leads to the observation that, although the sites of the Town and Abbey of Arbroath formed part of the old parish of Aberbrothock (St Vigeans) long previous to the foundation of the Abbey, still there is no reason to believe that after that event the Abbey precinct, namely, the sacred plot of ground enclosed within the high walls, properly formed a part either of the parish of St Vigeans or the more modern parish of Arbroath. Like the precincts of other large monastic establishments, the precinct of this Abbey was held as extra-parochial, and free from tithes or other parochial burdens—in other words, this piece of ground formed a small parish by itself, of which the great fabric erected on its northern boundary was the Parish Church. There appears to be no other reason than the contiguity of this ground, and the grounds of Barngreen, for their being held as parts of the parish of Arbroath since the Reformation.

We have thus traced the process of formation of the streets of Arbroath from 1303 till 1536, when the published Chartulary terminates. Like many other old Scottish towns, Arbroath seems to have increased very little during the two succeeding centuries. With the exception of a few houses at Hamilton Green and Townhead, and some houses erected on the recently-formed streets in the Abbey precinct, the description given of Arbroath, as existing in the year 1742, by the Town Clerk, might almost suit its condition as to size in the days of Cardinal Betoun. He states that the town consisted of two parallel streets (High Street and Marketgate), with three or four bye-lanes or wynds, and a small street on the west side of the water (Millgate). " On the water there are two bridges of stone, one near the north end, another near the sea. The town doth contain about 250 houses, and 2500 inhabitants."

V.—LOCAL TERMS IN THE TOWN AND NEIGHBOURHOOD.

A few farther remarks on the titles of places in Arbroath and its neighbourhood may here be added.

It is very doubtful whether the now obsolete name of the lower part of the High Street, *Covgate* or *Cowgate*, has any relation to the name of cow. There is much more probability that it is derived from an ancient word *Ghov*, from which have flowed our terms *Cove*, *Covey*, *Cover*, *Covert*, *Covin*, *Couch*, and also our verbs *to Cow* and *to Cower*, with the word *Coward*, and the old Scotch epithets *Cowclink* and *Cowhubie*,—all these terms being descriptive of something hollow, hidden, low, or depressed. This is suitable enough to the character of the Cowgate of Arbroath, and also to the Cowgates of Forfar, Dundee, and Edinburgh, each of these Streets being in a hollow or low situation, under the shelter of neighbouring heights.

"That part of the High Street called the *Rottenraw*," is a phrase descriptive of the properties on the west side of the High Street from the Kirk Wynd to Lordburn. It was literally a row of houses facing the high wall of the Abbey which lined the street on the east, as may be seen in an old engraved view of the Town; and it first appears in the Chartulary in the year 1496 under the name of "the Rattounraw." The term *Rotten* is evidently a corruption of some older word. There are numerous instances of the same name, Rottenrow, in old towns and villages both in Scotland and England. The term has also been applied to farm tofts or hamlets, such as those of that name in the Parishes of Panbride and Arbirlot, and it is the name of a favourite drive at Hyde Park, London. Various solutions of the term have been given, but none of them are altogether satisfactory. It was suggested to Dr Jamieson that it might come from the German *Rot*, from which is derived their *Rotmaster* or master of processions, and might be equivalent to *Routine*, or *Retinue* Row, from the street being traversed by religious processions. But the name is found in situations where there was little chance of monkish processions being ever seen. A learned friend has stated to us that a similar term is derived from the Hebrew *Roshen*, which in Chaldee becomes *Roten*, and signifies "chief or principal;" and also that the Hebrew has *Rotzen* or *Rotzeen*, which appears in Chaldee as *Roten* or *Rotun*, and signifies "pleasure or delight;" and that he thinks it probable that the first derivation may be the real one, and that the second in course of time may have been combined with it, as has very often happened in the history of words. Without expressing a decided opinion, we would remark that this old word *Rotten* is only found in conjunction with *Row*, and never, to our knowledge, with *gate, vennel, road, street*, or *wynd;* and that the houses in Arbroath bearing that combined title seem to have been erected more continuously, and in a more regular manner, than those above and beneath them. Continuous rows of houses, as already remarked, were rarely found in ancient Scotland; and it is possible that the term Rottenrow takes its origin from some old word, whence have also flowed the German Rot (retinue or procession), and our words Rote and Rotation; and that Rottenrow signifies a row of houses or trees (as in an avenue) following one another, by rotation or in regular succession.

Lordburn is very probably a contracted form of *My Lord Abbot's Burn*, having reference to the stream which traverses it after passing near the residence of the Lord Abbot. It was formerly called Lordburn-gate, or the street along which my Lord's burn flowed.

The name of the neighbouring small street, although of a much more modern date, the Abbey Path, is to be accounted for by the steepness of its ascent. The road leading up the bank from Millgate Loan to the Common was also styled "The Peth" in the Town records. The term *path* was applied originally to a road leading up a steep bank or hill, only fit to be used by foot travellers, and came to be applied generally to steep and hilly roads, such as Cockburn's Path, Path-Condie, Path of Struie, Path of Kirkaldy; the latter having as in other instances given the popular name to the village of Pathhead. The translators of the Bible have employed the term as descriptive of ways which, in a religious sense, lead both upward and downward.

The thrashing barns of the Abbey had stood on the high and once exposed piece of land on the north of the burial ground, which bears the name of *Barngreen;* although the teind barns and granaries would, as at other monasteries, be situated within the precinct. But this enclosed spot would be unfitted for the winnowing process required at the thrashing barns. The *Fisher Acre* is believed to have obtained its title on account of its having been possessed by the person whose duty it was to supply the Convent with fresh fish, of which, in Lent especially, considerable quantities were used. The level and swampy grounds to the east of the precinct, were termed the *Hay Meadows,* from their crops of meadow hay; hence their popular name of *The Hays.* The land behind Springfield evidently at one time belonged to the Abbey *Punder,* the officer who had the charge of their woods and forests, and who derived his common title from the exercise of one of his functions in *poinding* or *impounding* cattle found straying on his grounds. This elevated piece of land is styled in the Chartulary *Pwndirlaw* or *Punderlawfeild*. The Convent seems to have had a separate Punder in charge of their woods at Kingoldrum, as the *Punder's Cairn* is mentioned as situated on the Abbey Lands in that district. About the year 1563 the Town Council of Arbroath committed the charge of their grounds to two officers, under the same name of Punders. The Cellarer's croft and Graniter's croft will be afterwards alluded to.

The neighbouring lands of Tarry are invariably written *Terre* or *Terry* in the old monastic records. The houses which had been erected on the site now occupied by the farm-steading of *Warddykes,* evidently derived their name from their situation near the fences of those grounds, which were termed by the Abbots with emphasis as " Our Ward." In 1526 the Convent leased for nineteen years " that piece of land of *Varddykyshyll* (Warddykes-hill) between the Abbot's Vard to the west, and the king's way which leads to Northterre;" and in 1531 the lands of Damsdale are described as bounded by the " Abbot's lands, commonly called *the Vard,* and the king's way, on the east." The Ward may have derived its title from its being kept or reserved in the Abbot's hands as a home farm, or as pasture fields for the horses of the Convent; as it does not appear to have been let to tenants like the neighbouring lands. The little valley betwixt the Dale School and the remains of the Wardmill-hill, is very accurately described in 1531 under the Saxon name of *Damysdayll*, that is, Damsdale, from the dams or pools which it contained. It seems to have afterwards received the name of Dammindale or Demmindale, that is, the valley of the little dam; and now often appears under the semi-satanic title of Demondale. The *Cunnyngayr* or *Cunynghill* lay to the west of Damindale, and now receives the name of Wardmill-hill. The original name is to be derived from its vicinity to the Abbey kennel or doghouse. The Abbot was one of the great barons of the county, and as such was bound to keep dogs, so that at certain seasons of the year he might join the other barons under the direction of the Sheriff " to chase and seek the quhelpes of the woolfes and gar slaie them." This law seems to have given origin to our county kennels or packs of dogs. *Cairnie* was the common name of a fortalice or castle, according to the Gaelic speech; of which there are innumerable instances, either in its simple form, as in this instance, signifying " the Castle," or combined with other terms in the forms of *Cairn, Carn, Car, Cars, Kar, Kern, Ker*. The fort which stood at Cairnie is to be ascribed to a period anterior to the settlement of the Gothic races in the district of Arbroath.

An Abbey writ dated 20th October 1483, refers to a cross at Arbroath, commonly called *Maldgraym*, which afterwards gave its name to a piece of grass land, termed in the Burgh Court Book *Madie Gramis Croce*. The grass of this plot was let for many years about 1620–30, along with the grass of Boulziehill, Seagate, and Newgate. It is probable that the cross had stood upon or near Hill Place, but we have not learned its origin. Besides the above and other terms which are alluded to in these pages, the writings of the Abbey contain the names of many other places in its vicinity, which are not known to or not used by the present inhabitants. Some of them are as follows :—The *Cowchour Bank*, apparently on the east side of Copegate ; the *Sandypots* and *Madyr Croft*, near Hill Terrace ; the *Tansy Bank*, and the Constables' Croft, belonging to the Constable of Dundee, near the Old Market Gate ; the *Dunnekin Garden*, near the Abbey ; the *Durward's Yard*, which had belonged to the doorkeeper or warder of the Abbey Gate ; the *Guest Croft* or *Guest Meadow*, where the horses of strangers were sent to pasture ; and the *Goose Croft*, where the Abbey geese were allowed to feed in the vicinity of the *Guysdub* or *Guyspuyll*.

CHAPTER II.

CONSTITUTION AND RANK OF THE BURGH.—ARBROATH AT FIRST A BURGH OF BARONY AND REGALITY: MADE A FREE BURGH BY SPECIAL GRANTS: TEMPORARILY REPRESENTED IN PARLIAMENT A.D. 1579: MADE A PROPER ROYAL BURGH IN 1599.

THE period when Arbroath was first constituted a Royal Burgh has been considered a question of some uncertainty. A minute examination of the Abbey writings is fitted to lead to the conclusion that, although from the time of King David II., in 1351—at least Arbroath enjoyed several immunities similar to those of Royal Burghs—it did not hold the proper rank of a Royal Burgh, with right of representation in Parliament, till after the Reformation. The position of Arbroath in this respect was somewhat anomalous; and may be compared to that of its Abbots, who, although not Bishops, were still entitled to use the style and insignia of Bishops.

By two charters of David II. the regality of Arbroath and its burgh were declared toll free, or protected against such local impositions as were formerly levied on all merchandise; and also custom fee, and entitled to pass their exports of wool, hides, tallow, salmon, &c., by virtue of its own koket, as fully as was the case with the king's burghs. There are not many instances, after the dates of these charters, of the use of the phrase "*our* Burgh," by the Abbot and Convent; the usual phrase being rather "*the* Burgh." The older expression was still, however, occasionally used, and occurred so late as 1534—within thirty years of the dissolution of the Abbey. Another fact which militates against the idea of Arbroath being then a royal burgh is that, down at least till the beginning of the sixteenth century, the Chartulary occasionally contains both original feuing charters, and charters of confirmation of tenements in Copegate, Rottenrow and other parts of the original Burgh, to be held burgage for feu-duties to be paid to the Monks of the Abbey. A list of these duties was recorded in the Town's books so late as 1605. The Monks have very carefully preserved and recorded King David's grants as to the great customs and right of koket. They have also recorded the charter of King James I. in 1436, confirming their privileges of regality; with the charter of King James V., in 1529, confirming their rights of koket and custom; and even the charter of King James IV., in 1495, by which he erected their village of Torry, near Aberdeen, into a burgh of barony, under the Abbot and Convent. But none of these writs afford any indication that Arbroath was removed from under the Abbot, as its overlord of regality, to the immediate superiority of the king, so as to raise it to the rank of a proper royal burgh. And we cannot conceive that a change of so much importance to the Abbey could have taken place without its being recorded in the Abbey archives, and without the effects of the change being indicated more or less distinctly in such subsequent writs as related to the Burgh in its connection with the lord Abbot and Convent. The burghs of Arbroath and Brechin do not appear among the twenty-two royal burghs mentioned in the Chamberlain's accounts for 1330, although Forfar, Dundee, Montrose, and even Fyvie in Aberdeenshire, there appear as King's Burghs.

It has been already stated that the registering of writs in the Arbroath Chartulary, so far as yet found, terminates in 1536. Lord John Hamilton, Commendator of Arbroath at the Reformation, and for many years afterwards, was next heir to the throne after Queen Mary and her young son James IV., and his possessions were the greatest and richest in Scotland. It is not till the sudden downfall of the powerful family of the Hamiltons, in 1579, that we have any evidence of the Burgh of Arbroath being represented in Parliament; while the neighbouring Burghs of Montrose and Forfar appear to have been represented, at least for several years previous to that time, as shown by the records of such Parliaments as contain lists of members. Upon Lord John's outlawry, in May 1579, the Abbacy and Lordship of Arbroath was held as vacant, and fallen into the hands of the king, who thus became the immediate superior of the burgh and other dependencies of the regality. And the formal forfeiture of Lord John, his brother, and many more of the same name, was determined on and carried into effect in the Parliament which met on the 20th October of that year. The Commissioner of Arbroath for the first time appears in Parliament on that day, when it is recorded that "David Person" compeared by his attorney; and the "Commissioner" for Aberbrothock is again mentioned in the session or sederunt of 11th November following. This representative is "David Peirsone, burges of Aberbrothock," who after the Reformation obtained the lands called Barngreen, for a feu-duty of eight shillings Scots. No representative of Arbroath as a burgh is recorded as appearing in Parliament again for a long period after this year. It seems to have been practically unrepresented even subsequent to the date of the Royal Town Charter, till the Parliaments of Charles I. in 1643 and 1644, when John Ochterlony acted as Commissioner. It is likely that, according to the feudal principles which regulated the constitution of Scottish parliaments, David Peirson's short-lived appearance for Arbroath in the year 1579, arose from the Burgh being dependent at that time on the king directly, as its feudal superior, or lord of regality; and as the parliaments were in one sense equivalent to the king's regality courts, and as Arbroath could not then be represented, as formerly, by Lord John Hamilton, the former subject superior, it became both the privilege and the duty of the Burgh to appear by its representative in the Great Court or Parliament of its immediate overlord the king.

But this state of matters did not continue long. Within a few years afterwards the Hamiltons were restored; and King James having, in 1599, granted a formal charter to Arbroath, as to many other burghs, regularly constituting it into a corporation, holding of himself as its immediate superior, he the following year granted a charter of the Abbacy, with certain exceptions, to James Hamilton (afterwards second Marquis of Hamilton), in whose favour it was, by Act of Parliament, in 1606, erected into a temporal lordship. In the preface to this erection the Abbacy is described as "being in his Majesty's hands, be resignation made thereof by the Abbot and Convent of the same;" although many years previously such personages had existed only in name, if not perhaps rather in imagination.

This view of the former burghal rank of Arbroath agrees in general with that expressed by the Town Clerk in 1742, with the exception that we have not seen that the king's charter expressly refers to any "old evidences of royalty." His words are — " It was certainly the *Abbot's burgh* before the Reformation, although the charter of erection from King James the Sixth, in 1599, bears a novodamus [*i.e.*, a renewal of a former grant], and assigns a reason that these old evidences of royalty [?] had been abstracted by the Bishop of Murray. Yet even before the Reformation the burgesses had considerable privileges, being under the immediate jurisdiction of two bailies, whereof one was chosen by themselves and the other named by the Abbot."

The Town Charter of Arbroath is commonly termed a Charter of *Novodamus*, although it contains something more than a mere renewal of former grants. This peculiarity is confirmatory of the views already expressed. The charter narrates very fully that "the village of Aberbrothock, *lying within the regality* of Aberbrothock, with the houses, buildings, lands, &c., of old, was erected, confirmed, and endued with all liberties pertaining to a *free* burgh, by our most noble progenitors." But it does not indicate that it had before that date held the rank of a royal burgh. After narrating the robbery of its ancient evidences from the Abbey, "where the said infeftments, ancient erection, and confirmations of the said burgh for the time were set in order," the king proceeded to "confirm the ancient erection of the said burgh into one *free* Burgh, with all privileges, &c., of which the burgesses and inhabitants, at whatsoever times bypast, were in possession." This part of the charter is thus only a *confirmation* of the old privileges of a free burgh of regality, with freedom of customs, &c., as formerly enjoyed. It is by the succeeding portion of the king's charter that Arbroath is made a *royal* burgh. In that part he says —"WE OF NEW *constitute, create, erect,* and *incorporate,* all and haill, the village and burgh of Aberbrothock, with all and sundrie buildings, lands, &c., in one free Burgh *and Burgh-Royal* of Aberbrothock, in all time coming." The framers of this Act had been well acquainted with the previous position of Arbroath, namely, that it had not been a royal burgh but a regality burgh, with free privileges of custom and other immunities.

The conclusions to which the various documents bearing on the point are fitted to lead is, that Arbroath, like several other Scotch towns, rose step by step from the lowest to the highest rank of burghs; in other words, that it was first a burgh of barony, then a burgh of regality, and latterly a royal or parliamentary burgh. This is illustrated by the manner in which the town is described, many years after it was known to have been a royal burgh, in the title-deeds of the families of Hamilton and Panmure. In some of these writings Arbroath is occasionally styled a burgh of *barony*, and at other times a burgh of *barony and regality*, the bailies of which the Earls of Panmure are stated to have the privilege of appointing. In illustration of the municipal position of Arbroath, it may be remarked that the neighbouring town of Brechin, although dignified with the title of city, in reference to its bishop and cathedral church, was not properly a royal burgh till so late a period as 1695, or nearly a century after Arbroath received its royal corporation charter. Before this time it appears to have been merely a burgh of regality, holding of the bishop as its overlord or superior, notwithstanding a charter of erection granted by Charles I. in 1641. While existing as a burgh of regality it had privileges of trade like Arbroath and other burghs which held of great church lords, and had the *burden* of sending a commissioner to Parliament. Its erection into a free royal burgh was under a reservation somewhat similar to the case of Arbroath, namely, a privilege to the Earls of Panmure of choosing one of the bailies of the burgh, who shall be "constable and justiciar therein."

The power of nominating one of the bailies of Arbroath was held by the Abbots till the Reformation. For some time after that event the Councillors of Arbroath elected annually a bailie for the *Town* and another bailie for the *Place* (the Abbey.) From 1617 to 1636 this bailie was nominated by a Commissioner of the Marquis of Hamilton; and he was, during several years thereafter, elected by the Councillors, till the power was resumed by the Earls of Panmure, as proprietors of the Abbacy. They retained this privilege till about the middle of last century, when it is said to have been renounced. The Act of Parliament abolishing the Scottish heritable jurisdictions in 1748 would be a sufficient cause for the renunciation of such a power, as that Act limited the functions of magistrates thus appointed to a fraction so small as to render the retention of such a prerogative almost worthless.

CHAPTER III.

SOCIAL STATE OF ANGUS IN THE TWELFTH CENTURY.—CONDITION OF RURAL AND URBAN POPULATION AT THE TIME OF THE FOUNDATION OF ARBROATH ABBEY: SLAVERY OF THE RURAL POPULATION: POWER OF THE BARONS: BURGHS AS FOUNTAINS OF LIBERTY AND PROGRESS: EMBLEMS OF BURGHAL FREEDOM IN ARBROATH AND OTHER BURGHS: EARLY STATE OF URBAN INHABITANTS.

WE, in this nineteenth century, can form but a very faint idea of the important privileges which the inhabitants of Arbroath five or six centuries ago would derive from the place having been created a free burgh of regality, nearly equal to the rank of a royal burgh. With this view, it is worth while to take a cursory view of the state of the population of Scotland before the erection of burghs, and of those who for sometime afterwards continued to live beyond the reach of burghal privileges. And, in connection with this subject, it may be allowable to allude to a few of the many bygone marks which served to denote the wide distinction which formerly existed betwixt the rural and urban populations. The following description applies chiefly to the eastern counties betwixt Forth and Spey, which formed the ancient kingdom of Scotland, and the centre of which was occupied by the district of Angus, rather than to the Saxon people of ancient Lothian, or to the then pure Celtic inhabitants of the Highlands, Galloway, and Nithsdale.

With the exception of the barons and the clergy, the extra-burghal inhabitants, about the time of the foundation of Arbroath Abbey, were, in every sense of the word, slaves. They bore the distinctive name of "thralls," or bondmen, in public documents. They were born slaves, and as such they lived and died. They were unable to hold any property in land; but they could be, and often were, conveyed along with the lands as part of the purchase. Several of the older grants to the religious houses conveyed lands, with all the men upon them, just as a conveyance or sale of land at the present time includes (if it does not express) all the hares, partridges, and grouse that may be found on it. They were also sometimes bestowed on religious houses separate from lands, and distinguished by their names, as slaves are still transferred in America. Cristine, daughter of Walter Corbet, gave to the Canons of St Andrews, to be held on their lands of the village of Maurice, Martin, son of Vnieti, with his sons and daughters *(nativi* of the late Walter Corbet), and that in perpetual servitude, with all generations of their posterity. (Reg. St Andrews, p. 262.)

The goods, liberties, and even the lives of these bondmen were as completely at the disposal of the barons or landholders as those of Russian serfs are at the disposal of the Czar's nobility at the present day. Their condition was even worse, for the kings of Scotland never possessed that power of controlling or meliorating baronial oppression which the Czar is now exercising. These barons often held the lives of their bondmen at little value; and they were enjoined by the old laws to have always in readiness pit and gallows, or gibbet and drawwell, for the more convenient hanging of men and drowning of women.

The powers of life and death over their vassals were retained and exercised by the great Scottish barons until a comparatively recent period, in their characters of judges and feudal superiors, long after they lost the proper powers of slaveholders over the persons of their dependents. Many memorials of the stern enforcement of this judicial power still remain in the names of the Gallow-towns, Gallow-dens, Gallows-knowes, Gallow-hills, and Widdie-hills, which are to be found near the seats of the old barons. The executioner was accordingly in those days an indispensable officer in every baron's court; and the piece of ground which formed his proper patrimony still bears in some places the name of the Hangman's Acre, or the Hangman's Croft. Although Scotland now possesses a population probably six times more numerous than in some of the periods to which we have referred, it is at the present time totally destitute of such an official. Hence the complaint which has been ironically put into the mouth of the Society for the Protection of Scottish Rights that, among other wants, Scotland does not possess so much as one hangman, and could not put a capital sentence into execution without borrowing such a functionary from England.

The state of bondage in which a large proportion of the inhabitants of Scotland were formerly held was more complete, and can be much better established than is generally believed. As in the Southern States of the American Union at the present day, laws were enacted containing punishments on all who connived at or abetted the attempts of the unfortunate "thralls" to escape from their bondage. Thus, one of the laws of King William, the same monarch who founded Arbroath Abbey, was passed for restoring back to their slave masters born serfs or thralls who had fled from their bondage. It provides that, "if any man holds a bondman who is kind-born (i.e., born a slave) to another, after he be asked of his true lord, he sall yield the bondman with all his goods and cattle, and sall give to the lord of the bondman double of all his scaiths by him sustained, and be in the king's mercy for his wrangous withholding." Even King David, the great patron and protector of the burghs, had no idea of giving liberty from bondage to his poorer subjects, unless within the ports of his royal burghs. One of the laws of this King, who was, in many respects, in advance of his age, reminds us of some of the American Negro laws. It provides that, " Gif ony man be fundin in the king's land that has nae proper lord, after that the king's writ be read within the king's mutes *(i.e.,* the king's courts), he sall have the space of fyfteen days to get him a lord. And gif that he, within the said term, finds nae lord, the king's justice sall tak of him to the king's use aught kye (eight cows), and kepe his body to the king's behoof till he get him a lord." Thus it appears the bondman was held bound to provide a slave master for himself. Not only was the poor thrall doomed to slavery all his lifetime, but his children were born slaves, and transmitted their thraldom through unlimited generations. The last remains of this state of things were found among the colliers and salters on the shores of the Firth of Forth, who remained in slavery till they were emancipated by Acts of Parliament not more than a hundred years ago. The following singular statement of a case, and the solution given to it, found among our oldest laws, exhibits a resolution to perpetuate the stigma and misfortune attendant on slavery to the slave's wife and children, even where the mother of his children did not belong to the doomed class of thralls. It bears the title of " A gude were of law," and proceeds in these set terms —" Twa sisters (freewomen) has an heritage as richteous heirs,—the tane taks a thrall *(i.e.,* marries a bondman) ; the tother taks a freeman : She that taks the freeman has all the heritage *(i.e.,* she shall possess the whole heritage) ; for this, that ane thrallman may have nane : The thrallman begets a bairn with his wife : The bondman dees : The bondman's wife, her husband (being) dead, gaes till her heritage, and enjoys it for her lifetime : The wife dees : (The question then arises,) May the son recover the heritage ? (The answer is,) Na, he shall nocht, for this (cause), that he was begotten with that thrall's body that is dead."

At the period of which we are speaking, the class of our population known by the name of farmers had no existence. For centuries afterwards, agricultural tacksmen were only known as "the puir people that labour the ground." They were almost all tenants at will; and such leases as they could obtain were looked upon as mere private arrangements, to be set at nought on any change in the proprietor's position, or any transference of the property. Their goods were liable to be seized for the proprietor's debt, because they were situated on his lands, and were also liable to be carried off, for the same reason, by escheat or forfeiture if he was convicted of rebellion or other crimes. Even in the case of a private sale of the estate, the purchaser had power to disregard the leases of the tenants, and turn them off as soon as he entered on possession. This continued to be the case down till the reign of King James II., in 1449, when the Parliament "ordained, for the safety and favour of the puir people that labours the ground, that they and all others that has taken, or sall tak, lands in time to come frae lords, and has terms and years thereof, that, suppose the said lords sell or annalie that land, the takers sall remain with their tacks unto the issue of their terms, whas hands soever these lands cum to, for sicklike mail as they took them for." A short view of the principal steps by which the emancipation of the Scottish peasantry from their original state of feudal thraldom was effected, will be given in a note appended to this volume. (See Appendix No. I.)

Barbour, the old Scottish poet, understood something of the condition of Scottish serfs, whom he terms "thrylls," as appears from the following lines:—

> "And thryldom is weill wer than deid,*
> For quhill a thryll his lyff may leid,
> It merys† him, body and banys,
> And dede anoyis him bot anys:
> Schortly to say, is nane can tell
> The haille conditioun of a thryll."‡

* Well worse than death.   † Mars or ruins.   ‡ Barbour's Bruce, Book I.

Such was the state of the rural population of the Lowlands of Scotland about the time that Arbroath came into historical notice by the planting of King William's princely Abbey in its vicinity. But it is well known that the barons and great landlords of Scotland often made their powers to be formidably felt by the monarch on the throne, their professed superior, as well as by the poor vassals, who were both really and professedly their slaves. To obtain a counter-balance to these powers, and having witnessed the wealth and enterprise which the free towns of the Continent had introduced into the states where their liberties were protected, King David made it his object to establish as many such corporations as possible in his kingdom. He erected many of his towns and villages into free burghs, holding of himself, and hence styled burghs royal. From the influence of his example, the Abbots and other great lords of regality formed their villages into burghs, holding of them, and styled burghs of regality; while the barons erected the hamlets near their castles into burghs of barony, with privileges more or less extensive.

The nature of the inducements held out by King David for men to settle in his burghs, as well as the contrast between the freedom of a burgess, and the bondage of what was then styled an upland man or thrall, will be best understood from the following two specimens of his enactments. The first provides that, "Gif ony man's thrall, baron's or knycht's, comes to burgh, and buys a borrowage, and dwells in his borrowage a twelvemonth and a day withoutyn challenge of his lord or of his bailie, he sall be ever mare free as a burgess within that king's burgh, and enjoy the freedom of that burgh.' Another is in these terms: King David statutes that all burgesses "suld be free through all his kinrik, as weil be water as be land, to buy and to sell, and their profit for to do, withoutyn ony disturbance, under full forfeiture: the which are under his firm protection."

From these, and many other illustrations which might be given, we may come to understand something of the force and point of such expressions as " the freedom of the burgh," and " the liberties of the burgh," which occur so frequently in the documents connected with every municipal corporation in Scotland. At the time when these phrases were adopted, they truly described the existing state of burghs as distinguished from the extra-burghal territory. Within the bounds of the burgh was the domain of liberty and freedom; beyond these boundaries lay the domains of thraldom and servitude. The burgesses were both proud and jealous of their liberties; and to mark these the more distinctly, they built ports or arched gateways over the public thoroughfares at the points where they crossed the burgh boundaries. Of such gateways the inhabitants of Arbroath are still reminded by the names of the North Port, Guthrie Port, and West Port, erected apparently some time after the Reformation; and such ports remained in many burghs till within the last century. The town treasurer's accounts for 1608 contain various charges for the repairs of the North Port during a pestilence which was then prevailing. The ports were not intended to serve as defences against assaults from without, so much as to be visible badges of the political and social distinction between those who lived on either side of the structures, for very few of our Scottish towns appear to have been surrounded with walls or fortifications fitted to withstand a siege.

These ports were frequently associated with spectacles of a nature so loathsome and melancholy that the recollection of them makes us less to regret the demolition of our town-gates. These were, first, the lepers (" the lipper folk"), who were not " tholed to thig" within the burghs, but were allowed on certain days of the week to sit at the ports and receive alms from the passers-by. This continued to be the case till the reigns of the Jameses. They were also the places where the heads and limbs of malefactors, offenders against the State, were exposed to rot and blacken in the sun. This barbarous practice continued till the Revolution of 1688. The heads and hands of the Covenanters, smeared with tar, were the last of these dismal relics which were publicly exhibited at our burgh ports; but this was done in the southern and western districts of Scotland rather than in Forfarshire.

Another distinctive badge of the burgh was its market-cross, or according to the ancient orthography, its *mercat croce*. While only a portion of our Scottish burghs possessed ports, every burgh, even the smallest burgh of barony with its seven or eight score inhabitants, had a cross. And the cross, like the freedom of the burgh, was in those days not a name but a reality. It was not a mere circle of stones in the pavement, but a pillar with its upper part formed like a Latin cross, and often having for its basement a series of three or four stone-steps, either round or polygonal, and arranged in a pyramidical form. The most primitive market-cross now existing is perhaps that of the village of Dull, in Perthshire. In the more important burghs the steps supported a building of considerable size, generally octagonal in form, and containing a staircase leading to a platform, surrounded by a parapet or railing. These buildings sometimes exhibited considerable taste, as in that of Aberdeen still existing, and in that at Edinburgh foolishly demolished. The proper cross or pillar in such cases was erected in the centre of the platform; and the platform was a convenient position for heralds, officers, and public speakers. When crosses fell into disrepute, at the Reformation, the arms of the cross were cut off, and the stone generally now appears (where market-crosses yet remain) in the simple form of a round pillar surmounted by a unicorn. The mutilated stone unicorn which is said to have surmounted the cross of Arbroath was very lately, if it is not still, to be seen in the garden of Mr Andson of Friockheim. We have not been able to learn the precise construction of the

Cross of Arbroath, which stood, not at that part of the High Street where three successive town-houses have been built, but almost at the foot of that street, not far from the Old Shore Head. When printing was unknown, or but sparingly used, town crosses were objects of importance. They were the points from which all edicts and proclamations were published. The acts of the Scottish Parliament had to be read and proclaimed at the crosses of at least all the King's burghs, until which time they were not held to be in force; and (which appears strange to us) they were not even then considered to have full legal effect if the proclamation was met at that moment by a counter protest, at the instance of any party who considered his rights to be compromised by the law so proclaimed. Our history affords several instances of stealing marches in order to get an obnoxious law proclaimed before its opponents could be ready with their protest.

In the vicinity of the market cross were the merchants' shops, then termed booths, with their fronts open to the street. The goods were withdrawn into the inner part of the building at night, and reëxposed in the morning. Arbroath does not now seem to possess any houses built on this plan, although numerous instances may be found in some other towns. One of these booths was always used as the place for collecting the tolls or customs of the burgh, from which use the name of Tolbooth is derived. The magnates of the burgh naturally assembled at the Tolbooth for public business; and the place of confinement for delinquents, as a matter of convenience, was constructed there. Hence the original term, first formed to denote an open shed or booth for the receipt of custom, came afterwards to be the name of a town-house, and is now known as the old-fashioned and somewhat obsolete title of a Scotch jail.

To us who have seen the peculiar privileges of burgesses accounted of so little value as to have been abolished by Parliament without a solitary voice raised in favour of their retention, it is interesting to look backwards through a period of seven hundred years to the time when these privileges were first obtained, cherished, watched over, and guarded with such jealous care. The apathy with which we have witnessed their abolition might have been caused by a knowledge of evils arising out of the abuse of such privileges, greater than the advantage derivable from them, or from indifference to the cause of liberty and freedom itself. A better reason can however be assigned for the modern depreciated estimate of burghal privileges. In early times the burghs, like wells and reservoirs in a dry and thirsty land, were highly prized and carefully protected, as the only fountains of freedom in the midst of an enslaved and depressed population. But when the wilderness becomes a pool of water, and the dry land is turned into water springs (to borrow a metaphor from the Sacred Scriptures), when water can be readily obtained anywhere and everywhere, then particular fountains will necessarily lose their comparative high value, and cease to be objects of anxiety. So, in like manner when, in consequence of the merciful spirit of Christianity, and the diffusion of wise and liberal political principles, the inhabitant of every village and hamlet now enjoys as much personal and political liberty as could be secured to an ancient burgess, these corporation privileges, however valuable in themselves, and venerable as the first fruits of freedom, have lost their comparative importance, and have ceased to stand in need of statutory protection,—not because the burgess has in any respect sunk down from his proud position to the lower level of the upland man or thrall, but because every upland man throughout the kingdom has risen to the level of the once envied platform of the burgess or king's freeman.

If the condition of the Scottish peasantry generally about the time of the formation of burghs was, as we have seen, very melancholy, the state of the inhabitants of these burghs themselves was not by any means to be envied by us who live in times of greater freedom and higher civilisation. The glimpses we obtain of their manners exhibit that jealous care of small possessions, and vindictive punishment of the least aggressions upon these, which is characteristic of a poor people, together with the comparatively little value put upon human life which characterises a barbarous people.

The following excerpts from the burgh laws will help to illustrate the first part of this remark. By one of these it is provided that—" Gif a burgess or ony other halds swine or other beasts through the whilk the neighbours taks skaith, the swine fundin in the skaith withouten ony keeper following them, may weil be slain, and made escheat, and eaten after the law of the burgh." Another provides that—" Gif ony finds gait or geese in his scaith (*i.e.*, doing mischief to his property), he sall tak the heads off the geese, and fasten the nebs in the yird, and the bodies he sall eat,—the gaits, forsooth, he shall slay and hald the bodies for escheat." The "statute of theft" is an illustration of the low value of human life in former times. It exhibits an extraordinary gradation both in the crime and the corresponding punishment, in the following terms—" Gif ony be tane with the laff of a halfpenny in burgh, he aught to be dung through the toune; and frae a halfpenny worth to four pennies, he aught to be mair sairly dung; and for a pair of schone of four pennies, he ought to be put on the cukstool, and after that, led to the head of the toune, and there he sall forswear the toune (*i.e.*, he shall swear to leave the town for ever); and frae four pennies till aught pennies and a farthing, he sall be put upon the cukstool, and after that, led to the head of the toune, and there he that took him aught to cut his ear off; and frae aught pennies and a farthing to saxteen pennies and a halfpenny he sall be set upon the cukstool, and after that led to the head of the toune, and there he that took him aught to cut his other ear off; and after that, gif he be tane with aught pennies and a farthing, he that taks him sall hang him. Item, for threttie-twa pennies one halfpenny, *he that taks a man may hang him.*"

There are documents found among our old laws showing similar gradations as to crimes against the person. By one of these the life of a man may be compounded for by "nine score kye; and another contains the following item in a valuation put upon all sorts of assaults—" For a man's life, twelve mark." There is more agreement between these two apparently contradictory modes of valuing human life than is seen at the first view. By the first, the life of a poor thief is forfeited through his stealing thirty-two pence halfpenny. By the second, the rich criminal is allowed to redeem his own life when forfeited for murder, by one hundred and eighty cattle. Two shillings and eightpence halfpenny were accounted of more value than the life of the thief who was unable to redeem himself; and one hundred and eighty cows were accounted fully equivalent to the life of the victim if his murderer was wealthy enough to be able to give them.

CHAPTER IV.

ARBROATH FROM 1440 TO 1640.—DEPRESSION OF SCOTLAND IN THE FIFTEENTH CENTURY: CIVIL BROILS: CHAMBERLAIN AIRES: SUBJECTS OF INVESTIGATION: CONDITION OF CRAFTSMEN: ARBROATH AT THE REFORMATION, AND AFTER ITS ERECTION INTO A ROYAL BURGH.

WE have to regret the scanty notices afforded for the history of Arbroath during the dominion of the Romish Church, when the little burgh was overlooked in consequence of the contiguity of its gorgeous neighbour the monastery. Boyce, the historian, who was born in Dundee about 1465, does not even so much as name Arbroath in his general description of Scotland.

The period which intervened from the reign of Robert Bruce till the Reformation may be fitly termed the dark ages of Scottish history, when, instead of the surplus wealth with which the country abounded before the death of Alexander III. (as shewn by the sumptuous abbeys and cathedrals erected previous to that melancholy event), the demon of war ravaged the land, followed by its never-failing attendants, famine and pestilence. During these unhappy times, the population decreased, trade became almost unknown, lands formerly cultivated were allowed to run waste, all improvement was arrested, and the central government became weak and contemptible through the poverty of the royal estate, and the short reigns and comparatively long minorities of the kings of the Stuart line. And, as the royal power was diminished, the irregular and usurped powers of the great barons increased; and they, being generally wholly illiterate, unable to fill up their spare time by reading or other polite studies, and despising, through fashion, every peaceable occupation, were never pleased except when engaged in the prosecution of some feud or broil.

One of our historians, Lindsay of Pitscottie, in describing the state of matters about 1439, during the minority of James II.,—a melancholy period,—says, " Albeit thir three plagues and scourges reigned amongst us [dearth, pestilence, and war], yet nevertheless some men made them never to mend their lives, but rather daily became worse; diverse others that complained upon the enormities that they sustained got little or no redress; wherefore the people began to weary and curse that ever it chanced them to live in such wicked and dangerous times." That Arbroath did not want its full share of these calamities may be fairly concluded from the occurrence of the fierce and bloody skirmish which took place, on a Sabbath day in January 1445-6, at its gates, between the partizans of the Lindsays and Ogilvies, when contending for the Bailiery of the Abbey, of which an account, often quoted, is given by the same historian. It was occasioned by the Convent having removed Alexander Lindsay, eldest son of the Earl of Crawford, afterwards known as the "Tiger Earl," or "Earl Beardy," from the office of Bailiery, on account of his expensive habits, and the substitution of Alexander Ogilvy of Inverquharity in his room. Besides that given by Lindsay, there are several other original accounts of this barbarous specimen of Scottish party warfare. But perhaps none of these are more quaint or graphic than the following, which Mr Innes has transcribed from the Doric vernacular of the Auchinleck chronicle :—
" The yer of God MCCCCXLV., the XXIII. day of Januar, the Erll of Huntlie and the Ogilbeis with him on the ta part, and the Erll of Craufurd on the tother part, met at the yettis of Arbroth on ane Sonday laite, and faucht. And the Erll of Huntlie and Wat Ogilbie fled. And thar was slane on thair party, Schir Jhon Oliphant, laird of

Aberdalghy, Schir William Forbes, Schir Alexander Barclay, Alexander Ogilby, David of Aberkerdach, with uther syndry. And on the tother part, the Erll of Craufurd himself was hurt in the field, and deit within viij. dayis. Bot he and his son wan the feild and held it; and efter that, a gret tyme, held the Ogilbys at great subjeccioun, and tuke thair gudis, and destroyit thair placis." It has been said by some writers that upwards of five hundred men fell in this encounter. Sir James Balfour (Annals A.D. 1445) gives the number of soldiers slain as two hundred on Ogilvie's side, and one hundred on Lindsay's side. Their graves have been, from time to time, found below the surface of the ground on both sides of the Brothock. The skulls and other bones which were recently disinterred in the course of excavations made at Orchard Street, were probably the mutilated remains of some of these combatants.

The following account of the Battle of Arbroath, extracted from a MS. account of the family of Hamilton, in Panmure House, contains some particulars not given elsewhere:—" About this tyme that great difference fell out between the Earle of Crawfoord and the Ogilbies: for the Earle his eldest son, Alexander Lyndsay, purchased from the Abbott and Convent of Abberbrothock ane right to the Bailliary of that Abbacy, but was keept out of the possessione thereof by Alexander Ogilbie, whose tytle theirto was said to be equall if not better than his. This enmity kendled to such a flame, that upon aither side they assembled their friends in armes. The Ogilbies calleth the Lord Huntley to their assistance and the Lyndsays called the Hamiltons to theirs. Frequent meetings having been made to calm and reconcile maters betwixt them, and nothing being aggreid upon, it was resolved at last to decyde the cause by ther swords. The Earle of Crawfoord, being then at Dundee, posted in all haste to Aberbrothock, and came there just as both parties are ready to begine the fight; and he, designing by calmness to take up the quarrell, went too forwardly to demand a parlic with Alexander Ogilbie for his sone. But before he could either be known or heard, he was encountered by a commone soulder, who thrust him in the mouth with a spier, which laid him dead upon the ground. This sudden accident did excite both parties, the one for victory and the other for revenge, which occasioned a most cruel and bloody fight. The victorie fell to the Lindsayes. Alexander Ogilbie, being sore wounded, was taken and brought to the Castle of Fenheaven, where he dyed. The lord Huntley escaped by the swiftness of his horse. Ther wer slaine on the Ogilbies syde John Forbes of Pitsligoe, Alex. Barclay of Gartlay, Robert Maxwell of Tilling, William Gordoune of Borrowfield, and Sir John Oliphant of Aberdagie, of the better sort. Ther wer few of qualitie lost on the other syde, besyde the Earle himselfe, whose loss wes extreemly regreatted."

Referring to the same period, Lindsay adds :—" After this there followed nothing but slaughter in this realm, every party ilk one lying in wait for another, as they had been setting tinchills for the slaughter of wild beasts." A later historian (Tytler) justly asks, " What must have been the state of the government, and how miserable the consequences of those feudal manners and customs which have been admired by superficial enquirers, when the pacific attempt of a few Monks to exercise their undoubted privilege in choosing their own protector, could involve a whole province in bloodshed, and kindle the flames of civil war in the heart of the country ?"

In such a period it were vain to expect much prosperity in a place like Arbroath, which at that time did not exceed the size of one of our ordinary villages, although enjoying the rank of a burgh of regality, with commercial privileges equal to those of royal burghs. From its singular position in these respects, it is not easy to ascertain whether or not it was placed under the jurisdiction of the Chamberlain of Scotland, and was subject to his periodical visitations, like the proper royal burghs. As these burghs were considered in a special manner under the king's superintendence, the actual exercise of that superintendence was committed by him to his chamberlain, one of the great officers of State, whose office has been long since abolished. He had power to investigate into and redress all known grievances and corruptions within the royal burghs. For this purpose he made regular circuits or journeys, which were termed the Chamberlain Aires, most probably from the corruption of the Latin word *iter*, signifying a journey.

In those times, previous to the invention of printing, there was no publication of *blue-books*—these ponderous, voluminous, and expensive reports, in which are detailed at great length the results of Parliamentary Committees and Royal Commissioners on almost every department of enquiry in our own days. But we have fortunately a singular document still preserved; believed to have been compiled about the end of the thirteenth century, detailing the manner in which the Chamberlain was to conduct his investigations; with an account of the points to which his attention was to be directed, and the faults and delinquencies of all classes (from the bailies down to the beadles) which he was to enquire into. The records of the Chamberlain Aire are valuable, chiefly on account of the views they afford to us of the manners and customs of our fathers. It has been said that the Chamberlain Aire was not well liked by the burghs, and we are not surprised at their dislike.

We cannot resist the temptation of giving a few notices of the points into which the Chamberlain enquired, leaving it to modern burgesses to decide for themselves how they could stand the ordeal of a Chamberlain Aire at the present time. Although some of the following excerpts have been printed in a popular form, they are in general unknown except to antiquarian lawyers; and it is hoped that those to whom they are familiar, will excuse their repetition for the sake of the many to whom they are new. Thus—" Of the manner to challenge the bailies" —the Chamberlain was to examine whether they stood chargeable with such delinquencies as—" That they do nocht richt evenly to puir and rich : That they let them to do richt (they prevent themselves from doing justice), through favour, hatrent, or love of persons : That they tak gifts for the richt and law to be done, or left undone : That they seek (search) nocht the burgh lauchfully for lipper folk to be furth put : That they gar nocht walk the burgh on the nicht be sufficient walkers : That they gar puir folk walk and nocht rich." The two last points refer to the old " watch and ward," the tenure or service which burgesses were bound to render for their possessions; and which are highly indicative of the insecurity of life and property during the early history of our burghs. In explanation of this waking or watching, one of the old burgh laws provides, " that of ilk house within the burgh, in the which there wons ony that in the time of waking aught be reason to come furth, there sall ane wachman be halden to come furth, when that the wakstaff gais frae door to door, wha sall be of eild (of age), and sall gang till his wach with two wappons, at the ringing of the curfew ; and sae sall wach wisely and busily till the dawning of the day. And gif ony hereof failzie, he sall pay four pennies — out-tane widows ;" meaning that widows shall be exempted from this duty.

There were no excise laws in Scotland for a long time after this period. But as the brewing of ale was largely carried on, a set of officers named " aill tasters" were appointed to taste the ale of every brewing ; and thus, having put it to assize or trial, were to pronounce whether or not it was fit to be sold at the standard price. The Chamberlain was to enquire into their conduct on the following points :—" That they are nocht ready at the forthputting of the token for to taste aill ; That they are nocht ready to taste as oft as the brewster tuns: That they fars (fill) their wames in drinking within the house, whereas they should stand in the middle of the street, before the door, and send ane of their fallows in with the beddel, that sall choose of what pot he will taste, the which he sall present till his fallows, and they sall discern thereupon after the assize put to them: That they mak nocht the assize of aill, but say, simply, it is gude or it is evil." These officers were also called "gusters," from the old word *gust*, signifying taste. It was likewise a fault attributed to them, "That, whereas they suld but ance taste the aill, they drink our meikle, through the whilk they tine their gust and are drunken." Then follow some of the faults of brewsters. "They gar nocht the aill be tasted or it be sauld: They put nocht furth their aill wand to certify the tunners of the aill as they sauld: That after the aill be tasted by the tunners they tun new again: That the pots that they have contains not sae meikle clear aill withoutyn berme."

The gentle craft of shoemaking was also to be enquired into. But it is necessary to bear in mind that in these primitive times the shoemaker purchased his hides in a raw state, and tanned and curried them for himself. The points of enquiry regarding "soutars" were:—"That they buy bark and make schone otherways than the law has ordained, that is to say, that the horn and the ear should be like lang: That they mak schone, boots, and other graith of the lether or it be barked (*i.e.*, before it be tanned): That they sew with false and rotten thread, through the whilk the schone are tint before they be half worn: Whereas they should give their lether guid oil and taulch, they give it but water and salt: They work it or it be curryed in greit hindering and skaith of the king's lieges."

If the sutar was addicted to the above five faults it appears that the tailor stood chargeable with the following seven sins:—"That they mak our meikle refuse and shreds of mens claiths, sometimes for haste and sometimes for ignorance: That they tak pieces and shreds to sleves or other small things: That they mak men's garments otherways than men bids them: That they sew with false graith: They brek men their days, or (as it is sometimes written), They keep nocht their day to ilk man: They mak them maisters before they ken the craft in great skaithing of the king and the people: They work on haly days, against the law of God."

Of the challenge of wobsters (weavers), it is found:— "That they mak our lang thrums: Whereas they tak in with weights, when they give it out they mak it donk and weet with water, casting things thereon to gar it weigh, and there-through halding out of it to themselves a grit quantity: That they tak ae man's yarn and puts in another man's web for haste." In some old burghs almost every third or fourth tenement is described as having been at one time a malt work. Malt was made to a very large extent, both for home-brewing and for exportation. The malt-makers were to be challenged among other points, that "they steep nocht their bear enough for grit haste in the makin of it: That they reik it on the kill." Saddlery was an important branch of business in former times, when there existed no mode of travelling except on foot or on horseback. The Chamberlain was to enquire as to saddlers as follows:—" That they mak saddles of green timmer, whereas they aught to be made of withered and dry: That they fasten them nocht fast, nor binds them with leather and glue, as they aught to be: That they knit to their saddles evil harnessing, false bridle-bits and stirrups, through the whilk mony men are hurt or slain: That they hald nocht their days that they mak to men."

There is reason to believe that at this period the little town of Arbroath was honoured with the presence of much more aristocratical society than it now possesses in these days of its bustling commercial activity and increasing population and wealth. The high rank of its abbots, and the constant visits which it received from kings, ecclesiastical dignitaries, and nobles made it a fashionable winter residence for many of the more opulent neighbouring landed proprietors, whose "lodgings" are often incidentally referred to in the Abbey records, and may be yet identified on consulting the titles of properties situated near the middle of the town. Some of these mansions were enlarged or reconstructed subsequently to the fall of the Abbey, which was largely used in the furnishing of materials.

About the time of the Reformation the municipal affairs of Arbroath were managed by two Bailies and a Common Council, which varied from nine to fifteen members, elected every year at Michaelmas. At the same time various other sets of officers were elected or appointed, and filled by members of the Council and other burgesses. These were called Lyners, Dykprisers, Flesh-prisers, Tunners of Ale, Punders, Depositors or Treasurers, and "Kepars of the kees of the comon kest." The Burgh Court of Arbroath was at that time regularly held every fortnight, and in which a great amount of business was transacted. In these courts the Magistrates, sometimes by themselves, at other times with concurrence of the Council, and on important occasions with advice of the "haill neighbours," enacted laws and regulations regarding the burgh lands and grass, the state of the streets, the prices of provisions, measures to prevent pestilence, and other matters concerning the welfare of the burgesses. They tried offences against these laws, matters of debt, and disputes of all kinds, for which they impanneled juries consisting of nine, eleven, thirteen, or fifteen members; and visited offenders by injunctions to ask forgiveness of the injured party at the market cross, and sometimes by fines, banishment from the town, or loss of burghal freedom and share of the common lands. These proceedings are very distinctly detailed in a Court Register Book, extending from 1563 to 1576, which affords an interesting picture of the state of the burgesses at that time. This record gives a favourable view of the moral condition of the inhabitants of Arbroath at the period in question. The criminal charges tried before the Magistrates consist chiefly of calling names and menacing one another, or disturbing the town or the neighbours, with numerous instances of that old-fashioned specimen of ill nature, *lawburrows,* and a few instances where the quarrel had come to blows. About forty years afterwards, however, a considerable number of fines (unlaws) were exacted from persons convicted of drawing swords or dirks in their quarrels, and sometimes for shedding blood. But we have found no instance of an offender being tried for theft or drunkenness, or any of the more serious crimes.

After Arbroath was made a royal burgh it was during many years governed by two Bailies and other twelve Councillors, assisted by Lyners, Dykprisers, Flesh and Skinprisers, Overseers of the flesh and meal markets, Shoremasters, Constables, and Officers, while the lord of Arbroath was represented by his resident chamberlain. These burgh officials were elected annually at Michaelmas, when the bailies had " laid down the wand of justice and removed themselves furth of judgment." The Burgh Court became a court of record for the registering of deeds, but ceased to contain entries of those petty trials of offences which render the earlier records interesting. The Convention of Royal Burghs met at Arbroath in the year 1611 ; and, besides other expenses, cost the town £6 Scots for wine, £4 Scots for ale, fourteen shillings Scots for a peck of flour baken into bread, and five shillings Scots " for ane pund of butter to the bread." The clock (knok) and bell seem to have been placed in the church steeple about the same period. When the town was visited by noblemen, ladies of rank, or provosts of other burghs, they were treated with wine and boxes of confections; and the burgesses were entertained by minstrels on St Thomas' Day and other festivals, at the public expense. The Town Records at this time are chiefly filled with entries of the admission of burgesses. These entries shew that all the neighbouring landed proprietors, as well as many in Fifeshire and Kincardineshire, with the ministers in the vicinity, and numerous freemen of Edinburgh, Cupar, Dundee, Forfar, Montrose, and Aberdeen, became burgesses of Arbroath during the period after it attained the rank of a royal burgh till about 1639, when the civil commotions commenced. After 1647 a long blank of nearly seventy years ensues, during which the Town Records seem to have been lost. The existing Council Minutes are believed not to extend continuously farther back than the early part of last century.

PARISH CHURCH—OLD TOWER AND SPIRE.

CHAPTER V.

ERECTION AND STYLE OF THE ABBEY BUILDINGS.—DATE OF COMMENCEMENT: MIXTURE OF NORMAN AND EARLY ENGLISH ARCHITECTURE: STAGES IN THE PROGRESS OF BUILDING: SUCCEEDING STYLES OF ARCHITECTURE SHEWN IN THE BUILDINGS.

IT has been generally supposed that the erection of the buildings of the Abbey of Arbroath was only commenced in the year 1178, but it is probable that the commencement was one or two years earlier. King William, the founder, returned from his eighteen months' captivity in England on 8th December 1174. Thomas á Becket, an early friend of William's, was killed on 29th December 1170, and was canonized in 1173; and we find that by 1178 a church was built at Aberbrothock, which, in that year, was dedicated to his memory; and a company of Tyronensian Monks of the rule of St Benedict, with an Abbot, were brought from Kelso, and solemnly installed in the Abbey, in presence of the King, the Bishop of Aberdeen (the bishopric of St Andrews being vacant), with the Archdeacon of St Andrews,—" to bless the Abbey"—the Bishop elect of Brechin, the Prior of Restennet, and many other grandees. All this could not have taken place in the year 1178, as is stated in the Abbey writs, unless the eastern part of the great church, and certain houses for the dwellings of the Abbot and Monks, had been previously erected. Wynton, the Prior of Lochleven, in his " Cronykil," says that the Abbey was founded by King William, on the 9th day of August, although he is otherwise mistaken by placing the event nineteen years too late. His words are:—

> Of August that yhere the nynde day,
> Of Abbyrbrothoke the Abbay,
> The Kyng Willame, in Angus,
> Fowndyt to be relygyws.
> In the honoure of Saynt Thomas,
> That Abbay that tyme fowndyt was,
> And dowyt alsua rychely,
> Thare Monkis to be perpetually.

By this time the King had conferred on this Abbey of his favourite Saint (whose aid he was in the habit of invoking in the time of his captivity) the village of Arbroath, with the lands now forming the parishes of Arbroath and St Vigeans and the Parish Church. It is probable also that the church and parish of Ethie (Athyn) were granted about the same period. The best idea of the progressive gifts to the Abbey is to be obtained from the papal bulls granted in 1182, 1200, and subsequent years. (Chartulary, vol. I. pp. 151-160.) We also learn from Hollinshed and others that the greatest nobleman of the district—Gilchrist, Earl of Angus—having, under the influence of jealousy, strangled his wife, who was the sister of King William, was proclaimed traitor by the King, and deprived of his great possessions, a considerable part of which was soon afterwards conferred on the Abbey. These gifts probably consisted more or less of the territory of Athenglas (near Kinblethmont), and the estates or shires (now the parishes) of Dunnichen and Kingoldrum, and which, with the parishes of Aberbrothock and Ethie, continued to form the principal part of the Abbey possessions during all its history; for the numerous grants of lands, churches, teinds, fishings, saltworks, tenements in burghs, &c., subsequently made by King William and his nobles, and by kings and subjects in the three succeeding reigns, although very valuable, were not equal to these tracts of fertile lands given by him at the time of the foundation.

These large grants of land had enabled the erection of the Church and other Abbey buildings to be completed in a comparatively short space of time. King William in a journey from the north, "came by the Abbey of Aberbrothoke to view the work of that house, how it went forward; commanding them that were overseers and masters of the works to spare no costs, but to bring it up to perfection, and that with magnificence;" and afterwards he "was earnestly occupied in the advancing forward of the building of Aberbrothoke." (Hollinshed.) The consequence was, that the Church begun previously to 1178 was sufficiently advanced in 1214 to be the burial place of the royal founder, who died on 4th December of that year, and was interred in the choir before the high altar; and the erection of the south transept was completed in time to admit of the interment, in that part (before the altar of St Catherine), of Gilchrist Earl of Angus, who was advanced in years at the date of the foundation.

It was the general custom in buildings of this kind to begin with the east end, and finish the choir with as little delay as possible, for the performance of worship. The central tower and transepts, or cross arms, were then added; and a temporary wall being built toward the west, between the tower and nave, the extension of the church was often arrested at this point, for a time, or (as in the case of the late Trinity College Church in Edinburgh), for ever. The architects then added the greater part of the nave or western portion of the Church, and commonly made another pause before completing it, by the erection of the west front with its towers. The point where such a pause occurred in the construction of Arbroath Abbey, may be yet easily discerned on the south wall of the nave, at the west end of the cloisters.

The Abbey Church was probably finished in 1233, or about fifty-five years after its commencement; in which year, during the reign of Alexander II., it was again dedicated. It may be remarked that the neighbouring cathedral of St Andrews was in course of construction during no less than one hundred and sixty years, having been begun about the year 1158, and not finished till the year 1318. A comparison of the remains of the Cathedral with the great Church of Arbroath affords a curious confirmation of these dates, and would almost by itself demonstrate, to one versant in Gothic architecture, that the church of St Andrews was commenced at least twenty years previous to the church of Arbroath, and continued a considerable way according to the earlier style, and that its western part was constructed long after the magnificent western front of Arbroath church had been finished. The substitution of what is termed early English for Norman architecture, including as a principal feature the substitution of tall lancet-headed windows (without stone mullions) for round-headed windows, took place during the last quarter of the twelfth century; and these twenty-five years are accordingly termed in England the transition period. This period witnessed the erection of very many splendid ecclesiastical fabrics, and a great improvement in the style of masonry. Thus the eastern part of St Andrews Cathedral, being planned and commenced before this period, had only round-headed windows (nine of which were in the east gable), according to its obvious original construction, while Arbroath Abbey, not being commenced till the change began, has narrow lancet-headed windows without mullions, intermixed occasionally with the older round-headed arch, from the east gable even to the great west door; shewing that the transition period of intermixture of the two styles had been continued in Scotland later than in England, and during the early part of the thirteenth century. The cathedral of St Andrews exhibits three separate styles in succession—first, the latest Norman, then the early English, and lastly what is termed the decorated style. The style of the Abbey Church of Arbroath, on the other hand, is wholly of the "transition period" betwixt the first two styles here mentioned, and consists of the remains of the Norman style, with the early English prevailing. The church also exhibits a marked improvement in the quality of the masonry during the fifty-five years which elapsed between the erection of the chancel and the western towers, as may be observed on examination of the beautiful masonry of the great buttresses in the court behind the Abbot's house.

At the time of the erection of Arbroath Abbey, Gothic architecture was in the full vigour of its early manhood. The early English style is specially marked by grandeur, dignity, and simplicity in its general design. Its decorations were limited in number, and severe and chaste in character; and it was not hurt by an overload of meretricious and useless ornaments which have often marred the beauty of expensive Gothic churches constructed in later periods. The Abbey Church of Arbroath possessed most of the grand features which may yet be seen in many of the Abbey and Cathedral churches in England, of which a noble specimen is exhibited in Westminster Abbey, an erection begun in the reign of Henry III.

The small fragment of what had evidently been the Chapter House (vulgarly called the *pint stoup*) shews that it was erected in a style similar to that of the church, and at the same time. And it is to be supposed that other indispensable buildings, had they remained—such as the refectory and fraters' hall—would have exhibited further specimens of the same style. But every vestige of these buildings has been swept away.

The Abbey Church was finished some time previous to the introduction of what has been termed the third or decorated style of Gothic architecture, of which a modern specimen is supplied to Arbroath in the new Episcopal

Chapel. But the remains of the great gate called the *Pend*, exhibit in several features an approximation to that style, and show that this building was erected some time after the completion of the Church. The vestry (commonly called the Chapter House) was built by Abbot Walter Paniter, betwixt 1411 and 1433, and its south window is in the decorated style, with mullions; and can easily be distinguished from all the windows of the original Church. By this time the fourth or perpendicular style of Gothic architecture had been adopted in England, where many beautiful specimens of it may be seen. But its introduction into Scotland was retarded by the poverty and misery into which the country had been plunged by the wars of independence, which almost put an entire stop to the erection of great and costly churches similar to those founded in earlier and happier times.

RUINS OF ARBROATH ABBEY.

CHAPTER VI.

HISTORY OF THE ABBEY BUILDINGS.—ACCIDENTS TO GREAT CHURCH DURING THE ROMISH PERIOD: CONTRACT FOR ROOFING THE CHOIR: DAMAGE DONE AT THE REFORMATION: GREATER DESTRUCTION SINCE THAT PERIOD: OTHER CONVENTUAL BUILDINGS, ECCLESIASTICAL AND CIVIL: PRECINCT WALLS AND TOWERS: RUIN OF THE BUILDINGS.

THE buildings of Arbroath Abbey had to contend with many enemies, even during that period which may be termed their lifetime of nearly four hundred years, from 1176 to 1560, among which, besides the tear and wear incident to a period of such length, we must reckon the elements of wind and fire, accidental and intentional, and assaults both from English shipping and from the fierce barons of Angus.

During the melancholy year of 1272, on Saturday of the Octaves of the Epiphany, at midnight, a sudden and violent wind from the north, with hail, tumbled down houses and lofty buildings; and fire breaking out in consequence, burnt the church of Arbroath and many others. Hector Boyce adds that church towers were burnt, and that the bells (made of precious materials) were partly broken and partly melted, the most remarkable of which were the bells hanging in the towers of the church of Arbroath, and that the church was consumed along with them.

We do not know if the difference of form in the upper parts of the western towers of the Abbey Church is to be traced to this event. Whether they were both originally constructed after one model in their upper parts it is now impossible to say, but it is evident that, at a comparatively remote period, the upper portion of the north-western tower had either fallen or been taken down, and that this tower was rebuilt and carried up to a greater height than the southern tower appears to have reached, while the remains of the south tower exhibit no traces of a change from its original construction.

During the troubles of the wars of independence, and the contentions between David Bruce and Edward Baliol, the situation of the Abbey exposed it to the inroads of foreign enemies from the sea. One of the writs in the Chartulary also incidentally states that Abbot John, the immediate predecessor of Abbot Bernard, was carried captive to England as a prisoner of war. In the narrative of a grant, connected with the church of Monifieth, made to the Abbey by William Bishop of St Andrews, of date 11th May 1350, he stated that the "church of the monastery of Arbroath, placed on the brink of the sea, had suffered almost irreparable injuries from the frequent assaults of the English shipping," and that the grant in question was made to enable the repairs to be completed. Connected with these vindictive attacks by the English, it must be recollected that it was Abbot Henry of Arbroath who courageously delivered to Edward I. of England, in 1396, John Baliol's renunciation of his allegiance, and that it was in the buildings of this Abbey that King Robert Bruce assembled that famed Parliament, the members of which asserted the independence of their country, and declared their resolution to maintain their freedom at all hazards. It is not surprising, then, that the King of England's naval commanders had a quarrel with the Abbey of Arbroath.

In the year 1380 the great church was again set on fire. The Bishop of St Andrews ascribed it to the instigation of "the Devil, the enemy of the human race;" and authorised the Abbot to distribute the monks of the convent among other religious houses, until their own church should be repaired in the roof of its choir, nave, and transepts. The roofs thus destroyed by fire, were most probably those of the high central aisles, as the side aisles bear marks of having been arched or vaulted with stone. Resistance to this ordinance was to be visited with excommunication and imprisonment; and two monks and two squires were appointed to collect and levy the dues and rents of all the lands and churches of the monastery beyond the Mounth (that is, beyond the Grampians), and in Mearns, Angus, Fife, and Strathearn, to be expended in repairs by the master of the works, under the advice of the Abbot. The Abbot was also enjoined to restrain his own expenses, to receive no guests, but to live solitarily and privately in his own chamber; and each monk was to be content with twelve merks yearly for food and clothing.

It was several years afterwards, however, before these repairs were finished, and not at least previous to 1395, the year succeeding that on which Abbot John Gedy contracted to build the harbour. This is shown to have been the case by a document in the Scottish language, being a contract betwixt Abbot John and the Convent, and William of Tweeddale, plumber, burgess of St Andrews, for "theking the mekel quer with lede." The great choir was probably the wide part of the church immediately to the east of the transepts, opposite to the vestry. This contract is dated 16th February 1394, or, according to our reckoning, 1395. The contractor is taken bound to thatch the great choir, and gutter it all about with lead, for which the Abbot shall pay him thirty-five merks at sundry terms as he is working, but five merks shall remain in the Abbot's hands till the choir be thatched and parapeted with stone; and, when this is done, he shall "dight" it about with lead sufficiently, as his craft asks; and he is then to be paid the five merks, and a gown with a hood. The contractor and the Abbot are each to provide a labourer till the work is ended. The

Abbot is to find all the material, and the contractor is to have threepence, and one stone of each hundred, for his trouble in fining the lead; and each day that he works he is to have a penny for his luncheon. The indenture was then cut into two parts, and one-half given to each of the parties, after receiving the seal of the other party.

This is the earliest document in the Chartulary expressed in the Scottish dialect; and it possesses no little interest, not only as shewing the condition of workmen at that time, but also as exhibiting a genuine specimen of lowland Scotch nearly five hundred years ago; during which long period it is surprising to find that it has undergone so few changes. After making allowance for antique spelling, there are not above three words in this indenture, which are not still in ordinary use. As an excellent specimen of old Angus Scotch, we give it entire:—" This endentur boris wytnes that the yer of grace MCCCXCIIII. [1394-5], the xvi. day of the moneth of Feveryer, this *cunnande* [covenant] was made betwene Johnne Abbot of Aberbrothoc, of the ta part, and Wilyam Plumer of Tweddale, burges of the cite of Andirstoun [St Andrews], of the tothir part; that is to say, That Wilyam Plumer sal theke the mekil quer wyth lede, and guttyr yt al abowt sufficiandly wyth lede, for the quhilkis thekyn and gutteryn the Abbot sal pay till him xxxv. marcis at syndry termys, as he is wyrkand; and of the xxxv. marcis, v. marcis sal dwel style in the Abbotis hand quhillys the quer be thekyt and *alurryt* [battlemented] al abowyt with stane, and quhen it is allurryt about with stane he sal dycht it abowt wyth lede sufficiandly, as his craft askys; and quhen he has endyt that werk he sal be payt of v. marcis and a gown with a hude till his rauarde. Quhilk Wilyam Plumer sal fynd a man on his awn cost, and the Abbot and Convent a man alsua of thar cost quhil the werk be fullyly endyt. The Abbot and the convent sall fynd al maner of gratht that pertenys to that werk quhil is wyrkande. Willam sal haf alsua for ilk stane fynyne that he fynys of lede iijd. [three pennies], and a stane of ilk hynder that he fynys til his travel; and that day that he wyrkis he sal haf a penny till his *noynsankys* [luncheon]. In the wytnes of this thyng to the ta part of there [thir] endentur to the Abbot and the Convent for to dwel the selis of John Brog and of John Prechurrys, burges of the burgh of Abirbrothoc, are to put; the tothir part anens Wilyam of Tweddal, plummer, the comoun scle of the chapyter of Abirbrothoc remanys selyt. Dowyn and gyffyn the yer and the day of the moneth before nemmyt." William Tweeddale finished his plumber work about fifteen months after the date of this contract. On 21st May 1396 he granted a receipt to the Abbot for £20 sterling, paid to him for the "architecture of the great choir," and in full of all his claims for purifying or fining the lead, for his "nonesankys," and the gown with the hood, as specified in the indenture. The Latin words "architectura magni chori" in this receipt seem to be used as equivalent to "theking the mekil quer" in the Scottish indenture. Did the term *architecture* at this period denote the art of constructing arched roofs?

It has been said that the Abbey Church was again more or less damaged and burnt in 1445, on the occasion of the encounter between the partizans of the Lindsays and Ogilvies already referred to. The Hamilton papers (Maitland Miscel., iv. 96) bear that the English council reported to King Henry VIII. that one Wishart, among other enterprises, undertook that a body of troops, to be paid by the English King, "joining with the power of the Earl Marshall, the master of Rothes, the laird of Calder, and others of the Lord Gray's friends, will take upon them to destroy the Abbey and Town of Arbroth, being the Cardinal's, and all the other bishops' and Abbots' houses and countries on that side of the water thereabouts." It appears that King Henry, in his rage against the Cardinal, gave them every encouragement " effectually to burn and destroy ;" but there is no evidence that the undertaking was accomplished.

We have not seen any statement from a writer cotemporary with the Reformation that the *buildings* of this Abbey suffered at the hands of the Reformers, although it is probable that, as was done elsewhere, they burned the wooden images, beheaded and defaced the stone ones, knocked down the crosses and altars, and damaged the tombs. Neither have we seen any *authentic confirmation* of the popular tradition that the church was pillaged and then burnt by Ochterlony of Kelly at that period, in consequence of a feud with the Abbot; and from the great power of the Hamilton family, one of which held the Abbacy at the time, such an occurrence is far from being probable. Had such evidence been accessible, it was not likely to have escaped the editor of the second volume of the Chartulary, who is altogether silent as to any conflagration of the church at the period in question. The desiderated evidence may possibly yet be obtained; but, in the meantime, we think it possible that the story of the final alleged burning of 1559 or 1560 may have been derived from, or have been confounded with, some of the earlier burnings. We may also remark that those parts of the walls which remain do not exhibit any of that calcined appearance which we would expect to find in a building destroyed by fire; although the lapse of time may have been sufficient to obliterate such marks.

As to the Reformers, there is much truth in the following words of one who did not hold them in the highest respect: " I need only remark of the burning of the town of Dornoch and the Cathedral, in 1570, that here, as at Elgin, and in the case of many of our monasteries and churches demolished in the English wars, the disgrace does not rest on the Reformers, often blamed for what they did not as for what they did destroy." (Maculloch's letters on the Highlands, ii. 478.) In justice to them, we may add that it will be difficult to point to a single parish or town church, the walls of which were injured by them, farther than, perhaps, by the loss of crosses or statues ; and the latter class of ornaments does not seem to have been a large one in Scotland. There is no evidence that the walls of the great churches north of Scone, including those of Dunkeld, Dundee, Arbroath, Montrose, Brechin, New and Old Aberdeen, Elgin, and Kirkwall, suffered any damage at their hands. While we know that, to the English is to be attributed the destruction of much of the Abbey Churches of Haddington, Kelso, Dryburgh, Melrose, and Holyrood.

The statements made by Spottiswood and many others on this subject are very exaggerated. In regard to the year 1599, they speak as if a mob had in a few hours " razed to the ground" great monasteries and churches, a feat not so easily performed ; whereas, at Perth, where the spoliation of monasteries was the completest of any, the walls at least were left standing. The Act of Council passed in 1561 had reference to the destruction of *monuments of idolatry*, within the churches and monasteries, rather than to the buildings ; and although Knox writes that the Act was followed by the burning of the Abbey of Paisley, and the demolition of those of Failford, Kilwinning, and part of Crossragwel, without doubt because they belonged to Popish dignitaries, Mr D. Laing has shewn (Knox i. 167), that the destruction was far less complete than the words used would lead one to suppose. A fair idea of this purging process at the large churches may be obtained from the letter by Argyle, Moray, and Ruthven, in which they order the [wooden] images of Dunkeld Cathedral to be burnt, and the altars to be cast down, with the following caution—" Tak guid heyd that neither the dasks, windocks nor durris be ony hurt or broken—eyther glassin wark or iron wark." A few facts are worth more than whole pages of declamation. After Darnley's death, in February 1567-8, the Privy Council ordered the lead to be taken off the roofs of the cathedrals of Elgin and Aberdeen for payment of wages to soldiers. But when the power of the Presbyterians was very high, the General Assembly of 1587-8 sent a petition to the king regretting the decay of the cathedrals of Glasgow and Dunblane, and the Abbey Church of Dunfermline, " which are ruinous, and without hastie [immediate] repaire are not able to be remedied ;" and asking him to cause the Abbot of Dunfermline and the Bishop of Dunblane to repair their respective churches, and to order the falling lead of Glasgow Cathedral to be employed in bearing the cost of slating that church.

The walls of St Andrews Cathedral, Elgin Cathedral, Arbroath Abbey, the chancel of Brechin Church, and the choirs and transepts of the churches of Dunfermline and Old Aberdeen, seem to have been left to go to ruin as useless erections. The choir and transepts of Holyrood Church were recommended by the Bishop of Orkney to be taken down as "superfluous ruinous parts," in the year 1570. The funds which ought to have been employed in their repair having been appropriated by the monarchs and their favourites, many of the walls of these great buildings fell by their own weight, assisted by the frosts of winter, the rains of summer, and the mattocks and pickaxes of every one who wished to obtain stones. The Reformers ordered the church of Restalrig to be destroyed " as a monument of idolatry," after the nave of St Anthony's Church, in Leith, had been assigned as the more convenient place of worship for the people of that parish, the other portions of that church having been destroyed at the siege of Leith ; but the demolition of Gothic architecture in the time of the Reformers bears a very small proportion to that which was witnessed during last, and the early part of this century. Instances of this may be seen in the ruin of Melrose Abbey, after public worship ceased to be held in it, the ruin of the nave of Holyrood Church, by an absurd stone roof laid upon it, the substitution of the Gothic Town Churches of St Andrews, Cupar, Dysart, and Brechin, by the present lumpish buildings which were put in their place; not to mention the recent destruction of the noble Trinity College Church of Edinburgh, to make room for a railway shed.

It is time that the memory of our Reformers should be vindicated from the aspersions cast on it in regard to this subject. It cannot be denied that mobs at that, as well as at any other time, have committed unjustifiable excesses; but any one who has read Knox's lamentation on the burning of Scone Abbey will see that the more learned among them were proud of their ecclesiastical buildings; and the existence of St Giles, Greyfriars, and Trinity College Church, Edinburgh, St Michael's, Linlithgow, the Abbey Church of Paisley, the Greyfriars Church of Stirling, the cathedrals of Glasgow, Dunblane, and Kirkwall, the churches of Perth, Dundee, and Aberdeen, shew that they efficiently maintained those churches where there were congregations to be accommodated; and if the supernumerary erections, such as St Andrews Cathedral, Arbroath Abbey, and other monasteries, went to ruin, that ought not to be charged against the Reformed Church (which never had any spare funds to expend on what to it were useless walls), but to the nobility and gentry, and the Scottish Exchequer, who grasped the rents and lands endowed for their support, and not a shilling of which they ever thought of employing in their repair till the present century had considerably advanced.

We have little information as to the erection and repairing of the subsidiary buildings of the Abbey, nor is this to be expected. The Chartulary scarcely contains a reference to any individual building except the church and its altars, the chapter house and vestry, the dormitory, and the "Abbot's Hall," which we believe to be the modern Abbey House. The dormitory contained in its upper storey the sleeping apartments of the monks. It is described as in course of renewal in the year 1470, and is referred to in several of the monastic writs. In a lease of that year, by Abbot Malcolm to John Chepman, styled "our familiar," the Abbot let to him, "for his labour for bringing wood from Norway for the use of our dormitory, a toft in our elimosinary, and four acres of land in Pondirlaw, for five years: and when the said John is in our service he shall have the toft and four acres for his reward, and when he is not in our service he shall pay for the elimosinary (toft) twenty shillings, and for the four acres of Pondirlaw four bolls of wheat yearly at two terms." On 20th May of the following year, Abbot Richard leased the teinds of the church of Inverness to David, Bishop of Murray, for six years, at the rent of £53, 6s. 8d. Scots, "for the building of our dormitory erected of new." The dormitory formed the upper storey of the range of building which has the line of its roof so distinctly marked on the gable of the south transept of the church. It had a private door (now built up) through the transept wall for access to the church at midnight masses. There are indications in the Chartulary that at this period the restoration of roofs and other wood work about the Abbey had not been confined to the dormitory, but was carried out on a more extensive scale. The buildings were nearly three hundred years old, and we may easily suppose that the wood work of the twelfth century stood in need of much repair by the fifteenth century.

On 25th July 1474 the Abbot and Convent entered into a contract with Stephen Lyell, of St Andrews, to act as their carpenter in all kinds of wood work to be required within the monastery, or wherever it pleased them, during his lifetime. He was to receive twenty merks Scots annually for his wages, and his meat and drink. If he worked for the Abbot and Convent beyond the monastery, at the repair of their churches, he was to be allowed four pennies for his expenses each working day. He was to begin work every day at five o'clock forenoon, and finish at seven o'clock afternoon, except in winter. If he continued at work all day he was to have " ad gentaculum suum" [?], and his servant was to receive a small loaf from the hall, and a drink with the convent servants, and have his afternoon [four hours] for his refreshment. And he was not to work beyond the monastery without the license of the Abbot.

Below the dormitory there still remain the vestiges of an arched passage running from east to west, adorned with seats on each side, doors at each end, and having the roof supported by ribs ending in ornamented or flowered corbels. This passage led from the cloisters to the chapter house lying to the east, and of which only a fragment of the south-east corner remains. The chapter house was a lofty and spacious erection fit for convening the chapter, with room for deputies, visitors, &c., having arches springing from the walls, and meeting most probably in a pillar at the centre of the floor, as was the usual mode of constructing chapter houses of large monasteries. The Abbey of Arbroath could not have wanted such a necessary building as a chapter house during the 230 years that elapsed before Abbot Panter erected the much smaller building for a vestry adjoining the church, which is now erroneously styled the chapter house, but which could not possibly have ever served that purpose. The south wall of the chapter house remained till 1780, and exhibited a large arched door to the westward of the existing fragment.

The lower flat of the building, which abutted on the south transept wall may have been the refectory or dining hall of the Abbey; or it may possibly have been the frater hall, or place of meeting of the monastic brethren, in which case the refectory would probably occupy the space betwixt it and the Abbot's house, on the *south*, or that building which had run southward from the nave of the church, on the *west* side of the inner or cloister court,—so that the great church on the north, the transept and dormitory on the east, the refectory and Abbot's house on the south, and the building referred to on the west, formed what was termed this inner or cloister court of the Abbey. The Abbot's house was originally a square tower (forming the south-eastern portion of the present structure), the basement floor of which was a great kitchen with groined arches and pillars, and a gracefully-moulded door, which still remain, and are well worth a visit. The cloisters or covered walks, as in most great monasteries, appear to have run along the interior of the four sides of the square court which lay on the south side of the nave of the church. A door led into the church at the north-west corner of the cloisters, and another door entered the church at the north-east corner. This door bears marks of a great degree of ornament, the mouldings being enriched with carving of open filigree work of a kind superior to any other part of the remaining buildings. It was the private entrance of the Abbot and monks into the church. The great western door was only opened on high festival occasions; while the ordinary entrance into the church for the public was by the north door of the nave, which still remains close to the north-west tower, and exhibits much fine taste and beautiful specimens of plain mouldings.

The Abbey buildings erected to the westward of the great portcullis gate were more specially appropriated to the civil department of the conventual establishment. The arched apartment, now almost demolished, which extended from the gate to the corner tower, is believed to have been the regality court-house. The square donjon tower still remaining served the purposes both of fortress and prison, and on that account this part of the buildings

I

was sometimes termed the *Castle*. The lower apartment was a dismal dungeon, without light, and seems to have been accessible only by a hole in the vault, through which the unhappy prisoner was let down. This was the massimore of the Abbey, or the *vade in pace*, so called from the irony of the sentence, "Go in peace." The apartment next above this vault was also probably used as a prison; but the upper apartments of the tower contain fire-places and recesses, and exhibit such signs of comfort as lead to the conclusion that they were intended for other inmates than prisoners, and were most probably rooms for the safe custody of the Abbey records. This building was finished at the top like other towers of the period, with a bartizan and parapet surrounding a centre sloping roof rising several feet above the parapet. This upper part, with the bartizan, has been taken down, apparently from fear of accidents by its falling.

At the south-west corner of the tower may still be traced the height of the western precinct wall, which started from this point and ran straight down along the east side of the High Street till it approached near to Allan Street, and then turned a little way to the east, and again to the south, and terminated at the south-west corner of the modern Parish Church. It had a round tower at the point where it left the High Street, and the old Church steeple was the square tower which stood at its southern extremity. The line of the wall betwixt these towers forms the boundary of the burgh, and runs southward behind the houses of the High Street and School Wynd. At the Church steeple the precinct wall turned to the east and ran up to Hay's Lane, at a few yards' distance from what was then the high road to Montrose, the intervening strip of ground (on which the Parish Church, the houses in Academy Street, and others are built) being known by the name of the "Derngate Rig;" while this part of the wall was styled by the Abbots "our Red Wall." The Dern Yett, or private gate, stood at the south-east corner of the precinct. Part of the stonework of this gate existed till within five or six years ago. From the Dern Yett the wall ran northward along Hay's Lane, where a portion of it may yet be seen, and continued along the east end of the gardens of East Abbey Street, and the east side of the Convent Green, till it reached the south-east corner of the buryingground, where it turned to the west, along the line of the present wall, and joined the east end of the great church. The church and other conventual buildings still existing formed the defence of the monastery along the remaining part of the northern boundary.

The history of the Abbey buildings during the last three centuries may be stated in a short paragraph. In regard to monastic edifices, the first two hundred and fifty years of that period were "a time to break down" as the former centuries had been "a time to build up." It is probable that, not long after the roof of the church was removed, the upper portions of the east and west gables would fall by their own weight, in consequence of being rent by frost and rain. The north walls and transept adjoining the cemetery seem to have been industriously levelled to the ground at an early period. The dilapidated state of the walls would lead, under the pretence of safety to lives, to the undermining and fall of the great central tower (of the form and termination of which we have no record), and of the great columns with their superincumbent arches, *triforium* and *clere* storey. Many cartloads of the stones of these columns and arches were recently found at the demolition of an old mansion removed to make room for the British Linen Company's Bank in Arbroath.

The upper part of the north-west tower was blown down by a storm in 1739. Part of the south-west tower fell in 1772, and another part fell in 1799. In 1800 the Town Council of Arbroath demolished the groined arched roof of the great gateway, with the centre wall where the hinged gate and side wicket were placed. The Magistrates of the burgh had acquired from King George I. a feu grant of the ground within the precinct lying to the south of the Abbey buildings. They formed this ground into streets, and sub-feued it to private parties, up to the walls of the church; and this led to the removal of the greater part of the boundary wall, and of the walls of the other conventual buildings, excepting the few fragments which still exist. In the beginning of this century the Scottish Court of Exchequer began to take some steps toward the conservation of these remains; and about 1835 the Commissioners of Woods and Forests cleared out the area of the Church, and repaired and partially restored those parts of the walls of which the original form could be correctly traced. These repairs have been continued till the present time under the direction of the Commissioners of Works, by virtue of parliamentary grants, which it is earnestly hoped may soon be resumed on a scale so liberal as to admit of the purchase of the Abbot's house, the only portion of the original buildings now in the hands of private parties. Although this house has been denuded of its antique internal furnishings and its battlemented exterior, it is still well worth careful preservation, not only on account of its general form, and fine vaulted basement storey, being the patchwork of several ages, but also on account of its being the frequent residence of the patriot King, Robert Bruce.

CHAPTER VII.

ALTARS IN ABBEY CHURCH.—1. ALTAR OF ST CATHERINE: 2. ALTAR OF ST PETER: 3. ALTAR OF ST LAWRENCE: 4. ALTAR OF ST NICHOLAS: 5. ALTAR OF ST MARY THE VIRGIN: 6. ALTAR OF ST JAMES: APPEARANCE OF CHURCH ON FESTIVALS.

BESIDES the great or high Altar, dedicated to the patron saint Thomas á Becket, which stood at the upper end of the chancel, the Church contained various other altars or chaplainries founded in honour of other saints, male and female. We have ascertained the existence of at least six of these altars, although it is probable that a far greater number existed, of which we have as yet found no trace.

1. The Altar of ST CATHERINE the Virgin is understood to have been situated in the south transept of the church, under the conspicuous Catherine-wheel window. It seems to have been nearly coeval with the church itself, as Hollinshed states that Gilchrist, Earl of Angus, and both his sons, "are buried before the altar of St Catherine, as the superscription of their tombs sheweth." They were large benefactors to the Abbey. There are certain marks on the basements of the two southmost columns of the south transept which were probably caused by the erection of this tomb, if not of the altar in its vicinity. This altarage was largely endowed by Margaret Stewart, Countess of Angus and Lady of Abernethy. By her charter (confirmed by King David II. on 31st October 1344), she

granted to the monastery her lands of Braikie, Bollischen, (Bolshan), and Kenbraid, with the muir called the Frith, and common pasturage in the King's muir, called Montrithmont, for the celebration of mass every day perpetually for the soul of her late husband John Stewart, Earl of Angus, and for her own soul and the souls of their progenitors and heirs, at the Altar of St Catherine the Virgin, in the Monastery of Aberbrothock. This is the principal and almost the only accession of lands acquired by the monastery after the death of King Robert Bruce. Lady Margaret Stewart's valuable gift had obviously reference to the burying-place of the Earls of Angus near this altar.

2. The altar of ST PETER is mentioned in connection with an erection called a chapel, which stood within an aisle of the church. On 29th August 1465 Abbot Malcolm granted a charter of a tenement near the house now called Hopemount to Simon Tod, burgess of Aberbrothock, for eight shillings Scots, to be paid yearly to the younger monks serving the altar of St Peter in the church of the monastery for the repair of the altar and chapel thereof.

3. The altar of ST LAWRENCE is mentioned in the Chartulary as within the Abbey church in the fifteenth century.

4. The altar dedicated to ST NICHOLAS, bishop and confessor, had right to five shillings of ground annual from a garden at Lordburn called the green yard (now occupied by the Tanwork), the property or ground of which belonged at the same time to the other altar of St Nicholas, in the Lady Chapel at the bridge. A piece of ground on the north side of Lordburn belonged to this altar, and was called the lands of St Nicholas. And in a charter of a tenement on the north side of Homlogreen the feuar is taken bound to pay five shillings Scots yearly for the sustentation of wax lights to the altar of St Nicholas.

These four altars were dedicated by George de Brana, bishop of Dromore, on 26th August 1485, immediately after he had dedicated the chapels and altars of Hospitalfield and St Ninian, and the church of St Vigeans with its altars, as stated in a certificate signed and sealed the following day, and duly recorded in the Abbey register.

5. The altar of the Blessed VIRGIN MARY stood on the south side of the choir, close to the door of the vestry, now incorrectly called the chapter house, where the remains of the piscina or stone basin in which the vessels were washed, may still be seen. This altar is noticed at an early period; and its existence—not far from the great altar—seems to account for the circumstance that, in the twelfth and thirteenth centuries the names of God, the Virgin Mary, and St Thomas the Martyr are often joined together in grants to the Abbey. The oldest of the conventual seals, besides containing the martyrdom of St Thomas in front, represents the Virgin and babe on the reverse. Previous to 1219 King Alexander II. granted the yearly rent of a stone of wax from his toft beside the market of Aberdeen for lighting the altar of the blessed Virgin. In 1245 Abbot Adam granted the Mill of Conveth (near Laurencekirk) to John Wishart for ten silver shillings, to be paid yearly for lights to this altar. The document which indicates its position was a grant made on 28th April 1521 by the Abbot to Thomas Peirson, of a small piece of land called Guysdub, for the yearly payment of four shillings Scots to the chaplain of the " altar of the Blessed Virgin Mary, near the door of the vestry, in the church of the monastery, for the sustentation of the lights thereof."

6. The altar of ST JAMES was termed the altar Divi Jacobi. Its exact position is not indicated. On 10th April 1531 the Abbot confirmed to Adam Pyerson and his son, Thomas Pyerson, a tenement in the way or street of the Almory, lying to the south of the Almory House, and to the east of the chapel of St Michael the

archangel, for the yearly payment of six shillings Scots, to the monks of the Almory, and of ten shillings Scots to the monk or chaplain of the altar of St James, " situated in the monastery."

The greater part of these and other altars which existed in the Abbey church were probably founded by private persons in performance of vows, or for delivery of the souls of themselves and their friends from purgatory; and their endowments seem to have been latterly supplemented by the provision of small payments to them out of lands feued by the Convent.

At this period every great church was studded with altars devoted to saints and angels. For example, the Trinity Church, now the Town Church of St Andrews, contained, on the authority of the late learned Principal Lee, perhaps not much fewer than a hundred such altars, and we have the names of more than twenty of their tutelar deities. Each altar was lighted by wax candles, and was surmounted by the image of its patron saint, clothed in gaudy robes, and glittering with tinsel of silver and gold—the i-doll of the shrine. Beside it stood a priest, especially on festivals, extolling the virtues and power of his divinity, every one " crying for their offerings," and holding out peace and pardons in return. The more fashionable altars were surrounded by crowds of worshippers on their knees, presenting their gifts, offering up their paternosters and *Ave Marias*, and telling their beads, while incense and music lent their aid to enliven the solemnities. It was such a scene that Sir David Lyndesay satirises in his poem of the *Monarchie*, when he makes the Courtier enquire of Experience as follows :

> " Father, yet ane thing I wald speir,—
> Behald in every kirk and queir,
> Through Christendome, in burgh and land,
> Imagis, maid with mannis hand :
> To quhome bene gevin dyvers names :
> Sum Peter and Paull, sum John and James;

> Sanct Peter carvit with his keyis;
> Sanct Michaell with his wingis and weyis;*
> Sanct Katherine with her swerd and quhil;†
> Ane Hynd set up beside Sanct Geill."

And, after a description of the images of St Frances, St Tredwall, St Paul, St Appolline, St Roche, St Eloise, St Ringan (Ninian), St Duthow, St Andrew, St George, St Anthony, and St Bride, he concludes:—

> "Ane thousand mo, I might declair,
> As Sanct Cosma and Damiane,
> The Soutars Sanct Crispiniane.
> All thir on aultar staitlie stands—
> Priestis cryand for thair offerandis—
> To quhome, we commounis on our kneis,
> Dois worschip all thir imagereis;
> In kirk, in queir, and in the closter,
> Prayand to them our Paternoster:
> In pilgramage from toun to toun,
> With offerand and with orisoun:
> To thame ay babland on our beidis,
> That they wald help us in our neidis;
> Quhat differis this, declare to me,
> From the Gentilis idolatrie?"

Let the reader imagine himself placed in the great Church of Arbroath as it stood in its grandeur, on some 17th of July, beneath its "long drawn aisles and fretted vaults," among its massy Gothic pillars and arches, and in the solemn light admitted by its stained glass windows, while the rites here described were being performed at many surrounding altars, whose artificial lights threw a mystic glare upon their idols, priests, and worshippers, and on the tombs, gilded statues of abbots and kings, screens and crosses, and gold and silver vessels; and he thus may be able to form some faint idea of the festival of St Thomas á Becket as it was annually celebrated at Arbroath for nearly four hundred years.

---

* With his wings and scales. This was Michael the archangel, the tutolar deity of the chapel of the Almory of Arbroath.

† Sword and wheel. The wheel, an instrument of her martyrdom, is commemorated by the St Catherine or wheel window (now called the round O), above her altar.

CHAPTER VIII.

DISTRICT CHAPELS IN ARBROATH AND NEIGHBOURHOOD.—1. CHAPEL OF ST VIGIAN AT CONON: 2. CHAPEL OF ST JOHN BAPTIST AT HOSPITALFIELD. 3. CHAPEL OF ST MICHAEL IN THE ALMORY: 4. CHAPEL OF ST NINIAN AT SEATON DEN: 5. LADY CHAPEL OF ARBROATH, WITH THE ALTARS OF ST NICHOLAS AND ST DUPTHACUS: 6. CHAPEL OF ST LAWRENCE AT KINBLETHMONT: 7. CHAPEL AT WHITEFIELD OF BOYSACK: 8. CHAPEL AT BOATH, PANBRIDE PARISH: 9. CHAPEL AT PANMURE CASTLE: 10. CHAPEL AT KELLY CASTLE: 11. CHAPEL OF ST LAWRENCE AT BACKBOATH. 12. CHAPEL OF ST MARY AT CARMYLIE.

UNDER this head it is intended to give some notices of several chapels which existed in Roman Catholic times at Arbroath and in the neighbouring parishes, so far as authentic information has reached us. But it is not to be understood that these embrace the whole number of such chapels, even in this district. For example, chapels are said to have stood at Inverpeffer and Bolshan, and they probably existed at other places, concerning which few or no reliable statements can be made. And a number of chapels were connected with the large possessions of the Abbey elsewhere, which cannot be here specially alluded to.

Almost the whole of these chapels were of a later foundation than the parish churches of the Ante-Reformation period; and in some instances, as at Carmylie, the chapel has formed the nucleus of a modern parish. The chapels here noticed seem to have depended on the Abbey of Arbroath, excepting two or three which were dependent on the bishopric of Brechin; and, with the exception of the chapel of Grange of Conon, and perhaps also the chapel of Kinblethmont, they were founded after the establishment of Arbroath Abbey. Their endowments were generally very limited. They were small in size, perhaps hardly extending to forty feet in length, and twenty in breadth, and were generally surrounded by a small burying-ground, often circular in form, and a field of a few acres, which served as a glebe to the incumbent, who, in those chapels which depended on Arbroath, was a monk of the Abbey. The duty of the incumbent of such a chapel, in the earlier periods, was chiefly to conduct religious services for the inhabitants of the barony or district with which the chapel was connected, on Sabbaths and holidays when they were not disposed, or when the distance, or the then impassable state of roads in winter, did not permit them to attend public worship in the parish church.

As the Romish doctrine of purgatory gradually obtained belief in Scotland up to the first quarter of the sixteenth century, many of these chapels came into view in the chartularies, in consequence of the foundation of altars within them by persons who had made vows while under distress, or in the prospect of death. These writings conveyed lands or rents to be employed in payment of priests to sing masses for the delivery of the souls of such benefactors and their friends from the pains of purgatory, on certain days throughout the year, in all time thereafter, according to the missals and other rules which were specified in the letters of foundation. The next half century witnessed the complete alienation of every one of these endowments from the original purposes, which had often been prescribed with much care and anxiety.

I.—CHAPEL OF ST VIGIAN AT CONON.

During the reigns of the Kings Kenneth III., Constantine IV., Grim, and Malcolm II., according to the concurrent testimonies of several historians, Vigianus, a monk or hermit, famed for his merits as a preacher, "flourished" in the neighbourhood of Arbroath. The historian Camerarius states that he died in 1012, although he came into repute in the reign of the first-mentioned king, which closed about 994. The unvarying traditions of the district during many ages bear that St Vigian's residence, and the chapel in which he ministered, was situated on the estate of Conon, close beside the farm-steading which is now termed Grange of Conon. In the Chartulary of Arbroath he is termed St Vigianus the *Confessor*, indicating that he had suffered more or less on account of Christianity, which is not improbable, considering that several armies of Danes landed on and ravaged Angus during his lifetime. He appears, however, to have died in peace, and to have been interred in the burying-ground of his parish church of Aberbrothock, to which his name was attached two centuries afterwards. His monument will be alluded to in our notice of that church.

If St Vigianus had ministered at Conon during thirty-five years previous to his death, as we can easily suppose he did, his chapel must have been in existence at least two hundred years prior to the foundation of Arbroath Abbey. Like many other old churches and hermitages, it must at that time have stood in what was an oasis in the midst of a desert. It was placed on a piece of fertile ground, beside a copious spring, which still bears the name of St Vigeans Well. It was sheltered by a range of natural woods, afterwards known by the name of the "Park of Conan," on the north; and it was surrounded by muirs on the east and west, and by mosses on the south. It would also be under the protection of the baronial castle which stood on the hill to the westward. We conclude that this is the chapel mentioned in Bagimund's roll (1275) as connected with Aberbrothock Church.

It is scarcely possible that the walls which are still to be so distinctly traced can be those of the original chapel of St Vigian, which was erected more than eight hundred and fifty years ago. They are more likely to be the remains of a succeeding chapel, erected on the original site by the convent of Arbroath, in memory of the confessor to whom they had consecrated their Parish Church. A pigeon-house, standing immediately in front of the remains, bears the date 1721, and it is believed that the materials for it were supplied from the walls of the chapel, which have been demolished till within two or three feet of the surface of the ground. They may be estimated at about forty-six feet in length, by twenty-six feet in breadth, over walls. During the latter half of last century the labourers employed in digging a ditch a few yards behind the chapel, chanced to exhume a quantity of human bones, which had the effect of intercepting their further operations in the intended line. At the time that the existing trees were planted, in the year 1788, the floor of the chapel was laid bare, and was found covered with flagstones. The field in the corner of which the chapel had stood is believed to have belonged to it as a glebe. The Arbroath Chartulary does not contain any allusion to this, the most ancient chapel on the Abbey lands. But its remains have been more fortunate in regard to their preservation than those of others erected at much later periods; and we understand that the former proprietor of New Grange and Grange of Conon, in the long and peculiar lease which he granted of the surrounding farm, was careful to except and retain in his own possession the site of the chapel and burying-ground, as a fitting place for the intended erection of a mausoleum.

II.—CHAPEL OF ST JOHN BAPTIST.

This chapel stood near the mansion-house of Hospitalfield, a mile to the westward of Arbroath, and was erected in connection with the hospital or infirmary of the Abbey, established at this healthy spot at such a distance from the parent monastery as to relieve it from the risk of danger from contagious diseases. This was one of those hospitals which Spelman, the antiquary, says, " we now call a " *Spittal*," and which was possessed by every principal monastery. The hospital and chapel were erected in the thirteenth century. At least they were in existence previous to the year 1325, when Abbot Bernard leased the lands of " Spedalfeilde, belonging to the hospital of Saint John Baptist, near Aberbrothoc," to Reginald de Dunbradan and Hugo Macpeesis, for five years, at a rent of forty shillings, payable to the Almory of the monastery; and took them bound to build two sufficient husbandry houses—namely, a barn forty feet long, and a byre of the same length, within one year from their entry, and to leave the same in good order on the lands at the end of their lease—a noticeable instance of progress in the management of lands, and the wisdom of the Abbot's administration.

The hospital was connected with the Eleemosynary of Arbroath. In an inquest, made on 22nd November 1464, regarding the nature of the foundations of the Almory and Infirmary, the jury stated that " Spitalfelde" and this chapel were not distinct from the property of the monastery, and that the Monks of the Almory received annually two merks from these lands. The chapel was consecrated, and the altar of it dedicated, on 23rd August 1485, by the Bishop of Dromore. On 4th December 1490, the Abbot let the teinds of the church of Abernethy to John Ramsay of Kilgour, for a yearly rent, and a sum advanced for the repair of the chapel of the infirmary, which is described as in danger of falling into ruin. This is the last notice of the chapel found in the Abbey register.

The older or central part of the present mansion-house of Hospitalfield is evidently a part of the ancient Abbey hospital. This is proved by the remains of several old doors and other indications about the walls of the house; and especially by one side of an ancient door which was lately discovered during some alterations in the front wall, a few yards west from the modern door, and which the proprietor, with good taste, has caused to be repaired and left open for inspection. This door appears, from the depth and character of its mouldings to have been one of the principal entrances to the hospital, and to have been erected after the early English style of architecture had ceased to be followed. The spring of the upper stones shews that its head was either a pointed or semicircular arch, having the side mouldings carried round without alteration, and without capitals at the spring of the arch. If our view be correct, these marks denote the erection of the hospital to have been from fifty to a hundred years subsequent to the foundation of the Abbey. The remains of the chapel and burying-ground have not as yet been identified, and await discovery—we have no doubt, at some future day, in the vicinity of the mansion-house.

III.—THE CHAPEL OF THE ALMORY.

As formerly stated, this chapel was dedicated to St Michael the Archangel. It is frequently alluded to in the Abbey records; and was erected sometime previous to 1427. The situation of the Almory or Eleemosynary, and of this chapel, without the walls of the monastery, and separated from it by the public street, seems to have given rise to questions between the Bishop of Brechin and the Convent as to the exact nature and purposes of this establishment, and also as to the Hospital and Chapel of St John Baptist connected with it. These claims of the Bishop of Brechin gave occasion to the inquest which was held at Arbroath, in the "Abbot's Hall," on 22nd November 1464, in the time of Abbot Malcolm, by Master

Richard Guthrie, Professor of Sacred Theology (afterwards Abbot), and John Graham, Prior of the Preaching Friars of St Andrews, Commissioners of King James III., and James, Bishop of St Andrews. The names of the assize or jury were—John Ogistoun, apparent heir of the laird of Ogistoun (Hodgeton); Patrick Gardyne of that Ilk; Thomas Ogistoun; Henry Fethy of Ballisack (Boysack); John Strang, key-keeper to the King; William Scot, Walter Leys, and John Fermour, burgesses of Aberbrothoc; Alexander Peebles, Walter Butchart, John Durward, Thomas Ramsay, John Himlar, and William Stephen, diverse parishioners of the parish; Master John Clerk, Rector of Logy; Master Alexander Thorntoun, vicar of Nigg; Master John Fordyce, vicar of Garvock; Sir John Haruar, vicar of Banchory Ternan; Sir Richard Bennat, vicar of Aberbrothoc (St Vigeans); Sir David Bullock, chaplain; and Master Thomas Dikysoun, bachelor in decreets. They were asked to give their verdicts on numerous questions as to the constitution and condition of the Almory and its dependencies. Some of their answers were to the effect that the Almory was founded by the King or lord patron, to the end that, as at other monasteries, the poor and infirm might be daily sustained from the fragments of the tables of the Abbot and Convent; that they knew of no letter of foundation; that they knew of no rents of the house, except one garden and one croft; that the house and chapel were well adorned or furnished; and that they knew no reason wherefore the house and chapel are built without the monastery except that it pleased the builders to do so. They further stated that they saw no grounds for the common report that the Bishop of Brechin had any right over the Almory house; and otherwise they referred to the letter of foundation of the monastery. Many feuduties of the building-stances in the Almory were expressly made payable to the monks of the Almory, who performed service in this chapel and acted as almoners.

These feu-duties probably formed the rents, amounting in whole to £5 or £6 sterling, "called the Elymosinary, and payable from several houses and roods to the Kirk-Session for behoof of the poor," mentioned by the Town-Clerk in 1742, but the origin of which, he states, is *uncertain*. It may perhaps be yet discovered that the conveyance of these feu-duties to the Kirk-Session for the benefit of the poor was made after the Reformation. In the year 1574 the General Assembly proposed to the Regent Morton to "take a general order with the poor, and especially in the Abbeys, such as *Aberbrothe* and others." And as the Almory was originally founded for the poor, it was both just and natural that, after it was laid desolate, the rents payable to it should be received by the Kirk-Session for the same purpose.

IV.—CHAPEL OF ST NINIAN.

Close to the promontory called Arbroath Ness, and under the shelter of the high bank which at that point retires from the sea, the Abbot and Convent of Arbroath founded a chapel, which they dedicated to the honour of Ninian (*Scotice* Ringan), the famed Scottish bishop and confessor, who is said to have died about the year 437. The site of this chapel is a pleasing spot, marked by a spring which bears the name of St Ninian's or St Ringan's well. In the Arbroath register the chapel is usually described as situated at the den or valley of Seaton. St Ninian's chapel and altar were consecrated by the Bishop of Dromore, on 24th August 1485. Seven years afterwards, Abbot David Lichtone granted a letter of presentation to Dominie John Todd, during his lifetime, of the benefice of this chapel, vacant by the decease of Dominie William Gibson, the former incumbent. Religious services had been continued in the chapel till the early part of the sixteenth century. On 23rd February 1521 a presentation was granted by the Convent to

Dominic David Brown, presbyter, during his lifetime, of this chapel, vacant by the death of Master Richard Grant. The chaplain was taken bound to repair and adorn the chapel honestly for divine service, in such necessary manner as his predecessor had done.

The field in which the chapel and burying-ground stood formed the glebe of the chaplain, and has been long known by the name of St Ninian's Croft. After the Reformation it seems to have fallen into the hands of the proprietors of Seaton, and still forms part of that estate. All vestiges of the chapel have been removed, and the site subjected to the ploughshare. The memory of its patron saint was formerly kept up by an annual fair called St Ringan's market, which was wont to be held in Arbroath on the first Wednesday after Trinity Sunday, and which has given place to the present Whitsunday feeing fair.

V.—LADY CHAPEL OF ARBROATH.

The chapel of the Blessed Virgin Mary, commonly called Our Lady's Chapel, stood at the west side of what was formerly styled the West Bridge of Arbroath, now known, in reference to the memory of the chapel, as the Lady Bridge. The exact site was near the north-east corner of the inner harbour. It was sometimes styled the "Chapel of Arbrothe," and was more immediately connected with the burgh than the chapels of the Almory, Hospitalfield, and St Ninian. It is also spoken of as a "Chapel of Ease to supply the want of accommodation in the Parish Church of the 'Blessed Vigian.'"

From an old monastic Latin rent-roll now belonging to the Kirk-Session of Arbroath it appears that this chapel was, previous to 1455, founded by the Convent of Arbroath, who had granted for its support the greater part of the original feu-duties or annual rents payable to them from the old burgh of regality, as well as various portions of land within the burgh boundaries, on which the streets of Marketgate, Grimsby, and others now stand, and which had been afterwards feued out for behoof of the chapel. This roll is nine feet in length, beautifully written on parchment, and illuminated with red initial letters. Its title bears to be a " Rental of Lands and Annual Rents of the Chapel of the Blessed Virgin Mary of Aberbrothoc, and of the Bridge thereof, made the twenty-fourth day of the month of September, *anno domini* 1455 : the bailies of the said burgh at that time being discreet men, Thomas Prechoure and John Ayr : sergeands, John Wyntyr and John Fermory, procurators for the before written lands and annual rents: and the Chaplain thereof, Magister John Fordyce, vicar." It commences with " Imprimis, the Ladybink [a fishing bank], now let for 13s. 4d. with a boat ;" and then follows the description of no less than one hundred and fourteen separate properties or parcels of ground, arranged under the heads of " Neugate, Seygate, Neumarcatgate, Aldmarcatgate, Grymsby, Mylgate, Lortburngate, Appylgate, Ratounraw, and Cobgate." All these properties are described by the side of the street on which they lay, the names of their possessors, and of the proprietors of the grounds on both sides ; so that the names of most of the burgesses of that time may be gathered from this document. The annual rents payable from these grounds to the chapel were small sums, from three shillings and fourpence to sixpence ; and the rents of the lands were generally similar sums, or two or three firlots of corn. A property in Seagate was bound to " sustain one lamp yearly before Our Lady ;" and another in the same street was bound to " render to the Blessed Mary annually two shillings ; and for the fabric of the bridge thereof, twenty pennies ;" and was (like many others) held in feu of the foundation of Our Lady. It may thus be concluded that the first bridge was built at the same time as the chapel, to afford easier access to it from the town, and was upheld by a portion of the endowments. The Chartulary affords evidence of various other gifts to this chapel—such as a piece of ground between the Brothock and Gravesend, a part of the banks near the Saltwork, and lands near Toutie's Neuk, all termed the lands of *Nostre Domine* or Our Lady.

Notwithstanding all these gifts, the benefice of the chapel seems to have been small. John Fordyce, the chaplain, mentioned in the rent roll, became vicar of the Church of Ethie before 1460. It appears from the old burgh records that the ministers of Arbroath conducted public worship in the chapel for several years after the Reformation, and probably till the erection of the existing parish church. By this time the magistrates obtained the endowments of the chapel of Our Lady and its altar of St Nicholas,—as they are found about 1567 engaged in letting the lands, and farming out the annual duties of these endowments.

Besides the altar of "Our Lady"—which stood at the east end of this chapel—it contained an altar in honour of St Nicholas, founded by Charles Brown, burgess of Arbroath, conform to his charter, sealed on 14th November 1505, and confirmed by Abbot George Hepburn on 10th March 1505-6. The object is stated to be for the soul of the most excellent Prince James the Fourth, King of Scots, and his Queen; and for the salvation of the venerable father in Christ, George Abbot of Arbroath, and the convent thereof; and for the salvation of the souls of the founder, and Marjory Guthrie, his spouse, and his father and mother; and for the souls of his ancestors and successors, and all the faithful departed. He grants to God Almighty, the Blessed Virgin Mary, and the Blessed Nicholas, bishop and confessor, and to the altar newly founded by him to their praise and glory, and for the sustentation of a chaplain to minister at the said altar, situated in the Chapel of the Blessed Mary, at the end of the West Bridge of Arbroath, for ever, numerous lands, gardens, tenements, and feu-duties, or ground-annuals, in all quarters of the burgh, and described as situated in Copegate, Lordburn, Marketgate, New Marketgate, Boulziehill, Rattonraw, Applegate, Seagate, and Burghroods. On 13th April 1532, this foundation charter, and the confirmation of Abbot George Hepburn, were confirmed by Abbot David Betoun, who sanctioned certain ordinances made by the founder regarding the rights and duties of the chaplain, which Abbot George had not thought proper to confirm. He also confirmed a notarial instrument dated 18th April 1513, by which the founder gave additional portions of ground and ground-annuals within the streets of the burgh, and along the north side of Ladyloan. These ground-annuals seem to have been the original feu-duties formerly payable to the Abbey from the various properties described in Charles Brown's grant.

The Lady Chapel also contained an altar dedicated to St Dupthacus, founded by Robert Scot, burgess of Arbroath, on 4th January 1519, and confirmed by Abbot David Betoun on 18th January 1524. The introduction to the grant consists of the statement that by the prayers and masses of the pious, offered through Christ the Son of God to our Father, for our sins, they are remitted, and the souls of the departed are liberated from the pains of purgatory, and placed amid the joys of paradise: therefore in honour of the holy and undivided Trinity, Father, Son, and Holy Spirit, the most glorious Virgin Mary and Saint Dupthacus, patron, and all the saints of God, he of new founds and ordains a perpetual chaplainry in the chapel of Arbroyth, near the bridge of that town, that at the altar the chaplain may perpetually minister for an interminable catalogue of souls, and among others—" For the salvation of the souls of William Scot, my father, and Elison Clark, my mother ; for the souls of John Scot, my brother, and his spouse, Isobel Lamby, and their sons and daughters ; emphatically for the souls of Dominie David Scot, vicar of Tarlan, and Henry Scot, his brother-german, sons of the said John and Isobel; for the souls of Andrew Scot, my brother, and his spouse, sons and daughters; and specially for the soul of Dominic John Scot, principal chaplain of the Blessed Virgin Mary; for the souls of Dominie Thomas Scot, chaplain, David Scot, Thomas Scot, my brothers; for the souls of Duncan Spark, and his spouse, Marjory Scot, my sister, and their sons and daughters; for the souls of Thomas Scot, and his spouse, Isobel Scot, my sister, and their sons and daughters; emphatically for the soul of Master Thomas Nudere, archdeacon of Moray, and commendator of the monastery of Culross, proto-notary apostolical, and cubicular to our most holy lord the Pope; for the souls of Dominie Richard Scot, monk, and Robert Bower, John Bad, Patrick Murray, Andrew Scot, William Scot, Robert Aldinston, monks of the monastery of Arbroath; and also for the souls of all my ancestors and successors, benefactors and relatives, living or dead." The endowments consisted of lands about Toutie's Neuk, Grimsby, and Millgate, and tenements and lands in Marketgate, Copegate, Newgate, and Lordburn; and the foundation charter concludes with many minute rules and directions to be observed by the chaplains as to their masses and services at the altar. The term Dupthacus is identical with Duthac, Duthak or Dothess, the name of one of the early Bishops of Ross, in the north of Scotland, to whose memory King James III. founded a chapel, the ruins of which still exist near the town of Tain, in Ross-shire. This chapel, and the name of its patron saint, acquired celebrity from the annual pilgrimages which King James IV., the son of the founder, made to it, as acts of penitence for the share he believed himself to have had in his father's violent death. He sometimes rode unattended all the way from Stirling to Tain by the Cairn-of-Mount; and it appears probable that the same shrine had been visited by his son and successor, James V., at or some time after the death of Patrick Hamilton.

It is evident that the founder of this altarage was unable to discern the signs of the times. He did not foresee that in thirty years afterwards, the altar and masses for which he had so anxiously provided would be suppressed by the strong arm of law; that within other thirty years a parish church would be erected in Arbroath for teaching those doctrines which he without doubt abhorred as heretical; and that before the nineteenth century all remains of the chapel of the Blessed Mary, containing the altar of St Dupthacus, would be completely swept away.

It may be observed that the Latin title *Dominus*, so often applied to priests and monks at this time, was equivalent to the prefix *Sir*, by which many of them were styled, and which title, it will be recollected, was repudiated by Walter Miln, the priest of Lunan, when applied to him by his accusers on his trial, adding, " I have been ower long one of the Pope's knights." Sir David Lyndesay alludes to this title in the following lines :—

> " The pure Priest thinkis he gets nae richt
> Be he nocht stylit like an Knicht,
> And callit *Schir* befoir his name,
> As Schir Thomas and Schir Williame."

The title was applied to persons in priests' orders who had not taken the proper academical degree of Master of Arts, so as to entitle them to use the higher prefix of *master* or *magister*, which is applied to some of the clergy named in Robert Scot's list of souls. The title *Den*, prefixed to the names of several Arbroath abbots and monks in vernacular writings seems to have been the Scottish mode of writing Dean, as Lyndesay adds—

> " All monkes, as ye may hear and see,
> Are called Deanes for dignitie;
> Albeit his mother milke the kow,
> He must be callit Deane Andrew."

The titles *Sir* or *Den*, as applied to clergy, seems to have fallen into disuse after the Reformation. But as many Romish priests of the lower ranks came to be employed as readers and teachers, the term was after that event applied, in the old form of *Dominie*, to schoolmasters, and seems to have been familiarly used in addressing them; and that with more respect than is now generally attached to the term. An instance of this is afforded by a conversation which John Row, minister of Perth, had on his deathbed, in 1580, with " the master of the gramer schoole, commonlie called Dominie Rind," as recorded in the Additions to Row's Coronis, p. 456, Wodrow edition. Much information is collected on this point in Dr Jamieson's Scottish Dictionary (*voce* Pope's Knights); and some observations " On the title of Sir, applied to priests," are given by Mr David Laing in the appendix (p. 555) to the first volume of his Wodrow edition of Knox's Works.

VI.—CHAPEL OF ST LAWRENCE AT KINBLETHMONT.

The chapel at Kinblethmont was most probably in existence prior to the foundation of Arbroath Abbey. This chapel and certain endowments were conferred on the Abbey so early as during the reign of King William, betwixt the years 1189 and 1199, by a grant of Richard de Malville, the proprietor of Kinblethmont at that time. By that grant, he gave to the monks of Saint Thomas, the Martyr of Aberbrothock, and the chapel of Saint Lawrence of "Kinblathmund," ten acres in the plain of Kinblathmund, and half an acre in the village at the chapel toft, with the teinds of the mill at the village, and all rights belonging to the chapel, in perpetual gift, free from all secular exactions, with liberty of pasturage to the chaplain that serves the chapel for one horse, two oxen, four cows, and twenty sheep. The exact site of this chapel has baffled our search. It appears to have stood at a village where there was a mill, and it is not easy to identify such a site on the proper lands of Kinblethmont. In the map of Angus and Mearns, as supposed to exist in 1640, appended to the Chartularies of Arbroath and Brechin, "St Lawrence Chapel" is marked as a small church situated about half-a-mile south-southwest from the mansion-house of Kinblethmont, a little to the east of the old Brechin road, and nearly on a straight line between the houses of Kinblethmont and New Grange. This is fully a mile southward from the proper position of the village of Chapelton, which is not marked on the map. But this map is not an infallible authority.

There was also at Kinblethmont a house or hospital of the Knights Templars. In March 1621, Alexander lord of Spynie, is served heir (among other possessions) to the lands and hospital house of the Order of St German, called the Temple Lands of Kinblethmont, with the privileges. The well at Kinblethmont, sometimes styled St German's Well, and the name of the farm of Templeton, lying to the westward, are very probably to be traced to this establishment.

VII.—CHAPEL AT WHITEFIELD OF BOYSACK.

From several indications as to sites and other circumstances, we are in the meantime inclined to the conclusion that the chapel of Whitefield was an establishment distinct from the chapel of St Lawrence of Kinblethmont, although some have believed that both these names were applicable to the same place of worship. The chapel of Whitefield seems to have been the district chapel of the barony of Boysack, and the name of the village of Chapelton, where it stood, is derived from it. It may have been the chapel alluded to in Bagimund's roll, as situated in the parish of Inverkeillor. The venerable trees which once surrounded this chapel, and which now enclose the private burial place of the family of Kinblethmont, still continue to form a striking object on the old road from

Arbroath to Brechin. Among these trees the boundaries of the ancient burying-ground may still be traced; and a part of the back wall of the chapel forms the lower portion of the north wall of the modern burying-place.

It is probable that this was the "Chapel of the Blessed Virgin Mary of Quhitfcild," in which, at eight o'clock in the morning of the 17th of October 1470, Abbot Malcolm Brydy of Aberbrothock, by his procurator, ineffectually appealed to John Balfour, Bishop of Brechin, against the proceedings of Patrick Graham, Bishop of St Andrews. The Abbot complained of being detained in strait prison at the Castle of St Andrews by the Primate, and could not have been personally present in the chapel, although the Bishop of Brechin and his retainers were there on that occasion.

The patronage of the chapel of Whitefield, with the lands and teinds of the chaplainry, are repeatedly mentioned in connection with the lands of Border, Douglasmuir, and others, from 1615 downwards, as appears from the writings of the families of Spynie, Kinnoul, and Gardyne.

VIII.—CHAPEL AT BOATH, PANBRIDE PARISH.

By a charter of Adam Bishop of Brechin, in 1348 (Brechin Chartulary, p. 10), it appears that Walter de Maule lord of Panmure, granted the lands of Carncorty (Cairncorthie) to God and the cathedral church of the Holy Trinity at Brechin, for the sustentation of two chaplainries or altarages newly founded in that church in honour of the Blessed Virgin Mary and the Holy Cross, and for the chapel of "Boith," in the diocese of Brechin. Among other provisions, it was appointed by this writ that the vicar of Panbride was to minister at the altars according to the missal of the Blessed Mary, and the vicar of Monzcky [Monikie] was to minister according to the missal of the Blessed Marnoch.

By two subsequent confirmations of David II., in 1359 (Brechin Chartulary, p. 13, 14), it is stated that besides the lands of Cairncorthie given by Walter de Maule, Christina de Valon lady of Panmure, had granted to the chapel of Boith the lands of Botmernok [Both-Marnoch] with the pertinents, in the tenement of Panmure; and that the Abbot and Convent of Aberbrothock had granted two merks sterling from their lands of Breckis (Brax) toward the support of this chapel. The above reference to the missal of the Blessed Marnoch, with the name of the lands of Botmernok, which appear to have formed the first endowment of the chapel, make it probable that the patron or tutelar saint of the chapel was St Marnoch, and shows that the chapel was built about the middle of the thirteenth century. Commissary Maule states that the name Both was derivable from this chapel; and adds that about 1559 David Maule got it in feu from Hepburn Bishop of Brechin, "with the pendicles thereof called Carnekorthie, as we would say the hungry hillocks." It seems to have been the Barony chapel of Panmure previous to the newer chapel at Panmure Castle; and the patronage of this chapel, with the teinds, the lands of Boath and Cairncorthie, and a mill, are specified as part of the Panmure estate in retours of the years 1662, 1671, and 1686.

The chapel stood beside an aged and now solitary tree, not far from a spring which, after running a few yards, joins the Crombie-mill burn, where it descends, by a series of small cascades, into a deep, narrow, and finely-wooded den. On the brink of the den there is a very old pigeon house, with a dilapidated farm-steading, which exhibits some faint traces of former greatness. The moulded stones which had formed the sides and arched tops of the door and windows of the chapel may be recognised in the walls of some of the old houses, and the font is believed to be there, but covered by the falling ruins.

IX.—CHAPEL AT PANMURE CASTLE.

About eighty years, at least, previous to the Reformation a Chapel was erected at the old Castle of Panmure. The date of the first erection of this fortress is unknown. It was dismantled and partly destroyed during the war with England, after being made an English garrison. Commissary Maule thinks it most likely that it was destroyed by Sir Andrew Murray after he defeated the English in its immediate vicinity, A.D. 1338. It was afterwards rebuilt, altered, and enlarged by the Panmure family; and about the south-east corner of the great court stood the family chapel, which was consecrated to the Virgin Mary by a bull of Julian bishop of Ostia, in the time of Pope Innocent VIII., about the year 1487. Parts of the walls of this chapel were standing in 1611, when Commissary Maule wrote a minute and interesting description of the castle, which was then a ruin, but much more entire than it is now, as at that time the walls to the south and west stood fifty feet high above ground. The entry to the castle was from the north, where it was defended with a tower and a deep fosse. This must have been a strong fortress both by nature and art, previous to the invention of gunpowder. The last of its vaults, so far as recognisable, were demolished about thirty years ago to supply stones for drains. And the lines of its chief buildings, round a large quadrangle, are now only distinguishable by the mounds of rubbish and stones which excavators have left. The immediate successor of this fortalice was a house erected by Robert Maule previous to 1540. (MS. account of the family of Panmure.) This building was again succeeded by the large existing mansion which the Earl of Panmure erected in 1666, and which has been improved and beautified by the present noble proprietor at great cost.

X.—CHAPEL AT KELLY CASTLE.

The reasons for attributing the first erection of a fortalice on the bank of the Elliot water to Philip de Mubray, an Anglo-Norman settler, were stated in the Introduction. The Abbot and Convent, about 1208, granted license to Lord Philip to have an Oratory within the court of his place of "Kellyn," where divine service might be celebrated by a chaplain, on condition that the parish or mother church should not be deprived of its dues or other festivities; that Philip and his heirs with their families should attend the mother church on all principal solemnities, if not prevented by reasonable indisposition, and on various other conditions which are carefully inserted in the writing. The mother church must have been the parish church of Arbirlot, which had by that time been acquired by the Convent. This chapel is not again mentioned in the Abbey writings, and like many other private or family chapels its history is difficult to trace. The ruins of a chapel adjoining the Castle of Kelly, and situated in the garden, are recollected by persons still alive.

XI.—CHAPEL OF ST LAWRENCE AT BACKBOATH.

So early as the time of Abbot Walter (1250) a chapel, dedicated to St Lawrence, existed at the place now called Backboath, within the bounds of the modern parish of Carmylie. It is styled in the title of the writ after-mentioned in the Arbroath Chartulary, the Chapel of *Both*. By that writ Abbot Walter of Arbroath bound himself to Lord William de Mont-Alto, son of Lord Michael de Mont-Alto, to provide an honest chaplain from among the monks of his house for the Chapel of St Lawrence, within the lands of Konan-Mor-Capil (Conon-Muir-Chapel), to serve perpetually; for which Lord William granted to the Abbot and Convent the lands of

Konan-Mor-Capil in perpetual gift. The site of the chapel is still pointed out in a field called the Chapelshade, lying on the west side of the steading of Backboath, beside a well which has now been drained into a neighbouring ditch. The remains of the chapel walls—two or three feet in height—several tombstones in the surrounding burying-ground, and the enclosing fence of the ground, were cleared away about fifty years ago, and the site converted into arable land. A small part of the hewn work of the chapel, consisting of mouldings of doors, may still be seen built into the walls of the farm-steading.

XII.—CHAPEL OF ST MARY AT CARMYLIE.

The chapel of Carmylie was founded by David Strathauchin (Strachan) of Carmylie, on 5th March 1500-1 (Brechin Chartulary, vol. i., p. 223), and confirmed by King James IV., on 20th January 1512-13. David Strachan endowed his chapel with five merks out of his manor of Carmylie and mill, forty shillings annually out of his other husbandry lands, and four acres of land at the east end of Milton of Carmylie, an acre of sward or meadow on the south side of the mill-lade, a toft and garden in the Milton, and pasturage on the Common of Carmylie (Kermyle). Dominie Malcolm Struble was appointed perpetual chaplain. The chapel was styled after the Most Glorious and Blessed Virgin Mary of Kermyle, and the services were to be for the salvation of the Most Excellent Prince James the Fourth, King of Scots, and his ancestors and successors; for the salvation of the Most Reverend Father in Christ, William Bishop of Brechin; and for the salvation of the souls of the founder, and of Jonet Drummond, his spouse, and their children, fathers and mothers, ancestors and successors, and all the faithful departed. Among other conditions of his grant, David Strachan provided that the chaplain should, during all the time of his incumbency, keep a school for the instruction of youth.

The parish of Carmylie was erected by the Church Courts out of lands disjoined from the parishes of Panbride, St Vigeans, and Inverkeillor; and the erection was confirmed by an Act of Parliament passed in the year 1609. About the same time the present parish church was erected, on the site of St Mary's Chapel. But the chapel is often mentioned in the titles of the lands of Carmylie after it had merged into the parish church. Thus, on 16th Nov. 1616, Patrick Strachan of Carmylie was served heir to his brother in the estate of Carmylie, including, among others, the patronage of the chapel of the Blessed Virgin Mary at Carmylie. Again, on 1st April 1662, George Earl of Panmure, is served heir to the patronage of the chaplainry of Carmylie, called "Our Lady's Chapel," with the church lands which pertained to the chaplainry. The four acres at Milton of Carmylie which were granted to this chapel are very probably identical with what is called the south glebe of the minister of Carmylie, as that is held by him as an additional or special endowment to the incumbency, and was the only glebe he possessed previous to the year 1716.

The above notices help to illustrate a rather obscure passage in Friar William Airth's sermon, preached at St Andrews about 1534 (Knox's history):—" But now (said he) the greediness of priests not only receive false miracles, but cherish and fee knaves for that purpose, that their chapels may be the better renowned, and their offering augmented. And thereupon are many chapels founded, as that our Lady was mightier, and that she took more pleasure in one place than another; as of late days *our Lady of Kersgrange* hath hopped from one green hillock to another." There can be little doubt that our Lady of Kersgrange was a local title then given to the Virgin Mary, who had come into very great repute as the Queen of Heaven shortly previous to the Reformation.

CHAPTER IX.

CHURCH OF ST VIGEANS.—1. FABRIC OF CHURCH AND OLD MONUMENTS:
2. ALTARS OF ST VIGIAN AND ST SEBASTIAN: 3. PRIESTS AND MINISTERS
OF ST VIGEANS SINCE A.D. 1200.

THE Church of Aberbrothock, now called St Vigeans, held for a long period a prominent place among the parish churches of Angus, in respect of the peculiar construction of the fabric, as well as the extent of the parish and the richness of the benefice. It may not be unacceptable on that account to give in one view a short notice of the church itself, with its altars, and the ministers who served the cure as vicars of the Abbey, and during the earlier period of the Reformed Church, so far as these have been gleaned from the records of the Abbey and other sources.

I.—CHURCH AND MONUMENTS.

This was the parish church of the district or "shire" of Aberbrothock previous to the time of *Vigian* or *Vigianus*, the hermit or confessor, who died at Grange of Conon about 1012. The festival in honour of his death was held annually on the 20th day of January, old style, and gave rise to the fair termed St Vigeans market, formerly held on that day, now the winter market. This is one of the four annual fairs included in King James's charter of *novodamus*; but till about the beginning of last century it is said to have been held at a place near Smithy Croft, beyond the bounds of the burgh. Saint Vigian appears to have been interred in the cemetery of his parish

CHURCH OF ST VIGEANS.   145

church, as Dempster relates that his monument was there, and adds the fabulous statement that there stood in the cemetery a wooden cross (apparently in honour of the confessor) which could neither be destroyed by fire nor iron. The ancient carved stones in the cemetery are much more likely to have been parts of St Vigian's monument than to have belonged to any monument in honour of the architect of the Abbey, who has absurdly been also termed the architect of the church. One of these stones is carved in a style very similar to the stone at Pitmuies and the stones at Aberlemno, which are understood to have been erected in memory of the Danes slain in the flight after the battle at Carnoustie, in the reign of Malcolm II., about 1010. This invasion of the Danes was nearly coëval with the death of St Vigian. Another stone, now set up against the east wall of the church, is carved in a superior style, similar to the cross at Camuston, which is commemorative of the same conflict. These stones at St Vigeans church are obviously of a date considerably earlier than the foundation of the Abbey, but they agree in character and style with such a monument as would be erected shortly after the death of the hermit of Conon. The church of St Vigeans was certainly not erected by the architect of the Abbey Church, as it is evidently of a later and inferior style; perhaps not older than two centuries preceding the Reformation. The upper portion of the tower, and the extension to the north called the new aisle, are recent additions, made during the present century; which also has witnessed alterations in the walls and roofs of the original south and north aisles, by which the upper or *clere* storey windows have been shortened. The ancient doorway may still be seen on the west side of the tower; and there were probably one or more windows in the east gable before the galleries and stairs were erected. This interesting old church has been subjected to many changes during the last five centuries.

L.

II.—ALTARS.

The Bishop of Dromore certified that, on 25th August 1485, he dedicated the church of St Vigeans and two great altars, with the cemetery, at the instance of a devout man, John Brown, a parishioner of the church. The first of these altars appears to have been dedicated to the confessor Vigianus; but we have no distinct information as to the name of the other. In the beginning of the next century, however, the church contained an altar dedicated to St Sebastian, which was endowed with various tenements and rents in the High Street of Arbroath (Cobgate and Rattonraw), by John Brown in Letham in the year 1506. This was probably the devout parishioner to whom the bishop referred twenty years previously. He endowed the altar for the salvation of his soul, and for the soul of Jonet Lyn his spouse, and for his relations, parents, benefactors, and all the faithful departed; to the praise and honour of Almighty God, and the Lord Jesus Christ, and the Most Glorious Mary, and Saints Vigianus and Sebastianus. He states that a discreet man, Dominie Alexander Brown, his cousin, had been appointed by him to the office of chaplain at the altar. This foundation was confirmed by Abbot George Hepburn, on 5th July 1506. Some years afterwards the founder added various other tenements and ground-annuals about Arbroath, by a writing which was confirmed by Abbot James Betoun on 21st July 1521. This latter grant is more ample than the former; and is described as for the benefit of the souls of "Jonete Lyne, Elen Brown, and Jonete Brownche, my wives." The founder ordains that, out of the rents granted, the chaplain serving the altar shall receive fourteen shillings and eightpence annually, and shall celebrate every year perpetually an anniversary annually, viz., *Psalms* and *Dirigie*, with note and canto, at the feast of the Apostles

Peter and Paul, before the altar of St Sebastian, in the parish church, for the souls before-mentioned, with six priests and three boys; and shall give each priest ten pennies, and retain to himself two shillings, and shall give each boy eight pennies, and to the ringer of the bell four pennies, and for a collation to them two shillings; and shall give the remainder of the fourteen shillings to the poor and indigent; and he (the founder) ordains that this be done yearly perpetually, as the chaplain shall answer at the summons of the Judge on the day of judgment.

This document contains various other directions for the service of the altar on six holidays and two festivals —and provides that the chaplain shall have a silver chalice of twelve ounce in weight—that he shall have a missal (or mass book) of parchment written with a pen—two vestments, one for festivals, another for holidays—three tobals, and two phials. The founder concludes by a declaration which is significant of the state of morals of the clergy at the time, that if the chaplain or any of his successors shall be convicted by his judge ordinary of keeping a concubine or fire-lighter for the space of one month or forty days, then the founder or his successors shall have liberty to dispose of the chaplainry, notwithstanding anything contained in the grant. A part of the properties in Arbroath bestowed on this altar were commonly known by the name of St Sebastian's lands, about 1520. At this time St Sebastian, a martyr of the early church, had become a saint of great repute in Scotland. Sir David Lyndesay, in the *Monarchie*, says:

"To Sanct Sebastian they rin and ryde,
That from the schot he saif thair syde."

The legend states that the saint lived after he was shot full of arrows till Dioclesian put him to death.

In taking leave of these small endowments we would remark that a few such annual payments are still occasionally to be met with in the writs of properties about the eleemosynary and in the older burgh. The greater portion of them, however, are now lost sight of, and the causes of their disappearance cannot be better expressed than in the grant whereby King James VI., on 14th March 1585-6, let all the similar small duties about Brechin to James Erskine, vicar of Falkirk, during his lifetime; and which narrates "That there are diverse lands, tenements, houses, and annual-rents, which were mortified in time of ignorance to certain priests, prebendaries, and chaplainries within the citie of Brechin, for celebrating of masses, singing, and saying of dirigie, and doing of other rites, ceremonies, and papistical service, which now, by the Word of God, and laws of His Highness realm, are damnit [condemned] and alluterlie abolished; of the which nae commodity nor profit has nor will be reported hereafter, by reason the said annuals, in quantity small, and paid forth of diverse and sundry houses, lands, and tenements, *now forth of use of ony payment, and unknawin through the lang process of tyme*, cannot be applied again to nae godlie nor necessar use, according to the meaning of the first foundation, without great travell and expences." For these reasons, "and that ane certain knawin duty may be yearly paid therefore to the help and support of the poor, impotent, and decayed people within the said citie, or otherwise to be employed as His Majesty sall think maist meet," the whole duties were let to the vicar for the yearly rent of £6, 13s. 4d., payable to the collectors of the alms for the poor of the city of Brechin.

III.—MINISTERS OF ST VIGEANS.

We have but scanty notices of the priests of St Vigeans during the time of Popery, but they perhaps exceed the items of information which may be gleaned as to the early incumbents of almost any other Scottish church which did not rise above the rank of an ordinary parochial charge.

WILLIELMUS was probably the first parish priest of Arbroath under the monks, although, according to the custom of the time he was termed "chaplain of Abbirbrothoc," as the title of vicar does not appear in the district till about 1238. He was a witness to Earl Gilchrist's grant of the hospital, lands, and fishings at Portincraig in 1200.

RICHARD was chaplain of Aberbrothock in 1225, when he attested a grant to the Abbey by Bernard, the son of William.

ROBERT is the earliest priest that bears the title of *vicar* of Aberbrothock. He was a witness to Richenda de Berkelay's grant to the Abbey of lands in the parish of Fordoun, about 1245.

Thirty years after this period, namely, in 1275, the churches of Aberbrothock and Ethie, with the chapel, were entered in Bagimund's taxation at £70, shewing that they formed at that time the richest parochial benefice in Angus, except the church of Brechin, which was rated at £80.

After a considerable interval, we find the "perpetual vicar of Aberbrothock," styled Sir or Dominus MAURICE, in 1310. In that year he witnessed a grant to the Abbey by Michael de Monifieth. He is again mentioned as perpetual vicar on 20th December 1333, when his name occurs as witness to a deed.

Dominus WILLIAM DE CONAN is described as perpetual vicar of the church in the contract for building the port, dated 2nd April 1394, where he is named as a witness.

Dominus ROBERT STEILE resigned the vicarage about 1459.

On 1st August 1459 Abbot Malcolm granted a presentation of the perpetual vicar's pension of the parish church of Aberbrothock, namely, forty merks Scots, with the toft, as usual, vacant by Robert Steile's resignation, to Dominus RICHARD BENNAT, " our chaplain." Richard Bennat continued vicar at least till 4th November 1464, when he acted on the inquest regarding the house of the Almory and the chapel of St John Baptist.

Master PATRICK MACKULLOUCH was vicar on 18th September 1482, on which date the Abbot, sub-prior, sacrist, cellarer, and others, agreed to pay him five merks Scots yearly, as vicar's pension for his counsel, unless he resided elsewhere.

On the 9th July 1499 Master JAMES DOUGLAS, vicar of Aberbrothock, declared himself " to be bundin and oblist till David, Abbot of Aberbrothoc, and Convent in lawtay and service to be done and keepit to thaim for all the days of my lyif, be resone of ane certane fee and house-hald given to me by thaim; the whilk fee and househald I declaris be my conscience I have nocht be richt of my vicarage."

Dominus THOMAS HARROUR was pensionary vicar on 6th October 1512, when a dispute or process was pending betwixt him and the Abbot and Convent regarding the teind sheaves of the rood or croft of Arbroath, and the new pension thereof.

On 27th January 1524 Master ANDREW FOULAR was presented to the benefice of the perpetual pensionary vicarage, viz., thirty-two merks Scots, with the toft and manse, perquisites and oblations, according to the contract between the Abbot and Thomas Harrour, vacant by his resignation. Andrew Foular lived till about 1535.

On 13th December of this year the Abbot issued a presentation in the terms above noticed in favour of Dominus JAMES AUCHMUTHY to the pensionary vicarage of the parish church of " Abyrbroth," vacant by the death of Andrew Foular. James Auchmuthy is again mentioned as vicar on 20th August 1536.

After the Reformation, and till 1568, NINIAN CLEMENT was minister of " Aberbrothok Town and Paroche," with a stipend of 100 merks Scots. He was made a burgess and freeman of Arbroath on 2nd June 1564; and on 2nd March 1564–5 Jonat Boyis was ordered by the bailies to ask forgiveness in the chapel of " Nyniane Clament, mynister," for having slandered him. (Burgh Court Book.) After Ninian Clement's removal from St Vigeans, and previous to the year 1574, he had charge of the churches of Forfar and Restennet, Kinnettles and Tannadice.

Previous to 1574 Master JAMES MELVILLE, son of Richard Melville of Baldovie, was minister at St Vigeans. He was a person of learning, and possessed much influence in the councils of the Church. His name is sometimes mistaken for that of his nephew, James Melville, the minister of Kilrenny. It was during his incumbency, and about 1580, that the new ministerial charge was established in the town of Arbroath. In the Appendix No. II. a more extended sketch is given of the life of this worthy minister, who was the chief ecclesiastical personage about Arbroath for many years after the fall of the Abbey.

Master PATRICK LINDSAY, of the family of Edzell, was Melville's successor. He had previously been minister at some other church, and was a member of the Assembly in 1590. (Scott's Narration.) He was probably settled at St Vigeans about 1599, as he is stated by Calderwood to have been interested in the King's revocation of a grant of the teinds of the Abbey to Robert Bruce of Kinnaird in that year. In 1610 he was nominated a member of the court of High Commission for the trial of refractory presbyterians; and in 1613 was created Bishop of Ross. He was present along with other bishops at King James' extraordinary interview with Calderwood, the historian, in the Court of High Commission at St Andrews in July 1617; and, immediately afterwards, while Calderwood was being conducted to prison, " Mr Patrik Lindsay went up to him and

upbraidit him, but he sent him packing away from him."
(Wodrow Calderwood, vii., 268.) From this and other
instances of Lindsay's zeal for episcopacy it was not to
be expected that he stood high in the favour of the
presbyterians, although he possessed learning and various acquirements. He was promoted to the archbishopric
of Glasgow in 1633, and five years afterwards (12th December 1638) was included in the sentence of deposition
and excommunication passed on eight Scottish prelates by
the General Assembly at Glasgow. The chief complaint
against him was his activity in urging the service book
and other English innovations.

During a number of years, both previous and subsequent to Lindsay's removal from St Vigeans, DOCTOR
HENRY PHILIP was minister of the Town Church of
Arbroath, and held a conspicuous position in the public
affairs of the church. He was a supporter of prelacy,
and acted as clerk to the Convention or Assembly held
at Linlithgow in 1606, in which the preparatory step
of appointing constant moderators was carried. He was
named, as a decoy duck, along with the Melvilles, Scott,
Balfour, and other ministers, who were invited to London
by King James, to confer on matters relating to the
Church, but in reality to be delayed, and if possible
entrapped, until the establishment of bishops was ripe
for execution. The other eight ministers, fearing that
he might reveal their private sentiments to the King and
the bishops, refused to have him in their company.
(Forbes' Records, 1846, p. 552.) At all events, Philip
did not accompany them to London, and there was no
necessity for detaining *him* there, as he could serve the
King's purposes much more effectually by remaining in
Scotland. After this period, and down at least to 1619,
Dr Philip's name frequently occurs as a member of Conferences and of courts of High Commission under King
James, along with bishops and archbishops and other
supporters of that nondescript Scottish hierarchy which

existed from 1610 to 1638. He continued minister of Arbroath at least till 1629, and was generally named an extraordinary member of the Town Council of Arbroath, who paid him about £30 Scots in part of his stipend. His successor, SIMEON DURIE, was made a burgess of Arbroath, on 26th February 1630, and held the charge for at least the next ten years.

THOMAS ROY was minister of St Vigeans in 1618; as on 9th November of that year, he, along with the ministers of Arbirlot, Barrie, and Inverkeillor, were made burgesses and freemen of Arbroath. (Burgh Records.)

The famed Assembly held at Glasgow in 1638 had no representative from the Presbytery of Arbroath; but in the roll of Assembly held the following year, the Presbytery of Arbroath was represented by "Mr ALEXANDER INGLIS at St Vigeanes," minister, and John Auchterlonie, Cairnie, ruling elder; and the Burgh of Arbroath was represented by George Inglis, burgess. Alexander Inglis retained the charge during several years after this period.

After the restoration of King Charles II., and of Episcopal government, about 1665, PATRICK STRACHAN was translated from Carmylie to St Vigeans. He continued in the charge several years after the Revolution of 1688, without conforming to the Presbyterian government then reëstablished. In a preface to a small religious book, of which he was author, dated "From my Study at St Vigeans, 14th July 1693," after alluding to increasing bodily infirmities, he adds, "considering also the uncertainty of the times, not knowing how soon I may be *turned out.*" He dedicated the book to James Earl of Panmure, his patron, and entitled it, "The Map of the Little World Illuminated with Religion: Being a Practical Treatise directing Man to a Religious Scope and Right Measure in all the Periods of his Life, with Devotion suitable: To which is added an Appendix, containing a Gospel Minister's Legacie to his Flock." The "Little

World" is man viewed in a religious aspect at different periods of life. The book also contains prayers and hymns, one of which concludes thus :

> " From the first minute to ages all ;
> I will assert Thy Glore,
> In melodies sempiternal,
> To Trine Une evermore."

This publication shews that its author, although no great poet, was a good man, and a sound Protestant divine. During his incumbency the proprietor of Seaton, named Ochterlony, was twenty years under the discipline of the Church, of which he was an unruly member. Among other deeds he forcibly broke open the doors of Arbroath prison, in which his mistress had been incarcerated, delivered his favourite, and marched up the street with a drawn knife in his hand, setting all officials at defiance. The struggle betwixt him and the Church was ended by his sitting in the place of repentance at St Vigeans.

About the beginning of the eighteenth century Patrick Strachan was succeeded by his son, —— STRACHAN, who was soon afterwards deposed, most probably for nonconformity.

THOMAS WATSON, probationer, was appointed minister of St Vigeans in the summer of 1702, by the Presbyteries of Brechin and Arbroath, then united. He committed suicide in 1726, by hanging himself on a tree, some distance north-east from the church ; and was interred, not below the pulpit like his predecessors, but at the bottom of a turf dyke betwixt the lands of Newgrange and Newbigging. After some delay, arising from the opposition of the heritors, TOBIAS MARTIN, probationer, was ordained minister in the summer or autumn of 1727. His successor was JOHN BURN or BURNS — admitted minister on 14th May 1731 ;—died in 1734 : and was succeeded on 19th December of that year by JOHN HENDERSON. He died in 1753 ; and in 1754 the Rev.

JOHN AITKEN was appointed to the charge, which he held for sixty-two years. His successor, the Rev. JOHN MUIR, was ordained minister of St Vigeans in 1816; so that he and his immediate predecessor have held the benefice for more than a century.

To those acquainted with the times of James VI. it may be of interest to learn that St Vigeans Church contains the burial place of Peter Young, the King's tutor, under the learned Buchanan. The chief preceptor, notwithstanding his subsequent fame, "was a stoic philosopher, and looked not far before him;" and was allowed to live and die in poverty. But the tutor knew how to act the courtier. He was made a Privy Councillor and King's Almoner, and obtained Seaton and Dickmontlaw, with tithes and others which had belonged to the Convent of Arbroath, and was afterwards known as Sir Peter Young of Seaton. He died on 7th January 1628, aged eighty-two, and was interred in a vault at the back of the church, the new aisle of which now contains the tablet erected to his memory, bearing his titles, and that on account of his learning, prudence, and elegant manners he was dear to his king and countrymen, and to the kings and princes to whom he had been sent ambassador. The Latin version is:

PETRVS YOVNG
A SETON EQ. AVR. SERMO. AC.
POTMO IACOB. VI. BRIT. FRAN.
ET HIB. REGI A STVDIIS CONSIL.
ET ELEEMOS. PROPLER ERVDIT.
PRVDENT. ET MORVM ELEGANTIA
EXIMIAM DOMI REGI SVO CIVIB.
CHARVS FORIS REGIB. & PRINCIB.
APVD QVOS VARIIS LEGAT. FVNCT.
EST CELEBRIS HIO BEATORVM RESVR-
RECT. EXPECTAT.
OBIT. IAN. VII. AN. M.DC.XXVIII
ET SE. LXXXIII.

CHAPTER X.

POSSESSIONS OF THE ABBEY. — 1. LANDS, BARONIES, VILLAGES, &c. — IN ANGUS, MEARNS, PERTHSHIRE, FIFESHIRE, LANARKSHIRE, ABERDEENSHIRE, BANFFSHIRE, INVERNESS-SHIRE. 2. TENEMENTS IN BURGHS. 3. FISHINGS. 4. FERRYBOATS. 5. WOODS AND FORESTS. 6. SALTWORKS. 7. CHURCHES, TITHES, &c. 8. ORIGINAL ANNUAL RENTS. 9. BURGHS. 10. RENTS AT DISSOLUTION OF THE ABBEY.

WE have never yet seen any comprehensive state of the large and varied possessions of the Abbey of Arbroath. The best that have appeared are those contained in the Book of the Assumptions, and the account of the Collector General of the thirds of benefices in the year 1561; and in the " Charge of the Temporalitie" as annexed to the Crown in the year 1592. But these lists were drawn up subsequent to the Reformation, for special purposes, and after the Abbey had lost several lands, churches, houses, fishings, and others, which belonged to it for ages previously. The " Charge of the Temporalitie" contains an interesting description of certain lands, all of which had by that time been alienated as perpetual feus, but broken up into fragments, and arranged with respect to the feuholder only, and not in relation to locality, so that it becomes a difficult matter from such a document, to obtain a view even of the *lands* which had once belonged to the monastery.

It would require a considerably extensive knowledge of the topography of the northern counties, to be able to give a very accurate view of the Abbey lands in those districts; although the following list will enable any one acquainted with the boundaries of the baronies afternamed to trace them out with considerable correctness. It is impossible at this late period to give a *complete* view of the Abbey possessions, nor one into which errors will not intermingle. In the list here given these possessions are arranged under different heads, which will sometimes occasion more than one reference to the same tract of country, as the different kinds of endowments occur. The lands were at first almost wholly held by the Convent in *property;* but they were gradually feued out, till at last nothing except the superiority remained.

I.—LANDS, BARONIES, VILLAGES, &C.

In Angus.—1. The village and *schyre* of Aberbrothock, with the territory of Athynglas ; being nearly conterminous with the modern parishes of Arbroath and St Vigeans, including the lands of Guynd, Milton of Conon, and others, in the north-east part of the (modern) parish of Carmylie. The detached barony of Inverpeffer was held of the Abbey as superior.

2. The village and schyre or parish of Athyn or Ethie; which included the present estate of Ethie so far as now annexed to the parish of Inverkeillor, lying on the south side of the Keillor burn, or the middle of Balnamoon mire.

3. The village and schyre of Dunechtyn ; containing at first the largest or western portion of the parish of Dunnichen, and ultimately the estate of Dumbarrow, or the detached portion of that parish.

4. The village and whole schyre or barony of Kyngoldrum ; being nearly conterminous with the parish of Kingoldrum. Athynglas, Dunnichen, and Kingoldrum were given under burden of the liferent of Andrew bishop of Caithness.

5. The lands called the Abbacie or Abthanerie of Old Montrose, in superiority, with three stones of wax as feu-

duty. King William was the donor of the whole above-mentioned lands, except the lands of Conon, Dumbarrow, and certain lands at Kingoldrum, with the woods on these lands, which were given by his son King Alexander II. in forestry.

6. Thirteen acres of land near the church of Fethmuref (Barry); given by William Cumyn, Sheriff of Forfar.

7. Two oxgates of land at Rossie, in Gowrie; given by Hugo Malherbe.

8. Lands at Broughty or North Ferry, and hospital; given by Gilchrist Earl of Angus.

9. The land on the south side of the church of Monifod (Monifieth), which the Culdees had, with a toft and croft on the east side of that church; given by Maud Countess of Angus.

10. The davoch of Ballegilgrand; given by Donald Abbot of Brechin. These lands are believed by some to be those of Ballishan or Bolshan, in Kinnell parish; but there is not any direct evidence of this in the Chartulary. Bolshan was afterwards given by the Countess of Angus.

11. A toft and croft and two acres of land at Stracatherach (Stracathro), with the teinds of the fishing-net on North Esk; given by Turpin Bishop of Brechin.

12. Ten acres of land in the plain of Kinblethmont, and half an acre in the village at the chapel toft, with the oblations pertaining to the chapel of Kinblethmont; given by Richard de Maleville.

13. The lands lying betwixt Aldenkonkro and Aldendoven, in the territory of Kirriemuir; given by Malcolm Earl of Angus. These lands may probably be found in Glenprosen, or near the north boundary of Kingoldrum parish. Earl Malcolm stated in his grant that there had been controversy between him and the monks regarding them.

14. The lands of Brakie, Bolshan, Kenbraid, and Frithmuir, in the parish of Kinnell, and common pasturage in

the King's muir of Montrithmont; given by Margaret Stewart, Countess of Angus.

15. The lands of Hedderwick, near Montrose; the donor of which we have not ascertained.

16. The church lands of Inverkeillor, now the farm of Kirkton, with pasturage in the territory of Inverkeillor; granted, along with the church of that parish, by Walter de Berkeley, at the foundation of the Abbey.

17. The lands of Auldbar in the barony of Kethick.

18. The lands of Konan-mor-capil, now called Backboath; given by William de Montalto.

19. The lands of Cotside, Balskelly, Cowbyres, and Whitelums, in the parish of Barry; also the lands of Greenlawhill, Easter Barryhill, and Wester Barryhill.

The barony of Inverarity, near Forfar, has been said to belong to the Abbey, and to have been feued to Alexander Burnet of Leys, on 27th July 1500. This is a mistake. A liferent lease of Invercanny, near Banchory-Ternan, was granted by the Convent to Burnet of Leys on that day; but the Abbey never had lands near Inverarity.

In Mearns.—20. A ploughgate of land in Monethen or Mondyne, on the river Bervie; given by King William.

21. The lands of Balfeith or Belphe; given by Umfrid de Berkeley.

22. Two oxgates of land, called the Rath of Ketteryn (Katterline), on the coast; given by William Fitz-Bernard.

23. All the lands of Glaskeler, lying betwixt the church and the rivulet of Katteryn; given by John de Montfort.

24. A ploughgate of the lands of Balekelefan; given by Richard de Frivill.

25. The whole lands of Nyg, including the parish of Nigg, in the north-eastern corner of the county (excepting the kirklands of Nigg belonging to the bishops of St Andrews); given by King Alexander II. These lands were afterwards formed into the barony of Torry. The

Convent had a church or religious house at Torry called the Abbot's Chapel. This chapel probably stood at the spot now called Abbot's Walls.

26. The lands of Tubertachthas, Glenferkeryn, Kinkell, Culback, Auchinblae, Blairs, Catterlin, Miln, &c., in the parish of Fordoun; given by Robert Warnebald and Richenda his spouse. These lands were afterwards held by the Convent under the general title of the Barony of Newlands.

27. The lands of Conveth, Halton, Scotston, and Mill of Conveth, near Laurencekirk.

28. The lands and barony of Banchory-Ternan, on the river Dee.

29. The lands of Ardoch, in the parish of Banchory-Devenick.

30. The lands of Petmegartney were given by Stephen de Kinardley.

In Perthshire and Fifeshire.—31. The lands of Bellach and Petinlour were given by King William, along with the church of Abernethy. The Convent for a long period held the former lands (probably Ballow, near Abernethy). They also held for ages the *teinds* of Wester Pitlour, in that part of Abernethy parish which lies in Fifeshire: but they either never acquired or had given away the *property* right to the lands at an early period.

In Lanarkshire.—32. The lands between Ethkar and Calledouer were given by Thomas, the son of Thancard, in the time of King William. He stated that his father had received these lands from King Malcolm. This tract of land was of considerable extent, and was afterwards erected into the *Regality of Ethcarmuir*, of which the Abbot continued to be overlord till the Reformation, although the property or rents of the lands were feued at an early period for half-a-stone of wax, payable yearly at the messuage, if asked. The lands consisted of the eastern half of the parish of Cambusnethan, lying between the water of Auchter and South Calder river.

In Aberdeenshire.—33. The village and lands of Tarves, Cairnbroggin, Milton, Newton, Smiddichill, Brakcalaw, Tillicarne, Tulielt, Cairnfechill, Auchinleck, Kirktown of Tarves, Milns of Tulielt and Fechill, Cowlie, and others, in the parish of Tarves, afterwards incorporated into the barony of Tarves. A part, if not the whole of these lands, were given by King Alexander II., and they were formed into a separate regality by a charter from King Robert Bruce.

34. The lands of Ardlogy, Lenthendy, and others, in the vicinity of Fyvie. These, with the mill of Fyvie and the lands of Mondurno, were afterwards formed into the barony of Fyvie. In 1179 Fergus Earl of Buchan founded a religious house or priory for the Order of St Benedict on the banks of the river Ythan, within this parish. It was dedicated to the Virgin Mary; and was bestowed by the earl on the Abbey of Arbroath, of which it henceforth became a cell or dependent house. The grant was confirmed by Margaret Countess of Buchan, his daughter, who married Sir William Cumin, afterwards Earl of Buchan. In 1285 Reginald de Cheen granted to the Abbey of Arbroath "and to the monks of that monastery in the religious house constructed on the lands of Ardlogy, near the church of St Peter of Fyvie," all his lands of Ardlogy and Lenthendy; and his gift was on the same day confirmed by Henry Bishop of Aberdeen. Abbot Bernard appointed one named Albert to the office of custodier of the house of Fyvie in 1323; and in 1325 he addressed to him a letter as to the discipline, rules, and services of the house, which will be afterwards referred to. In the same year King Robert Bruce granted a writ for the settlement of the marches betwixt the Abbey lands of Ardlogy and his park of Fyvie; in which he refers to the burgesses of "our burgh of Fyvyne," and their claim to take peats from the lands of Ardlogy. Fyvie was once ranked among the royal burghs: it is now annihilated. The points in

dispute were decided by a jury of twenty-one men, most of whom were destitute of surnames. In 1361 Abbot William made Patrick de Firmatorio custodier of the house of Fyvie. Malcolm Brydy, afterwards abbot, was prior of Fyvie in 1451; and at the same time John of St Andrews was custodier of the house. In 1471 Alexander Masoun, prior of Fyvie, did much for the repair and enlargement of its buildings. He rebuilt the chapel and offices, and enclosed the garden with a wall. He was still prior in 1484, when he took a prominent part in the election of Abbot David Lichtone. This priory continued its dependence on the Abbey of Arbroath till the Reformation, when its revenues were given up in the various accounts as worth about £400 Scots. Beside some small remains of the buildings, the memory of this house is kept up by the name of the "Prior's Well" and the "Monkshill" in their neighbourhood. The patron saint of the church is commemorated by "Peterwell" in its vicinity.

35. A ploughgate of the lands of Kinnethmont, in Garioch; given by Earl David, brother of King William.

36. The lands of Mundurnach or Mondurno, on the river Don; given by Roger de St Michael.

37. The lands of Abbots Hall, at Futy, within the burgh of Aberdeen. The name of Futy is derived from "Fotinus," the patron saint of the church of Nigg and of the village of Torry, on the south side of Dee.

In Banffshire.—38. The lands of Forglen, with the custody of the "Brecbennach," or ancient consecrated banner of St Columba; granted by King William. Under this ancient standard the Abbey tenants were marched to war. The office of Keeper was always held by a family of distinction.

39. The Kirklands and Kirktown of Inverbondie; given by King William along with the church of that parish, now called Boyndie.

II.—TENEMENTS IN BURGHS.

King William granted to the Abbey a toft or tenement in each of his burghs, and where he had manors or residences. And from the Abbey writs it appears that, in consequence of grants from him and others, the Convent actually held such tofts—sometimes called hostilages—in the following burghs, viz.:—Forres, Aberdeen, Perth, Forfar, Montrose, Dundee, Crail, Kinghorn, Inverkeithing, Stirling, Edinburgh, Peebles, Berwick-upon-Tweed, and in the village of Auchterarder. The greater number of these tenements were feued away previous to the Reformation; the feuars being often taken bound to provide temporary lodgings for the abbot and monks when they visited the place. The "Charge of the Temporalitie" only takes notice of two tenements in Aberdeen, one in Perth, and one in Arbroath. The Convent also held lands at Linlithgow, and a granary in Leith.

III.—FISHINGS.

The Abbey possessed right to many fishings. The following may be specified:—1. A net fishing in Tay, called Stok; and 2. A net fishing in the North Esk, called St Thomas; both granted by King William. 3. A half-mark out of the fishing of Ur on Tay; granted by the Earls of Strathearn. 4. Fishings at Broughty on the Tay; granted by Gilchrist Earl of Angus. 5. Fishings at Banchory-Devenick, on the Dee. 6. Salmon fishings on the Dee, called Poldoun-Largat, in the barony of Torry. 7. A net fishing near the Bridge of Dee. 8. Fishings at Inverbondie, part of King William's gifts in that district; with right to a boat in "St Brandon's haven. 9. Fishing rents payable from Inverness in herrings, salted and in barrels.

IV.—FERRY BOATS.

1. The Abbey obtained from King William, and for a long period retained the right to the Batell or ferry-boat at Montrose, with the land attached to it. 2. They possessed the right to a ferry-boat at Kincorth on the Dee, where the bridge now crosses that river. This boat had probably belonged to the barony of Torry.

V.—WOODS AND FORESTS.

The Abbey possessed, 1. A right to take timber from all the king's forests; granted by King William and King Alexander II., and renewed by King Robert Bruce. 2. The wood of Trustach on the Dee; granted by Thomas de Lundyn, durward or door-keeper to King William. 3. The right of taking coals (charcoal) from the wood of Edale (Edzell); granted by John Abbe the son of Malise. 4. The rights of free forestry on the lands of Conon, Dumbarrow, and Kingoldrum; granted by Alexander II., as already mentioned. King Robert Bruce afterwards granted the Park of Conon and Dumbarrow in warrenry. 5. The right of free forestry in the King's Park of Drum; given by King Robert Bruce.

VI.—SALTWORKS.

1. King William bestowed on the Convent a saltwork in the Carse of Stirling, beside his own saltworks, with five acres of adjoining land and common pasturage attached. It is difficult to comprehend how a saltwork on the brackish waters of the Forth could have been a boon to Arbroath Abbey, situated close to the German Ocean. 2. A saltwork at Dun, with an acre of land, was granted by John de Hastings.

VII.—CHURCHES, TITHES, &C.

Not long after the establishment of the Abbey, it obtained right to forty-six churches, with the manses, glebes, church lands, and tithes attached to them. The greater part of these churches were obtained from King William. The remainder were granted by the Earls of Angus, the Bishops of St Andrews, Brechin, and Dunkeld, the De Berkeleys, and other grandees of the time. Some of the church lands extended to the size of considerable farms, such as the lands of Inverlunan and the Kirktown of Inverkeillor. The names of the churches were *(In Angus and Mearns)*—Aberbrothoc or St Vigeans, *St Mary of Old Munros or Maryton, Newtyle, Glammis, Ethie or St Murdoch, Dunnichen, Kingoldrum, Inverlunan or Lunan, Panbride, *Fethmuref or Barry, *Guthrie, Monikie, Monifieth, Muirhous or Murroes, Kirriemuir, Earls-Strathdichtie or Mains, Arbirlot, Inverkeillor, Ruthven, Clova, *Nigg, *Kateryn or Catterlin, Garvock. *(In Aberdeenshire and Northern Counties)*—Banchory-St-Ternan, Coul, *Tula or Tulunauth, Fyvie, Tarves, Inverbondie, Fetter-Angus, Gamery, Aberchirdor or St Marnoch,* Turriff, *Inverugie, Kinnerny, Bothelnie, Forg, Langley, Banff, Inverness. *(In Perthshire and Fifeshire)*—Abernethy, with the chapels of *Dron, *Errol, and Dunbog, which were dependencies on the church of Abernethy in the time of King William. *(In Nithsdale)*—*Kirkmahoe. *(In England)*—*Hautwisel or Haltwhistle, in Tynedale. Those to which an asterisk is prefixed were alienated or suppressed previous to the Reformation, leaving thirty-four churches in actual possession at that time. The church of Barry was acquired by the monks of Balmerino at an early period; and the church of Guthrie was given up by the Convent about the time when it was erected into a collegiate establishment previous to the year 1479.

VIII.—ORIGINAL ANNUAL-RENTS.

The annual-rents or ground-annuals given to the Abbey out of the lands of various proprietors were numerous; although it is not, in some cases, easy to distinguish such ground-annuals from the feu-rents, payable to the Abbey by the feuing out of their own lands. We may mention a few of the former class. 1. One silver merk, given by Fergus Earl of Buchan. 2. Two shillings from the lands of Balcnaus; given by Thomas Malherbe. 3. A half silver merk from the Mill of Haddington; given by William de Vallibus. 4. Two shillings given by Thomas de Lundyn, doorkeeper to the king. 5. One hundred shillings from the Manor of Forfar; granted by Alexander II., for behoof of thirteen poor persons. 6. Ten merks from the lands of Monifieth; given by the same monarch for augmentng the wax lights of the abbey church. 7. Four silver merks from the king's lands of Kinghorn; given by Robert Bruce, for sustaining lights round the tomb of King William. 8. Four beeves yearly granted by Maldoueny Earl of Lennox, with twenty beeves at his death, on condition that his name and the name of Aveleth, his brother, be inscribed in the martyrology of the monks, and that they be yearly absolved by the chapter on their anniversary. The four beeves were afterwards commuted for two silver merks yearly, payable at Cambuskenneth. 9. Ten merks from the lands of Redhall, Balfeych, and Mill, in the barony of Newlands, in Mearns, with a piece of ground lying in front of the cathedral church of Brechin; given by John Wishart of Pittarrow, knight, to the chaplainry and altar of St Thomas the martyr, in the cathedral.

About the year 1560, the Convent had also right to forty shillings annually from lands at Glammis; 12s. 6d. from a tenement in Perth; 6s. 8d. from a tenement in Dundee; 40s. from a tenement in Aberdeen; £4, 6s. 10d.

from the Grange of Monifieth ; 39s. 10d. from the lands of Balgillo ; and 13s. 8d. from the lands of Ballumby in the parish of Murroes.

IX.—BURGHS.

In virtue of royal sanction the Convent of Arbroath founded two burghs on their domains, viz.:—1. The burgh of barony and regality of Aberbrothock. At the Reformation the Abbey retained annual-rents amounting to £11, 10s. 1d. Scots, payable from the older portion of the burgh, and £13, 16s. Scots, payable from the feus of the Almory, which are not included in the rentals after referred to. By that time the greater part of the rents of the old burgh belonged to the Lady Chapel, the altarages of St Nicholas, St Sebastian, and the dirigie dues payable to the altar of St Dupthacus. 2. The burgh of barony of Torry, in the parish of Nigg, was erected by a charter from King James IV. on 11th December 1495, in honour of the blessed martyr Saint Thomas, and Saint Fotinus, patron of the village of Torry, and out of love and favour for David Abbot of Arbroath, and for the convenience and hospitality of all others who travelled beyond the Mounth to Aberdeen or other northern parts of the kingdom. The king conferred on this little burgh the right to buy and sell all merchandise, and to exercise all kinds of trade with the freedom of a burgh of barony ; and, with consent of the Abbot, to elect bailies and other officers ; to have a cross and weekly market, and an annual fair at the feast of St Fotinus and the four following days, with the tolls and customs leviable at the fair. In the year 1509 the Abbot and Convent appointed William Rolland, burgess of Aberdeen, to be the bailie and commissioner, to admit new burgesses, and to parcel out and dispose of roods and crofts in their burgh of Torry "newly erected" for the utility of the place.

X.—RENTS, &C., AT DISSOLUTION OF THE ABBEY.

In the end of the year 1561 the Privy Council passed an act that the rentals of all the benefices of the kingdom should be produced, in order that the third parts of their proceeds should be levied for the use of the reformed clergy and the Queen, leaving the remaining two-thirds in the possession of the popish incumbents. The rentals given up by virtue of this order and others enforcing it were formed into a list called the "Book of Assumption of Thirds;" and among the rents of the great benefices the income of the Abbey of Arbroath stands assumed, or supposed to be, £2873, 14s. Scots money ; 35 chalders wheat ; 156 chalders 2 bolls 2 firlots bear ; 200 chalders 3 bolls 2 firlots meal ; 27 chalders 2 bolls oats ; 37 barrels salmon ; 2 barrels grilse. This rental would, at that period, be nearly equal to what £9847, 14s. sterling is in the market at the present time. But these rents must either have been assumed at too high an amount, or the collector-general of the thirds had failed in getting payment. This will be seen by comparing the above quantities with those which the "comptare" or comptroller—Wishart of Pitarrow—charged against himself as having received out of the "Abbacie of Aberbrothoik" for the year 1561. When to these "thirds" actually received, other two-thirds are added, there arises a great defalcation in every item, excepting the oats. Thus :—Scots money, £2483, 5s. : Wheat, 26 chalders 9 bolls 1 firlot ; bear, 118 chalders 7 bolls 3½ pecks ; meal, 168 chalders 8 bolls 2 firlots 1¼ pecks ; oats, 27 chalders 10 boll 3 firlots 3⅔ pecks ; salmon, 15 barrels. It appears that £800 of the money, as "superplus of the thirds" of Arbroath Abbey, were paid to the Crown ; and that Wishart dealt out the remainder to the working clergy with such a careful hand as to lead to the proverb, "The good laird of Pitarrow was an earnest professor of Christ, but the meikle deevil receive the Comptroller."

The Book of Assumption gives the following general abstract of the "Temporalitie" or *lands* of the Abbey, viz.:—The baronies of Arbroath, Dunnichen, Ethie, Kingoldrum, Newlands, Torry, Banchory-Ternan, and Tarves ;' and in regard to the Church tithes to which the Abbey had right, and which were in those days termed the *Spirituality* of the benefice, it gives a list of the thirty-four churches remaining at the Reformation.

The following is an abstract of "the charge of the Temporalitie of the haill Kirklandis" of the Abbey "annexit to oure Souerane Lordis Crowne" in 1592, thirty years after the previous rent rolls were framed. By that time the whole lands of the Abbey, except the precinct, had been feued out; and the feu-duties are taken payable in Scots money, wheat, bear, meal, oats, salmon, poultry, &c. This long list however does not specify the feu-duties of the office of bailiary of the regality of Arbroath, nor the duties payable from lands at Fyvie, and office of bailiary of Fyvie and Tarves; and certain lands, such as those of Kenny Mekil and Middle Persie at Kingoldrum, are merely charged "with service used and wont." With these exceptions the whole feu-duties of the Abbey lands, described as lying in the counties of Forfar, Kincardine, Aberdeen, Banff, and Perth, are found to amount to: Scots money, £1499, 6s. 10d.; rynmart silver, £8, 12s. 6d. Scots; wheat, 8 chalders 14 bolls 1 firlot; bear, 35 chalders 14 bolls 2 firlots; meal, 19 chalders 14 bolls; oats, 20 chalders 6 bolls 1 firlot; horse corn, 9 chalders 3 bolls; 3 barrels salmon; 185½ capons—250½ poultry; 1 ryn wedder—1 sow; 23 carriages of hay, &c.; 151 loads of peat and turfs.

The whole of the duties above noted, except about £410, 10s. 7d., part of the Scots money, are leviable from lands situated in the county of Forfar. In order to obtain an approximation to the market value of these rents about the time when they were fixed—nearly three hundred years ago—the following calculations are given :—

1st. As a pound Scots would at that period suffice for the purchase of as much in the market as can now be purchased for a pound sterling, the whole money feu-rents, amounting to £1507, 19s. 4d. Scots may be stated as equal to the same amount in sterling money, viz., ... £1507 19 4
2nd. Wheat at 30s. per boll, . . . 212 7 6
3rd. Bear, meal, oats, horse-corn, at an average of 20s. per boll, . . 1365 15 0
4th. Capons and poultry at 1s. 6d. each, 32 14 0
5th. Other items at least, . . . 10 0 0

Amounting to . . . £3128 15 10

—That is to say, the Abbey rents, so far as set down in the list of 1592, would, about 1560, purchase as many commodities as could in 1859 be purchased for £3128, 15s. 10d. But in order to ascertain their actual market value at the present time, eleven-twelfth parts of the money-rents, or £1382, 6s. 1d. must be deducted on account of the depreciation of Scots money, which reduces the value of the rents in the market of 1859 to £1746, 9s. 9d. sterling.

Some idea of the present yearly value of the *lands* which were formerly bestowed on the Abbey may be learned from the fact that the rental of four out of the eight baronies or parishes which it possessed, viz., Aberbrothock, Ethie, Dunnichen and Kingoldrum, amounted, by the recent valuation, to £13,848, 16s.

CHAPTER XI.

SUBORDINATE OFFICERS OF THE ABBEY.—1. SUB-PRIOR: 2. STEWARD: 3. CHAMBERLAIN: 4. TERRARIUS OR LAND-STEWARD: 5. SACRISTAN: 6. GRANITOR: 7. CELLARER: 8. MASTER OF WORKS: 9. JUDGE OR DEEMSTER: 10 JUSTICIAR OR BAILIE: 11. MAIR AND CORONER.

IT is not very easy at this period, and in this country, which now possesses no original monasteries, to define the positions and duties of the various officers who are from time to time mentioned in the Abbey writings. In such an establishment these officers were numerous; although it is probable that the same office may have sometimes borne different names in earlier and later periods, while new offices may have been created as older offices became extinct or degenerated into sinecures. The writings of Arbroath Abbey allude to the Sub-Prior, the Steward, the Chamberlain, the Terrarius or Land Steward, the Sacristan, the Granitor, the Cellarer, the Master of Works, the Judge (or Deemster), the Justiciar or Bailie, and the Mair and Coroner.

1. The SUB-PRIOR was the Abbot's depute in religious and strictly monastic matters; and during the early period of the Abbey history appears to have borne the simple designation of Prior. He acted sometimes the part of a chamberlain; and rents and lands are stipulated to be paid to him. In the Abbot's absence he occasionally granted charters, and acted as his vicegerent in other matters. Sub-Priors of the name of Richard Guthrie were successively elected Abbots in 1450 and 1471, if these do not both denote the same

person. The latter was also styled Professor of Sacred Theology. The Sub-Prior presided *ex officio* at elections of the Abbots; and during the late degenerate time of commendams, pluralities, and absenteeism, the actual domestic government of the Abbey seems to have been practically left to him.

2. The office of STEWARD or Senescallus was held by John de Pollok about 1202, and then during a long period by a person named Adam, who is witness to numerous charters granted by Gilchrist Earl of Angus, and others. Rayner the son of Allan, was Steward in the time of Abbot Bernard. In 1387 the office was held by "Alexander Skrymchur of Aberbrothoc our Stewart;" and seven years afterwards this "Alexander Skyrmechur" is designed Justiciar of the Regality.

3. The CHAMBERLAIN is repeatedly alluded to in the monastic writs from the foundation of the Abbey till about the year 1521, as distinct from the bailie or justiciar. During the earlier period he seems to have been an officer of importance. He had charge of the Abbey rents, many of which are stipulated to be paid to him. For example, the rents of the teinds of Arbroath were on 30th April 1501, provided to be payable to the "Sub-Prior, Chamberlain, and Master of Works, for the sustentation of the fabric of our place." Afterwards certain rents are ordered to be paid to the Chamberlain, having the special mandate of the Abbot for that effect. The Bailie was sometimes styled Chamberlain; but it is probable that the duties of the office were actually performed by one bearing the title of Chamberlain, either as deputed by the Bailie, or appointed by the Abbot and chapter. The duties of the Chamberlain, like those of the Sacrist, Cellarer, and some other offices, were generally, if not always, performed by a monk.

4. The TERRARIUS appears to have been a land steward. He is only once mentioned, viz.—in a contract bearing the early date of 1240, betwixt the Abbot and

Alexander Cumin Earl of Buchan. One part of his duties was to keep a "Terrar" or rent book for the Abbey lands.

5. The SACRISTAN (now shortened to sexton) or vestry keeper, was an officer to whom certain rents were made payable, from the above-mentioned date of 1240 till 1534. In 1242 it is stated that an oxgate of land beside the Mill of Conveth, near Luther, had been given to the Sacrist of Aberbrothock, in the Eleemosynary, for sustaining a light at the altar of St Mary. This altar being at the door of the vestry, would naturally fall to the care of the monk who held the office of Sacristan, with the charge of the vestry and its contents.

6. The GRANITOR had charge of the grain and granaries, including flour, meal, barley, and malt brought to the Abbey as teind dues or rent dues. He was one of the monks; and "Den Richart Scot Sup-priour of Abirbrothoc" in 1488, seems to have also held the office of Granitor two years later, in 1490. The Granitor seems to have assumed the power of leasing the teinds due from lands, particularly those at a distance, such as about Abernethy, for a money payment. Abbot David, in 1489, recorded some "Ordinances for the regulation of the place," which afford an interesting view of the provisions annually made for the Abbey. He directs that the Granitor shall bring in and place within the girnals yearly, by Allhallowmas or "Mydlentryne," 82 chalders of malt, 30 chalders of wheat, and 40 chalders of meal, "and this rule to be observit and keepit for the gude and singular profit of the place :— the sum of all corns to ordinary expense within the place is 7 score and 12 chalders of wheat, bear, and meal." The Abbot provides "that naething be set to nae baron nor landed man without my lord's advice. Since the rental may sustain the place, that through the negligence of the Granitor the place [may] sustain nae fault, but that all the victuals be brought in as is

before written, and that nane be to crave frae Pais till Allhallowmas in the country, sen [since] God of his grace has given the place largely to live upon, and that slothness of officers gar [not] the place want provision; and that the Abbot, for the time being, that he be nocht slothful, nae [but] he tak cuir [care] upon him till gar all be fulfilled and inbrought in due time as said is; and that the counts of the officers be heard four times in the yeir." The field which lies immediately outside of the precinct walls, to the east of the Convent green, and styled the Granitor or Grantor's croft, formed part of the patrimony of this officer. After the Granitor's office had ceased, on the breaking up of the monastery, the Granitor's croft was set in feu to Patrick Hamilton, porter of the Abbey, in life-rent, for the yearly payment of one boll of bear, and three shillings and tenpence Scots.

7. The CELLARER was the title of the officer who had charge of the Abbey cellars with their contents, consisting of flesh, fish, poultry, spices, &c. He was the chief butler of the monastery, and is often mentioned in conjunction with the granitor. Den John Drybrugh, a monk of the Abbey, was cellarer from 1482 till 1487. Abbot David's ordinances give a view of the cellarer's office still more interesting than that given of the granitor's department. We take liberty to recite part of these regulations, not only to show the provision and economy of one of those establishments, which exerted no little influence on society in past times, and of which we now understand so little, but also to afford a view of the current prices of these indispensable articles of merchandise nearly four hundred years ago,—keeping in view that the prices are stated in Scots money, one shilling of which fell (ultimately, at least) so low as not to exceed the value of a penny sterling. The cellarer was to expend yearly on " wedders 800 [120 per hundred,] price of the piece 3 shillings—sowme, £144: in marts lardinar [beeves salted],

and fresh all the year 9 score, or 180, price of ilk piece 15 shillings—sowme, £135 : in keling lardinar [salted cod-fish] 1500, price per hundred, £3—sowme, £45. And of thir fish, where mister [need] is in winter, to be spended 500, and against Lentren 1000—sowme, £322, 6s. 8d. : in salmon lardinar betwixt Dundee, the Ferry, and Montrose [to be supplied from these places], 11 barrels ; and the cellarer to bring in the same by Lammas yearly ; and thereof in winter to be disposed of 5 barrels, and in Lentren 6 barrels : to be bought in dry haddocks and speldings, 12,000 ; price of each hundred, 16 pennies—sowme, £8 : by [beside] the teind and lardinar [fish], to buy fresh fish daily, £60 : to buy eggs and butter, 20 merks : to buy lambs, veals, gryces, and chickens, £20 : to buy salt, 20 merks : 4 lbs. saffron, £6 : 16 lbs. pepper, 8 merks : 2 lbs. ginger, 20 shillings : 2 lbs. cannel [cinnamon], 32 shillings : 2 lbs. cloves, 2 merks : 1 lb. *granis* [carroways ?], 1 merk : 1 lb. mace, 16 shillings : 100 lbs. almonds, £6—price per lb., 20 pence : 3 dozen *rys*, 24 shillings : candle in the year, £20 : in vinegar, 6 gallons, price per pint 4 pennies—sowme, 32 shillings : in honey, 6 gallons, price per pint 18 pennies—sowme, £3, 12s. : in the cellarer's office for the fuel bringing hame, £5 : 2 dozen swine and baris [boars], £10 : till his expense passing to the fairs, £8 : in habit silver, £5, 13s. 4d. : for the servitors' fees in the kitchen, £3, 10s. Memorandum, that the auld cellarer's charges was, the year of God, auchty and aucht years [1488], *the Kings Henes* [Highness] *being here twys, the Archebischop thrice, and the lords of the realm and all others hospitalitie kepit*, draws £500, 29s. 4d. And now the memorial extends [exceeds] that sowme £27." This "memorandum" affords a lively idea of the demands which were made on the hospitality of the Abbey. The two great personages who so liberally favoured Arbroath with their visits in the year 1488 must have been either the ill-fated James III., who was killed on 7th June of that year, or, more probably, his young successor, James IV., and William Schevez, Archbishop of St Andrews.

The high grounds betwixt Wardmill and the old Brechin road were in old times attached to the cellarer's office, and bore the name of the "Milhil" before they were leased to persons of the name of Guthrie, about the year 1501. This officer also possessed a croft known by the name of "the Cellarer Croft," till it was let, along with the Wardmill, about 1509, for a rent, to be paid to "our cellarer." This land is described as lying near the Brothock and the Wardmill, along with which it continued to be leased for many years afterwards. In consequence of this connection the term "Wardmill Croft" may have come to be applied to it, while the only vestige now remaining of the term Cellarer is to be found in the name of the neighbouring ford by which the Brothock was crossed at the south end of this field, and which can be traced from the original Cellarer-ford through the various forms of Cellery-ford, Sellery-ford, Sillery-ford, to Siller-ford, its modern and corrupted orthography.

On 6th May 1498 Abbot David Lichtone leased the half of the lands of Seaton for nineteen years to the Cellarer for the decent sustentation of his office, on condition that he, or other monks joined with him in the possession, should provide yearly at their expense a boat for fishing, with men and other necessaries required for it, near *the Maiden Castle* (le Madyn Castel), or wherever the Abbot and Convent might see expedient—the Cellarer to make yearly count of all the goods and commodities of the half part of Seaton and boat, and to have no power to let the said half without special license—sub-tenants and other necessary servants excepted." The Maiden Castle is a small rocky peninsula which projects into the ocean near Covehaven, and was defended by what is still a very high and conspicuous bank or *vallum*, with a deep ditch or fosse in front. This fortification was probably hastily thrown up as a last resource by some company of Danes or Norwegians after a defeat, whether at Carnoustie or elsewhere. If they were allowed to leave it, or managed to embark in boats before their enemies were able to take the fortification by force, it would from that circumstance, as in many similar cases, get the title of a virgin fort; or, as in the Abbey writings, "the Maiden Castle." It is proper, however, to mention that Chalmers and others have attempted to derive the term from more ancient sources.

8. The MASTER OF THE WORKS seems to have been a monk who had the charge of keeping the fabrics or Abbey buildings in repair. He is occasionally mentioned in the monastic writings during the period from 1490 till 1501, in both of which years the teind rents of the church of Abernethy were made payable to this officer: on the first occasion to Den John Dryburgh (formerly the cellarer), now *Magister Fabrice*, in conjunction with the granitor and cellarer, for the repairs of the chapel of the Infirmary; and on the second occasion, in conjunction with the sub-prior and chamberlain. Part of the patrimony of this officer consisted of the ground now called the Smithy Croft. This ground contained a building styled the Smiddy House or House of the Works, with a garden attached; and about the time of the Reformation they were all set in feu to Adam Pierson for 16s. 8d. Scots yearly.

9. The ancient office of JUDEX, now corrupted into Judge, is repeatedly mentioned in the Arbroath Chartulary. This officer also bore the Saxon or lowland Scotch name of Doomster, Deemster, or Dempster, from it being his duty to pronounce the doom or final sentence; and his functions seem to have gradually sunk down from that of deciding cases into a formal rehearsal of the sentence. In a writing of 1227, already referred to, one Adam is mentioned as "Judex of our lord the king," in conjunction with his brother "Kerald, Judex of Angus."

The Judex of Angus was probably the Deemster of the court of the great earls of Angus, but it is not easy to define the difference betwixt the king's Judex and the Sheriff at this early period. About 1230, or later, this Kerald is styled Judex of our lord the king, and obtained certain lands, which from him received the name of "Keraldstown," now "Caraldston," while his descendants took their surname of Dempster from the office; and for many generations the Dempsters of Caraldston held the office of Deemster to the Parliaments of Scotland. The office passed with the lands through the hands of the Earl of Crawford and other owners down till 1748, when it was abolished with the other heritable jurisdictions.

The family of Caraldston seem to have also held the office of Dempster of the courts of the Abbots of Arbroath, and to have possessed the lands of Kennymukard, near Kingoldrum, in free tenandry. In the year 1370, Andrew Dempster of Keraldston bound himself to Abbot John that he should serve the office of Judex in the Abbot's courts, by one man to reside in the shire of Aberbrothock, sworn faithfully to perform the office, for which he was to receive each year "twenty shillings of sterlings," besides the usual perquisites of the office. Ninety years afterwards (in 1460), David Dempster of Caraldstown, with consent of David Dempster, his son and heir, resigned into the hands of Abbot Malcolm his office of Dempster in the Abbot's courts, with the annual payment of "twenty shillings of usual money of the kingdom of Scotland," and others belonging to that office. This is the last notice of such a functionary in connection with the Abbey. We may remark that the last remaining Dempster in Scotland was that of the Justiciary Court, which, after existing long as a sinecure, was abolished within the recollection of persons still alive.

10. The extensive civil and criminal jurisdiction of the Lord Abbot of Arbroath was administered by a high officer termed the JUSTICIAR or BAILIE OF THE REGALITY.

Alexander Scrymechur, one of the witnesses to the contract for the erection of the harbour in 1394, is described as Justiciar of the Regality. This officer was sometimes styled in the Abbey writs " Justiciar, Chamberlain, and Bailie." Under this title, Abbot David Lichtone, on 26th November 1485, conferred the office on James Ogilvy of Airlie, Knight, and John Ogilvy of Ballindoch, his son and apparent heir, for eleven years. The office had become vacant by the death of James Ogilvy of Luntreith, Knight. In the year 1494, James Lord Ogilvy of Airlie, had a dwelling-house or " hospitium" in the burgh of Arbroath, within which his son, John Ogilvy, Baron of Fingask, Bailie of the Regality, held an inquest concerning the lands of Forglen. Whatever may have been the case at the time of the battle of Arbroath, 1445-6, when the bailiary was contended for by the Lindsays, it appears soon afterwards to have become virtually hereditary in the family of Airlie.

King James V., by a writing dated 10th January 1526-7, declares that " it is onderstand to us and the Lords of owr consall, that owr Abbay of Arbroyth and Abbotts tharof ar infeft of auld of free regality, and justice ayres to be halden be thare balyeis wythin thar lands passyt memor of man ;" and that although Abbot David (Betoun) had omitted to hold the justice aire of their regality before the king's justice aire in Forfarshire, " for ministracioun of justice upon personis replegyt be tham and thar bailye furth of owr said justice ayr, we wyll nocht that tha be hurt tharthrow in thar regalite in tyme cumyng, bot hald thar justice ayris tharin eftyr owr sayd nyxt justice ayr, syklyk and als frely as they or thar balye micht have dune," &c. From this and other documents we learn that the Bailie of Regality held circuit courts, and had power to repledge or redeem from the king's circuit courts persons dwelling within the regality when accused of crimes. In virtue of this right of regality, Abbot Walter Paniter in 1435, compounded with Andrew of Lychtoun, and granted him remission for the slaughter of James Gibsoun. Even after the Reformation, in 1570, we learn from Pitcairn's Criminal Trials that the commendator of Arbroath could rescue from the king's justiciar, and repledge into his own court, four men accused of the murder of William Sibbald of Cair, on account of their dwelling within his bounds.

The formidable powers of Bailie of the Regality of Arbroath remained in the family of Airlie till the abolition of heritable jurisdictions, when John, fourth Earl of Airlie, received £1400 sterling in compensation for his loss; and John and James Smith, the life-rented regality clerks, received each £41, 13s. 4d. sterling for their losses.

Like the old high-sheriffs, the bailies of regality executed parts of their functions by deputies. On 13th May 1476, David Herice de Dery, as "Depute-Bailie of the regality and lordship of Aberbrothock," granted a charter of resignation to Sir John Tody, chaplain, of a tenement near Hopemount, Arbroath.

The Abbey lands in the parish of Tarves, Aberdeenshire, were, by King Robert Bruce's charter of 26th February 1322-3, erected into a separate regality, with confirmation of all the privileges of "foss, furk, sock, sack, thol, them, infangthief," contained in King Alexander's original gift of these lands. But we have seen no indications in the Chartulary of a separate office of Bailie of *Regality* over that district; although in the list of feu-duties annexed to the Crown in 1592, George Gordoun is stated as the holder of certain lands in the lordships and baronies of Tarves and Fyvie, "with the *baillierie* of the saids baronies."

Besides the regalities of Arbroath and Tarves, the Abbots held, as already stated, the feudal superiority of a regality in Lanarkshire, called " our Regality of Athkarmoure," or Ethkarmuir, which, from 1476 at least to 1529, they committed to the charge of persons appointed by them, as "Justiciar, chamberlain, commissioner, and bailie,' with power to repledge men dwelling within the bounds from the King's justice aires or circuit courts held at Lanark.

11. The offices of MAIR and CORONER of the Abbey were probably held by separate persons in early times; but from the days of Abbot Malcolm they were combined in one person, and seem to have lost all those judicial powers which originally belonged to them, having retained merely the humbler executive department. They were latterly the macers or court officers of the Regality Bailie. On 11th February 1462-3 Abbot Malcolm Brydy conferred these offices on Master Thomas Deyksoun for life, with a salary of forty shillings Scots, 12 bolls barley, and 12 bolls oats, with the occupancy of a piece of ground called *Mairland*, on the north part of Cairnie, which seems to have been a special perquisite of this office. On 8th June 1528 David Betoun appointed Henry Guthrie, and John Guthrie, his eldest son, then tenants of Ruffys and the Park of Conan (Ruives and Parkconon), to the office of mairs and coroners of all his courts and justiciary or chamberlain aires, either of burgh or barony; and of notaries or clerks of court during their lives, with power to appoint substitutes, for the usual salary of the land—oats and barley before specified—except that in room of 8 bolls of the barley they were to get a chalder of a certain kind of oats, commonly called horse-corn. This grant was renewed in 1578 by Lord John Hamilton in favour of John Guthrie, son and heir of Henry Guthrie of Colliston.

The word "Dereth," a corruption of the Celtic term *Derach*, was the name of a similar office in the Abbey's regality of Tarves, Aberdeenshire. On 7th December 1463 Abbot Malcolm confirmed a grant whereby Abbot John Gedy, in 1384, had conferred " our office of Derethy of Terwas" on Thomas de Lochane and the heirs of his body in perpetuity.

CHAPTER XII.

THE ABBOTS OF ARBROATH.—1. INFLUENCE AND INCIDENTAL ADVANTAGES OF MONASTERIES IN EARLY TIMES. 2. SCOTTISH ECCLESIASTICS AT AND PREVIOUS TO THE FOUNDATION OF THE ABBEY. 3. BIOGRAPHICAL SKETCH OF THE ABBOTS OF ARBROATH, FROM 1178 TO 1606. 4. CAUSES OF THE DISSOLUTION OF THE ABBEY.

I.—MONASTERIES IN EARLY TIMES.

WITH the exception of Abbot Bernard and Abbot David Betoun, these dignitaries made little figure in our national history, and their memories possess an interest almost entirely local. But, notwithstanding the oblivion into which their names have fallen, it must not be forgotten that "the Lord Abbot of such a house as Arbroath, whether bearing crosier and mitre or buckling on more carnal armour; whether sitting in the high places of Council and Parliament, or taking homage and dispensing law among his vassals and serfs, or following his sovereign to battle, was, in virtue of his social position, his revenues, his followers, and actual power, by far the greatest personage of the shire." (Preface to Chartulary, vol. ii.) It may also be safely added, that in regard to education and intelligence, fairness as judges, mercifulness as feudal superiors, kindness as landlords, bountifulness as alms-givers, liberality as hosts, and general civilisation, the Abbots of Arbroath must have stood for ages many degrees superior to even the highest lay grandees of the district; and that their influential position—intimately connected as it was with the sovereign, the nobility, the clergy, and the neighbouring inhabitants, both urban and rural—was directly calculated to abate and modify the jarrings of these different classes, and to repress that barbarism which so much prevailed.

From a single glance at the magnificent buildings of Arbroath Abbey, with its large endowments of lands, teinds, fishings, tenements in towns, and numerous valuable privileges, it is apparent that it was intended to subserve many other purposes besides the support of twenty-five monks bound to celibacy. It may not perhaps be easy for us to understand all the objects which King William, nearly seven hundred years ago, had in view when he founded this monastery; but we may allude to a few of the then comparative advantages which flowed from such an institution.

The Abbey served as a caravansary or lodging-place for travellers of every rank—from kings and archbishops, judges on their circuits, legates and delegates, down to the poorest scholar who asked hospitality—where shelter and accommodation was to be had far superior to that of any feudal castle (for hotels had at that time no existence), and where sustenance was afforded to man and beast without fee or reward.

The Abbey was a school of letters at a period when, perhaps, the only other school betwixt the Tay and the Grampians was the Culdee College of Brechin. And there are indications that at the period in question the Culdees were becoming secularised in more senses than one. The knowledge of letters was entirely confined to churchmen; and the kings were obliged to employ ecclesiastics as judges and political ministers from the incapacity of the lay nobility through ignorance. We know from incidental notices that the Abbey possessed a library, and took land rents for its support; and that the Convent engaged pedagogues to teach the younger monks various branches of learning; and one of the sub-priors is styled Professor of Sacred Theology, and probably delivered lectures within the Abbey to the monks and clergy of the district. "And although the character of the theology there taught was low and puerile, and the state of the other branches of human learning deformed by superstition and error, yet without the feeble spark preserved in the religious houses, and the arts of life which were there cultivated and improved by the clergy, the state of the country during the period of which we are now writing would have been deplorable indeed." (Tytler's Hist., ii. 356.)

The Abbot and monks were in many cases the historians of the district, and of the kingdom in general. The registers of Paisley and other monasteries have supplied the most authentic accounts of many events in Scottish history; and the Abbey chartularies are almost our sole sources of information as to the social state of the country, and many usages and customs observed during ages preceding the Reformation. That part of the old register of Arbroath which was lately discovered at Ethie House contains many laws passed by King Robert Bruce during the chancellorship of Abbot Bernard, the authenticity of which historians and jurists had hitherto held as doubtful. The monasteries were at one period almost the sole places where books were composed; and what is perhaps of as much importance before printing was invented, they were the only places where books were transcribed, as many of the monks occupied almost their whole time in transcribing manuscripts. Even the numerous ancient manuscript copies of the Holy Scriptures must to a great degree be placed to the credit of the earlier monks.

The monks of rich Abbeys such as Arbroath were bountiful alms-givers. Each of them had an almory where provisions were weekly or oftener given to the poor with no sparing hand. And the conspicuous place held by the almory of Arbroath in the Abbey writs, and in the names of places in the vicinity of the monastery, shew that this, one of the most merciful and benignant purposes of its establishment, was by no means overlooked.

Convents were benefactors to this country in their promotion of horticulture. In former times gardens and orchards were scarcely to be found except at the monasteries; and those who have witnessed the privations and inconveniences, not to speak of diseases, sustained by the inhabitants of our Highlands and Western Isles, where the cultivation of garden vegetables and fruits was till lately, or is still, either unknown or neglected, will understand the value of those herbs and fruits which were principally introduced by the monks. They were likewise benefactors as intelligent landowners and agriculturists. From what we can glean they were the first landowners in this district who granted leases for a number of years certain, thus giving to their tenants a degree of encouragement and energy which tenants at will could never possess. The earliest leases recorded in the Arbroath register were granted by Abbot Bernard, in the time of Bruce, for periods of five or ten years, or for life. Our ordinary period for the duration of an agricultural lease (nineteen years) was adopted by the Abbots of Arbroath upwards of four centuries ago. And no landed proprietor of the present day guards more carefully than they did against the assignation, subletting, or subdivision of his lands while under lease. They had evidently much more respect to old tenants and their families than is now shewn by many modern landlords; and while they leased many of their farms at easy rents to the widows and sons of former tenants, they guarded themselves against the intrusion of strangers or unknown persons into their grounds by the singular provision that the widows should not marry again without the special license of the Abbot and Convent. Sir Richard

Maitland in his "Complaint aganis Oppression of the Commouns," alludes in complimentary terms to the churchmen as landlords, thus :

> "Sum commouns that has been weil stakit
> Under kirkmen, are now all wrakit
> Sen that the teind and the kirklands
> Came in gret temporal mennis hands."

Another very great advantage possessed by tenants of Abbey lands arose from the circumstance that their landlords were not subject to sudden and rapid changes by death, forfeiture, or sale ; upon any of which events the tenants of lay proprietors were subject to be turned away by new landlords, and exposed to want or beggary, besides suffering the loss of those advantages which they had expected to reap from improvements made by them.

These are a few traces of that progress in learning, and amelioration of manners, which we believe to have flowed from the monastic establishments of Scotland, before they fell into decrepitude and corruption about the year 1500. And we must add the important fact, that to them and the ecclesiastics in general at an earlier period is to be attributed much of the credit of effecting the emancipation of our rural population from that thraldom in which they were held by the barons previous to the erection of the great monasteries and the burghs.

II.—ANCIENT SCOTTISH ECCLESIASTICS.

Previous to the time of King Macbeth the whole of Scotland, excepting some large moorlands, had been divided into parishes by the old Scottish clergy and their bishops. These parishes were not in all instances conterminous with the modern parishes. Many old parishes, such as Aldbar, Burghill, Dunninald, Ethie, Meathie-Lure, and Kirkbuddo, have been since suppressed, and their lands added to other parishes, while at and after the Reformation, new parishes, such as

Carmylie were erected, and disjoined from neighbouring parishes. On the other hand the present churches of Fowlis, Dron, and others, in those early times, bore only the name and rank of *chapels*. These parish churches were originally served by the ordinary clergy, who came afterwards to be termed *secular* clergy. The state of the ancient parochial clergy of Scotland is involved in much obscurity. They appear in the early part of the Chartulary under the title of priests or parsons, and some of them had sons honourably mentioned as born in wedlock. Several of the churches came into the hands of the Culdees in the time of Macbeth, Malcolm III., and Edgar. The Culdees were secular canons, educated and trained in their ancient abbeys and colleges, such as those of Iona, Lismore, Dunkeld, Lochleven, Abernethy, St Andrews, Brechin, Scone, Murtlach, and Monimusk, and had the choice of the few bishops and prelates who then presided over the Scottish church. They first appear in Scottish history after 800. Their college at Abernethy was called a "University" in the time of Malcolm III., or shortly afterwards. They, and the old Scottish parochial clergy, held very little subjection to Rome, and many of them were married, and were succeeded in their offices by their children.

At the accession of Malcolm III. the Culdees had in many instances become ignorant and deteriorated, and the heads of their religious houses were rather lay barons than learned ecclesiastics. From their not being bound to any special rules of living and spending their time, these parish priests and Culdees were in course of time termed *secular* clergy; while the monastic orders, who ultimately supplanted the Culdees entirely, and even the parochial clergy to a large extent, and whose lives, habits, and studies were framed according to the regulations of their founders, and approved of by the Popes, were termed the *regular* or regulated clergy. These two classes had long contended in more southern countries, —the *regulars* to gain footing and power, and the *seculars* to retain their powers. The regular clergy first began to gain favour in Scotland through the patronage of Margaret the queen of Malcolm: and here, as in many other countries in Western Europe, the seculars, possessing neither papal nor regal partiality, had the worst of the contest, and were gradually, after a resistance of nearly two centuries, deprived of their power and influence, and stripped of their possessions; till in the reign of Alexander III., the order of Culdees seems to have become extinct, although their memories were long afterwards held in reverence in many parts of the country.

By the time of Malcolm III. the Normans had begun to erect in England those majestic cathedrals and abbey churches which have never been equalled either at an earlier or subsequent period; and Scotland, poor although it was, having some spare wealth at command, resolved to follow the example set by England. The Abbey Church of Dunfermline, erected in the Norman style, seems to have been one of the earliest of such buildings in Scotland. The simple and antiquated rites of the Culdees being deemed unworthy of these costly erections, it was found necessary to import the new monastic or regular clergy from England or the Continent, whose greater scholastic learning, gorgeous ritual, sanctity of manners, apparent or real, and courtliness of style, fitted them for occupying these buildings.

The various orders of monastic clergy who at different times were settled in Scotland during the five centuries which preceded the Reformation were very numerous. Their conventual establishments nearly amounted to two hundred, not including hospitals. Besides their distinction from the secular clergy they were themselves divided into two great classes, namely, the older or endowed monks, who lived on rents and lands bestowed on them; and the newer and begging friars (brethren) who lived on alms, with few or no endowments. Both these classes were again subdivided into various sections. Thus, the endowed monks were known in Scotland as monks of St Augustine, monks of St Anthony, as Red Friars, Praemonstratenses, Benedictines or Black Monks, Tyronensians, Cluniacenses, Cistertians or Bernardines, monks of Valliscaulium, Carthusians, Gilbertines, &c., from the framers of their regulations, the colours of their robes, or the places where they had first been established. The begging friars were subdivided into Black or Dominican, Grey or Franciscan, White or Carmelites ; so termed from the colours of their robes, their founders, or place of formation. Several of the endowed and mendicant classes had corresponding female orders, or nuns, who lived according to rules alleged to have been framed by St Augustine, St Benedict, or St Francis. Besides all these, the two orders of religious knights—viz., the Templars or knights of the Temple, and Knights of St John— held numerous lands and several establishments in Scotland. But the orders of monks who settled in this northern kingdom were few in comparison with those of Italy and the other Continental nations.

The great influx of the monastic clergy into Scotland began to take place in the reign of Alexander I., who reigned from 1107 till 1124 ; and it increased greatly during the reign of his brother and successor David I., when the canons of St Augustine and St Benedict were settled in many richly-endowed Abbeys, often after the expulsion of the Culdees or partial loss of their rights. Among other endowments they obtained from many kings and barons the patronages and teinds of parish churches which had previously been served by the secular clergy, who were in many instances younger sons of families of rank, and who being in right of the whole parochial tithes were termed rectors or parsons. Thus not only did the old monastic or college rents of the Culdees, but even the parish churches pass, from the hands of the secular into those of the regular clergy. And the latter (the monks) having thus obtained right to the parsonage or benefice, deputed one of their own order to serve the cure of the parish as their *vicar*, and assigned to him a portion (perhaps one-third) of the tithes as stipend or salary, while the remainder helped to endow their monastery. As already stated, the monks of Arbroath held at least about thirty-four parish churches in vicarage. The Chartulary shews that frequent questions arose between the Abbey and the bishops as to these benefices, and the stipends to be paid to the vicars.

The Tyronensian monks were the second or later section of those that followed the rule of St Benedict, a Roman Saint of the early church, born in Italy A.D. 480, and who died in A.D. 542. He founded many monasteries in Italy, and is styled the Patriarch of the Monks in the West. A set of seventy-three rules, sometimes called the *Inclosure*, is said to have been composed by him for the government of his monks, although some believe their author to have been Pope Gregory III. The monasteries of his order soon became very numerous and immensely rich. The second or reformed section of the monks who bore his name were first established at the Abbey of Tyron, in the diocese of Chartres, in France. They seem to have worn a black habit like the older section. David I. (before his accession) brought them to Selkirk, and then removed them to Roxburgh. After he became king he founded the Abbey of Kelso for them in 1128. They rose in importance, and obtained the small priory of Lesmahago; and the beautiful Abbey of Kilwinning was erected for them about the year 1140; till at last, about forty years afterwards, they reached the summit of their grandeur in Scotland by obtaining possession of the Abbey of Lindores, founded for them by David Earl of Huntingdon, brother of King William, in 1178, and by being installed at the same time in the still richer monastery of Arbroath. The Abbey of Kelso was the parent establishment of this order in Scotland; and on this account the first company of monks was brought from Kelso to occupy the Abbey of Arbroath at the time of its foundation.

III.—BIOGRAPHICAL SKETCH OF THE ABBOTS.

1. REGINALD, formerly a monk of the Abbey of Kelso, was the first Abbot of Arbroath. By a deed dated in 1178, John, Abbot, and Convent of Kelso relieved him from all subjection and obedience as elected Abbot of the Church of St Thomas at Arbroath, and declared that the Abbot of Kelso should never claim any authority over the Convent of Arbroath although monks had been taken from Kelso for it; and that mutual charity, friendship, and prayers should exist between the houses, but no dominion or power. This seems to have been done at Arbroath, and in presence of King William and others. Soon afterwards Abbot Reginald and the Bishop of St Andrews were sent by the king to present his obeisance to Pope Alexander III., and the Pope returned a rose of gold, and gave certain new privileges to the Scottish Church. Abbot Reginald died within a year of his appointment.

2. HENRY, also a monk of Kelso, was his successor. In 1179 John Abbot of Kelso granted in his favour a renunciation of all authority, in terms similar to that granted to Abbot Reginald, in presence of King William, David his brother, and Joceline Bishop of Glasgow. Henry was Abbot down at least till after the accession of William Malvoisine to the see of St Andrews in 1202, as he is a witness to a charter granted by that bishop relating to the church of Adnachtan (Nachton) in Fife.

3. RALPH or RADULPHUS was, according to the view of the late Mr Chalmers, the third Abbot of Arbroath, in 1202 or 1204. Mr Innes is doubtful whether there is sufficient evidence on the point. There is an agreement (recorded in the Arbroath Chartulary) betwixt William Malvoisine Bishop of St Andrews and the Abbot and

Convent of Aberbrothock regarding the kain and rents of Fyvie, Inverugie, and other lands in Aberdeenshire, entered into apparently about 1202 and at least prior to 1211. If the name of the Abbot appearing in this writ as "Rad" be correctly read it would seem to support Mr Chalmers' view. Hugo de Sigillo, who became Bishop of Dunkeld in 1214, is said to have been one of the monks of this Abbey previous to his elevation. Spottiswood says that he bore the good title of "The poor man's bishop," but did not survive his consecration a year.

4. GILBERT is the name of the next Abbot that occurs. He is mentioned in the chartularies of Moray and Lindores before the year 1214, and down to 1225; and is also alluded to in a charter of Abbot Ralph, his successor, as having perambulated certain lands of Kenny in the shire of Kingoldrum. It was in the year 1219 that the perambulation of the march betwixt the lands of the Monastery and the "Barony of Kynblathmund" took place before an assize or jury, who declared the division betwixt "Kynblathmund and Adynglas and Abirbrothoc" to be "Hathuerbelath unto Sythnekerdun, and so on to the head of Munegungy" (Magoungie), in presence of Hugo de Chambrun Sheriff of Forfar, and about fifteen neighbouring proprietors.

5. RALPH (RADULPHUS DE LAMLEY or LANGLEY) was Abbot on 30th March 1226. We learn from the chronicle of Melrose that in his time, on 18th March 1233, the Abbey Church was completed and dedicated. Abbot Ralph became Bishop of Aberdeen in 1239; when it is to be presumed he resigned the Abbacy, as in that comparatively pure period such benefices were not held in *commendam* or in plurality. "He was a man of great prudence, and painful in his calling; for he travelled through all his diocese on foot, preaching and visiting the churches, that he might know their true estate; and is said never to have changed his form of living that he used in the cloister." (Spottiswood, p. 102.)

6. ADAM would seem to have been the next Abbot. In 1242 he granted the lands of Conveth, Halton, and Scotston, near Laurencekirk, to John Wischard in feu. He gave the Mill of Conveth to the same person in 1245. In 1247 Peter Ramsay, one of the monks of Arbroath, succeeded Ralph as Bishop of Aberdeen. Hector Boyce states that "he was learned and pious, and that he composed a book of canons."

7. WALTER was Abbot in 1250 and 1255, as shown by his writing relating to the chapel of Backboath, and his grants of lands at Banchory-Devenich and Tarves. It was probably this Abbot who, in the Court of King Alexander II. at Forfar, on 17th February 1250, obtained the verdict of John Thane of Monros, and other Angus jurymen, in favour of the Abbey, against Nicholas of Inverpeffer, as to the service and superiority of the lands of Inverpeffer. Peter de Ramsay, then Bishop of Aberdeen, having procured a papal bull for the augmentation of the stipend of each vicar in his diocese to fifteen merks, the Abbots of Arbroath and Lindores, about 1250, convened a meeting of abbots and priors, who appealed to the Pope and obtained a reversal of the bull. During the time of this Abbot the Chartulary bears that, on the day of St Alban the martyr, in 1254, on account of a controversy betwixt the Lord Abbot and Convent of Arbroath on the one part, and Lord Peter de Maul, Lord of Panmure, and Christian his spouse on the other part, concerning the marches of the Convent's lands of Conon and Tulloch, these parties convened on Cairnconon for the mediation of prudent, noble, and discreet men, William de Brechin, G. de Hay, Robert de Montalto, and others, who perambulated the marches of these lands, and decided the points in dispute.

8. ROBERT was Abbot in December 1261. Fordun states that in 1267 his monks expelled him from the Convent, and that he appealed to Rome; but we have no further account of him. About this time (1260) Spottis-

wood speaks of one *Eustace*, Abbot of Aberbrothock, who accompanied Edward, a bishop of Brechin, in a pedestrian tour through the kingdom, preaching the gospel; but the monastic writs do not refer to any Abbot of this name.

9. SABINUS, Abbot of Arbroath, is witness to the foundation charter of the Mason Dieu at Brechin, by William de Brechin, about 1267. He seems to have held the abbacy not longer than one year.

10. JOHN was Abbot on the feast of the Assumption 1268, at which time he granted a writ regarding the taxation of the vicarage of the church of Frendraucht, in the diocese of Aberdeen. Fordun says in his Scotichronicon that this Abbot died in 1270.

11. ADAM OF INVERLOUNANE, according to Fordun, succeeded John in 1270, and died in 1275. The first burning of part of the great church happened during his rule in the year 1272.

12. WILLIAM occurs as Abbot in writings from 1276 to 1288. He granted the lands of Letham, in the shire of Aberbrothock, to Hugo Heem on 26th March 1284, in compensation for Hugo's right to some lands in Mearns. He was confirmed Bishop of Dunblane by Pope Martin IV. in January 1284-5. In a writing dated 1285, the Bishop of Aberdeen provided that the monks of Arbroath and Fyvie should allow to the vicar or chaplain of the church of Fyvie a stipend of a hundred shillings. The canons of the Scottish Church had, in 1242 and 1269, fixed the lowest stipends of vicars at ten merks. From this time till the appointment of Abbot Bernard the Chartulary contains very few notices of the Abbots. The monks had not begun to register the leases and other writings executed in the ordinary management of their lands and benefices, and the war of independence, by the confusion into which it threw the affairs of Scotland, is marked by the barren and meagre state of the register at this period.

13. HENRY was Abbot of Arbroath at the feast of Epiphany 1288 when he feued the Abbey lands in the village of Caral (Craill) to John Chaplain, son of William of Camboc (Cambo). No other writing in the register bears his name, except that he is incidentally alluded to by his successor Nicholas. Henry held his office during the humiliating period of homages to Edward I. of England in 1291, and afterwards became renowned for his courage. Provoked at the thraldom under which Edward was attempting to place the kingdom by means of its deputy king, John Baliol, whom he had appointed over it, the Scottish Parliament framed an instrument in which they made Baliol renounce allegiance to Edward, and refuse to appear in his English courts, on account of the many injuries inflicted by him on Scotland. It was a melancholy time; and Buchanan says that no man of any eminence would carry this message to Edward, because he was not only fierce by nature, but rendered more so by good fortune. Whilst every one was afraid to beard the lion, this dangerous task was at last undertaken by Abbot Henry of Arbroath, who is called by Fordun a bold-spirited man. He was attended on his embassy by three of his monks. Lord Hailes remarks that the instrument bears to have been presented " by a religious man, guardian of the Minorite Friars of Roxburgh, and his *socius*;" and that this *socius* was probably the bold Abbot of Arbroath, who may have wished to keep himself concealed in the train of his religious brother. This fact may be also probably connected with the safe conduct under which Henry passed to Edward. Meantime Edward had besieged and taken Berwick-upon-Tweed, and mercilessly butchered its inhabitants without distinction of age or sex, on 30th March 1296. Soon afterwards Abbot Henry presented himself before Edward, who is stated by Hailes and Tytler to have been still at Berwick, but who is said by Wynton and Hollinshed to

have been then at London. From what is stated as to Abbot Henry's risk on his return to Scotland, there is reason to believe that his perilous interview with the King of England took place at a much greater distance from Scotland than the camp at Berwick. Abbot Henry faithfully delivered the renunciation to Edward in council, and, together with his companions in the embassage, was treated in a manner unworthy of a king of Edward's pretensions. Various accounts bear that Edward made to Henry this answer in Norman French : " The senseless traitor ! of what folly is he guilty ? But since he will not come to us, we will go to him." Wynton, the prior of Lochleven, in his description of the embassage of " Abbot Den Henry," says that he was neither asked to meat nor feasting because he was disliked for his surly temper ; and that, after delivery of his message, he returned to Scotland without deigning to inquire whether or not his safe conduct had expired. This renunciation exasperated the English, and gave specious grounds for Edward's invasion of Scotland, which immediately followed. Langtoft, an English historian, exclaimed in reference to it, " Scotland whi ne mot I se be sonken to helle ground !"

What is stated will enable the reader to understand the following account which Wynton has given in his " Cronykil" of the character and mission of Abbot Henry :

> " The Abbot of Abbyrbrothok than,
> Den Henry than callyd, a cunnand man,
> Be cownsale he wes chosyn thare,
> Of this charge to be berare.
> For he wes rwyd,[1] of gret lowrdnes,[2]
> Wyth mony men he lathyd wes :[3]
> This message thai gert him tak for thi[4]
> And on he passyt rycht hastyly
> Wndyr cwndyt[5] of schort space.

[1] Rude. [2] Great surliness. [3] He was loathed. [4] *For thi*, *i.e.*, thereupon. [5] Safe conduct.

" Quhon he to Lwndyn cumyn wes,
To the Kyng intil presens
Of hys gret cownsal wyth reverens,
Hys charge he delyveryd thare.
The Kyng than made hym this awnsware.
' *A l ce fol felun, tel foly fettis.*'
In Frawnkis quhen this he had sayd thare,
In Frawnkis he sayd yhit forthirmare,
' *S'il ne voit venir a nos, nos vendrun a ly.*'
The fyrst Frawnkis in propyrte
All thus may understandye be ;
' Now may yhe se, that a fwle swne
' Here a fwlys deid hes dwne.
' Cum til ws, gyve he na wille,
' But dowt we sall cum hym til.'
" Set[1] this Abbot wes messyngere
This Kyng made hym bot lowryd chere :[2]
Nowthyr to mete na mawngery[3]
Callyd thai this Abbot Den Henry,
Set he was lathyd for lowrdnes,
A stowt man and a lele he wes ;
And in hys cownsale he wes wys,
And did this charge all at dowys.
And, for his cowndyt wes nere gane,
Langar cwndyt he askyd nane ;
But fra he this charge had dwne,
In Scotland hame he sped hym swn :
Nevyr-the-les he was in dowt,
Or his cwndyt wer worne out."

In the summer of this year (July 1296) Edward compelled Baliol to resign his mock-monarchy at Stracathro, and after proceeding as far north as Elgin, he came by Arbroath in his progress southward, and lodged at the Abbey on Sunday 5th August. As Abbot Henry's sovereign was by this time deposed, we may safely conclude that his bold ambassador was now displaced by King Edward, and a more complacent churchman appointed in his room.

14. NICHOLAS was Henry's successor. He granted a charter of the lands of Kedloch in 1299. The only other recorded deed of this Abbot is a charter of the Abbey hostilage in Stirling, by which he granted to Richard son of Christian, son of Lochlan, and his

---

[1] Sith or since. [2] But sorry cheer. [3] Feasting.

heirs, all the lands which the convent had in the burgh of Stirling for the yearly payment of four shillings and six pennies in silver, and on condition that he should provide for the Abbot for the time and his monks, friends, clerks, bailies, and attorneys when coming on the affairs of the monastery, and for their servants, an honest hall for meals, with tables, trestles, and other furniture; a spence with a buttery; one or more chambers for sleeping; an honest kitchen, and a stable fit to receive at least thirty horses; with sufficient fuel for the hall, chambers, and kitchen; Paris candles for light; straw for bedding; rushes for strewing the hall and bedchamber; and salt for food: he being bound not to provide fuel, candles, and others beyond three nights at each visit. The above affords a picture of a town lodging in the days of Bruce and Wallace.

15. JOHN OF ANGUS was Abbot on the feast of St Stephen 1303, on which day he granted the charter of building ground in the burgh of Arbroath already referred to. Edward I. lodged at the Abbey on 1st August of the same year in his journey to the north. On 21st October in the following year the monks of Arbroath contracted with the Bishop of Brechin that they should not be obliged to pay the vicars of their churches within his diocese higher stipends than ten pounds of sterlings. Soon afterwards this Abbot was carried captive and detained in England as a prisoner of war, and was ultimately loosed from his office by the Bishop of St Andrews on the feast of All Saints 1309, as mentioned in a writing under the hand of his successor.

16. BERNARD DE LINTON succeeded John of Angus. He had been parson of Mordington, in Berwickshire; and swore fealty to Edward I. on 24th August 1296. In 1307, the year after Robert Bruce assumed the throne, he made Bernard his Chancellor for Scotland. It is likely that at the same time he entered on pos-

session of the Abbacy of Arbroath, although not formally appointed Abbot till 1309, when his predecessor was loosed. Michael de Monifieth granted an obligation to the Abbot and convent in 1310, when Bernard was Abbot; and his name repeatedly occurs in the succeeding years. On 21st August 1312, he entered into an engagement with Adam Abbot of Kilwinning for the redemption of "brother John, late Abbot of the monastery of Arbroath, and now a simple monk," from his captivity in England, and also for the ransom and return of two or three of the monks. In 1315 Abbot Bernard granted a lease of the lands of Dunnichen beyond the Vinney (Vuany), except the lands of Craichie, to David de Manuel, for a rent of 12 chalders oats and 12 chalders barley, to be reduced by arbitration if the lands should be devastated by the common war; with liberty to construct a mill, and hold a court of the men dwelling on the lands for deciding actions among themselves. David de Manuel was taken bound to attend the three yearly head courts of the Abbot, and if amerced in these courts he was to pay five shillings or one cow: from which we learn that a cow was then sold for fivepence sterling. He was also taken bound to have on the lands a hostilage for the Abbot and his servants and monks, properly provided with fuel, fodder, bedding, and white candles. The deed contains other stipulations about burying the corpse of David Manuel at Arbroath. This writing has been sometimes misrepresented as a charter of the lands of Ethie to an imaginary David de Maxwell.

Abbot Bernard celebrated the battle of Bannockburn in a Latin poem, a fragment of which is still extant. (Fordun.) He continued Abbot and Chancellor till 1328. During these seventeen years the Abbey of Arbroath reached its culminating point of prosperity. It was the meeting place of councils and parliaments during one of the most interesting periods of Scottish history, when Bruce was effecting the deliverance of his kingdom from foreign domination and intestine foes. And the celebrity of the Abbey seems to have been extended to the small town under its walls, the houses of which now began to be erected according to a regular plan.

Among Bruce's many visits to Arbroath he resided at the Abbey in the autumn of 1317, when an interview occurred which is worthy of notice. Pope John XXII., after the battle of Bannockburn, was induced to send two cardinals to England with a bull commanding a truce for two years, under pain of excommunication of Bruce or whoever should disobey it. They despatched two messengers to Bruce, who, according to Spottiswood, gave them audience at Aberbrothoick, and allowed the Pope's open letters, recommending peace, to be read in his presence with all due respect. But when the sealed letters, addressed to "Robert Bruce, governing in Scotland," were presented, Bruce replied, "Among my barons there are many named *Robert Bruce* who share in the government of Scotland, these letters may possibly be addressed to them, but they are not addressed to me, who am King of Scotland. I can receive no letters which are not addressed under that title." Notwithstanding all the apologies of the messengers, Bruce not only refused the letters but firmly withheld his consent to the enjoined truce so long as the Pope and his legates, under English influence, withheld from him the title of king. The letter to the Pope from the barons assembled at Arbroath, on 6th April 1320, has been already alluded to.

Amidst Bernard's numerous duties he by no means neglected the Abbey: he executed many repairs on its buildings at considerable expense. In 1317 he feued the Abbey tofts in Peebles and Inverkeithing to burgesses of these burghs, on condition of their upholding halls or hostilages in each of them similar to that at Stirling; the feuar in Inverkeithing being also taken bound to supply vessels and wooden plates for the hall. A similar hostilage was provided at Aberdeen in 1320, and at Dundee in 1327.

Abbot Bernard's letter of 1325, addressed to Sir Albert custodier of the Priory of Fyvie, gives us a view of the corruptions among the monks of Buchan at that time, as well as of his determination to reform them. After alluding to the want of discipline and the disorder which existed at Fyvie, he commanded the custodier to hold within the chancel of the chapel a chapter three times each week—on Mondays, Wednesdays, and Fridays —to reform divine worship on Sabbaths and festivals ; to keep the fasts in terms of canonical institution ; and if any of the brethren should be found drunken, clamorous, abusive, rebellious, and disobedient, to reclaim him, if possible, by good counsel ; and, if otherwise, to punish each monk by silence and bread and water in a place of confinement, beyond access of the seculars ; and if he amended not, to transmit him to the monastery of Arbroath, with a statement of the delinquencies of which he stood chargeable.

The monastic writs of Bernard's time afford proofs of the destruction which flowed from the war with England. In March 1323, the official of St Andrews decided an action which had been raised by the Abbot against William, perpetual vicar of the church of Arbirlot, for non-payment of two merks per annum, appointed to be paid by an order of the Bishop of St Andrews in 1249, and which had been in arrear for twenty years, owing to the poverty, sterility, and destruction of the parish and its inhabitants, occasioned by the late war. The official found the vicar entitled to relief from a portion of the arrears. At this period, in obedience to a statute of the Lateran Council, general chapters or meetings of the monasteries of the order of St Benedict in each kingdom or province were held every three years. Abbot Bernard was cited by the Abbot of Dunfermline to compear in such a chapter, to be held at that Abbey on 21st October 1326, with one or two of his convent, most learned and expert in the customs and rules of the order, with procurators, under penalty in case of absence. The monasteries represented at such a chapter were those of Coldingham, Dunfermline, Urquhart, Kelso and Lesmahago, Kilwinning, Aberbrothock, Fyvie, and Lindores. Of the grants made by King Robert Bruce to the Abbey betwixt 1313 and 1325, four were given at Arbroath, two at Forfar, and two at *Fons Scocie* or Scotlandwell, a small village and religious house of the Red Friars, beside a spring once famed for its healing powers, in the parish of Portmoak, near Lochleven, to which Bruce had probably resorted for relief from the terrible disease of leprosy, with which he was afflicted in the latter years of his life.

There is little doubt that Bernard was the Abbot of Arbroath who went to Norway on King Robert Bruce's affairs; on which occasion the King issued a special letter of protection to the Abbey, against all injuries or vexations, during the absence of their Abbot. Mr Innes thinks that this may have probably been in connection with the negotiations which ended in the treaty of Inverness 1312. In 1328 Abbot Bernard was elected Bishop of Sodor (the Isles); and on 30th April of that same year, the Bishop of St Andrews, in a visitation of the monastery of Arbroath, assisted by the Abbots and fathers of the monasteries of Kelso, Dunfermline, St Andrews, Jedburgh, Lindores, and Coupar, taking into consideration Abbot Bernard's long government of the Abbey and services to the King, and in compensation for his expenses in repairing the monastery, and discharging his office of chancellor, granted to him all the teinds of the church of Abernethy, with the chapel of Dron, for seven years after the feast of Pasch 1328.

17. GEOFFRY (styled in the Abbey writs GALFRIDUS) held the Abbacy from 1328 till about 30th December 1342. He was one of those who submitted at first to

Edward Baliol in 1332. He feued the lands of Tulloch (Tulloes) to Fergus, the son of Duncan, on 29th March 1329, with liberty to hold a court called "Couthal," of the men residing on the lands, for deciding actions among themselves. We have not observed this term elsewhere. It is probably allied to *couth, couthie, couthily,* kindly or neighbourly, the reverse of which is *uncouth,* strange. The feu-duty of five chalders oats and five chalders barley was to be restricted if the lands should be destroyed in the common war betwixt England and Scotland. About the year 1336 Edward III. having resolved to fortify the town of Perth, ordered the same to be done at the expense of six of the richest Abbeys on the north side of Forth, of which Aberbrothock stands first on the list. This Abbot feued out the Abbey tofts in Perth, Auchterarder, Forres, and Colly [Cullen?], for small sums, with obligations to provide hostilages.

18. WILLIAM was Abbot on 17th July 1348, when he vindicated the Abbey's privilege from toll against the bailies of Dundee, who had presumed to levy a penny from his stallinger or stall-keeper at a fair in their burgh. This took place in the Justiciary or Circuit Court at Forfar. About two years after his appointment, notice is taken of the injuries which the Abbey buildings had sustained from the English shipping. This Abbot seems to have been both active and influential. He obtained various charters from King David Bruce confirming the Abbey's privileges of regality, koket, and great customs. A writ granted by him in March 1366 regarding the priory of Fyvie, is said to have been sealed at Aberbrothock in the *cathedral*. This term was probably applied to the great church in reference to the pontifical privileges at this time expected, if not possessed, by its Abbots. The last writing executed by Abbot William is dated 18th July 1366.

19. JOHN GEDY was Abbot in 1370, when he entered into an agreement with Andrew Dempster of Caraldston,

as to the ancient office of judge or doomster of the regality. As the builder of Arbroath harbour, the memory of this Abbot possesses more interest to the inhabitants of Arbroath than that of almost any other. It was in his time, previous to June 1380, that the Abbey Church was greatly damaged by fire. He lived to see the damage almost repaired. His seal is appended to the Act of Parliament, settling the succession to the Crown in 1371. The Pope's bull conferring the privilege of wearing the mitred crown and pontifical vestments was addressed to him, on 6th July 1396. It is difficult to ascertain how long he held the Abbacy during the next fifteen years.

20. WALTER PANITER or PANTER, of the family of Newmanswalls in the Mearns (within the regality of Arbroath), was the next abbot. He is named on 11th December 1411. The inquest held at Cairnconon on 4th April 1409, regarding the lands of Kennymykyl near Kingoldrum, was probably held in his time. He obtained from Pope Martin the privilege of conferring the minor orders by a bull, dated 5th June 1420; and he granted the first charter of building-ground in the Eleemosynary, near the lane now called Braick's Wynd, on 8th July 1423. He made a claim on one of the burgesses of Edinburgh who possessed the Abbey hostilage in that city; and the rights of the parties were adjusted by an indenture, executed at Edinburgh on 20th November 1428, which forms a good subject for those who love to read old lowland Scotch. After an introduction, the writing bears that "The said Jhon Vernour, moffit of consciens, has grantit the said annuale rent of twa schillingis to the forsaid abbay, in fee and herytagis, for euirmar, to be takyn of a crofft of his, lyand on southt half the town of Edinburgh, betuex the croft of Sanct Lenard on the est parte, and the croft of the hous of Soltre on the west parte: Alsua, the said abbot sal haf ostillary within the forsaidis tenement of John Vernour, that is to say, hal, chawmyr, kechyng, and butre, with swilk vtensele as the

said John Vernour vsis, for al the tym of the said abbotis lyffyng, as he repayris at consalis and assembilleis : and the said John Vernour and hys familiaris, als lang as the forsaid abbot beis within hym at innys, sal be on the abbotis cost for reuerencis, honour and courtasy of the forsaid lord abbot. It is accordit alsua, that fray the dissese of the said abbot the said John Vernour and his ayris sal be discharged foreuirmair of all suilk ostillary of his forsaid tenement, and neuir abbot of Abirbrothoc to challange na clam fra thyn furth ostillary within the said tenement. It is accordit alsua, that the said John Vernour sal be brothiryt in the forsaid abbay." This is the second monastic writ expressed in the Scottish dialect. The next is a note of the marches of Dumbarrow, in 1434, bearing the following title :—" Thir ar the merchis devydand Dunberrow on euery syde, that is to say, betwex the landis of Gardyn, Connansyth, the Boch (Boath), the lordship of Eidwy, Auchirmegyty, and the landis of Presthok." It is minute in its details, and interesting to one acquainted with the locality.

The first nineteen years' lease of a portion of the Abbey lands (viz., Muirdrum, near Kinnaldy) recorded in the Chartulary, was granted by Abbot Walter on 20th January 1434–5. He enters in the register the marches that bounded the Miltonmuir, the Easter Brax, and the "bishop's lands of St Andrews," in these terms, slightly modernised in orthography :—" In the fyrst, begynnand at the Ramdenheid, and fra thyne (thence), passand sowth-west to the tod-holis ; and sae furth to the aiken bush, and sae on to the blind or the beld stane, ondyr the dikys of the Brakkys ; and sae on to the denheid of Gutheryne (Guynd), ondyr the gait, as the induellaris of Gutheryn cummys and gays to Sanct Vigianis Kyrk." At that period the lands of Guynd were included in the parish of St Vigeans. This old march may be identified with the north boundary of Arbirlot parish, from the head of the Ram Den to the Elliot water. On 5th

November 1436 King James I. granted a charter in favour of the Abbey, confirming its possessions, privileges of regality, and other rights. On 15th April 1443 the Abbot feued the church lands of Brekko to John Ogilvy of Luntrethyn, Knight, for 8 merks Scots yearly, for which Sir John bound his lands of "Ballyshame (Bolshan), Brekkis, and Kenbrede." The skirmish betwixt the Ogilvies and Lindsays took place in Abbot Panter's time. The last writ granted by him is dated 6th March 1446. Abbot Malcolm Brydy afterwards states that—" Deyn Walter Panter was an auld man, and resignit the Abbacy till ane Deyn Richart Guthre."

21. RICHARD GUTHRIE, the Prior, thus succeeded Abbot Panter, and held the office previous to 2nd October 1450. The writings executed by him are few, and without public interest. He resigned the office on 18th December 1455. His successor, Abbot Malcolm, records of him that he "*was nocht active*, nor gave intendens for remeid of wrangs dune to the haly place." This statement is made in a long document, which affords a specimen of the Scottish language at the time, being a complaint by Abbot Malcolm to a Parliament held at Perth, relating to the lands of Caulte in the barony of Tarves, in which a smith had been allowed to squat. In this document the Abbot relates that " the wrangus occupatioun of owr said landis of Caute was movyt and begwn on this way : —For service of our landis, and aisiament of the said smyth, our predecessoris overlukit and tholyt the smyth till byg ane smyddy in the moss, because of his colys and fuell that was necessar to his office, to be won in time of yeir : the said smyth was called Ade (Adam) of Caute, and in skorne with the nychtbours was called laird of Caute in derisioun, because he set in the myddis of ane cauld moss, and through that skorne the land was callit Caulty ; and because he was callit sae laird of Cauty, howbeit it was bot for derisioun, our predecessoris thynk- and it onkyndlye tyll thole ane nominatioun of lairdschipe

of sic ane man in the said Caute, without rycht or resoun, thay removit and put the said smyth fra the said place, for dreid that percase the smyth, or ony of his, suld eftyr, be process of tyme, pretend ony clame of rycht till the said landis," &c.

22. MALCOLM BRYDY, formerly prior of the subordinate house of Fyvie, was Abbot on 27th July 1456, when he concluded an agreement with John Stewart, Lord of Lorne, and Baron of Inverkeillor, relating to the mire of Balnamoon recorded in an "Indenture" written in lowland Scotch. This Abbot does not appear to have been liable to the censure of negligence passed by him on his predecessor, so far as the temporalities of the monastery were concerned. In 1461 he obtained from Pope Pius II. a confirmation of the Abbey's exemption from attendance at the yearly synods of the clergy, and a declaration of excommunication against all who should trouble them on that point. He effected perambulations of the marches of Tarves, Dunnichen, Ochterlony, Kingoldrum, and Guynd. He vindicated the rights of the Abbey to the almory and the hospital from the claims of the Bishop of Brechin; and at various times obtained bulls in confirmation of the Abbey privileges. He obtained from William of Ochterlony, and Jonet his spouse, a charter empowering the Convent to quarry and win stones at their pleasure in any part of the lands of Ochterlony, called of old Kelly, under the penalty of ten merks Scots to be annually levied from the lands, and ecclesiastical censure, in the event of interruption. This charter is dated in 1466, and is followed by infeftment of the right granted by the baron to the Abbot, at his "mansion of Ovchtirlovny, alias Kelly," on 13th December 1468. In 1470 "Deyn Malcolm" is found in high contention with the Bishop of St Andrews, whom he accused of extortion and oppression, especially in visiting the monastery, not in a pastoral manner, and with lawful number of followers, but with one or two hundred horsemen. The Bishop

had by this time proceeded to extremities, and thrown Abbot Malcolm into his dungeon at St Andrews *(arctis carceribus)*. All this and much more is stated in an appeal made by the Abbot to John Bishop of Brechin, on 17th October 1470, within the chapel of Whitefield. This seems to have been Abbot Malcolm's last effort in his own behalf in connection with the monastery, for soon afterwards, on 3rd November of the same year, he is described as deprived of the Abbacy, and his successor was then appointed. The prelate against whom Abbot Malcolm complained so heavily was no other than Patrick Graham, then Bishop, and next year made Archbishop, of St Andrews, whose character, according to the united testimonies of all our historians, was decidedly the reverse of that given by the Abbot. He was Bishop of Brechin during the three years before his promotion to St Andrews in 1466, and, although not specified by name in the inquest regarding the Almory in 1464 procured by Abbot Malcolm, that measure seems to have been directed against him, and was probably an earlier stage of the quarrel between these dignitaries, which thus came to a height about six years afterwards. Spottiswood says, that in worth and learning Graham was inferior to none of his time, and that he was oppressed by the malice and calumny of the clergy, because they dreaded his intentions to reform their abuses. If his treatment of Abbot Malcolm was unjustifiable and cruel, he was soon afterwards subjected to a similar fate, from a combination of enemies; and which resulted in his imprisonment for life successively at St Andrews, Inchcolm, Dunfermline, and lastly at Lochleven Castle, where he died.

23. RICHARD GUTHRIE, Professor of Sacred Theology, and Prior of the Convent, was elected Abbot in room of Malcolm Brydy. It is probable that he is the same person with the Abbot of that name who resigned the Abbacy in favour of Malcolm, as both were styled Priors,

He granted on 20th May 1471 a lease of the teinds of the Church of Inverness, already mentioned, for the building of the dormitory. But he died, or demitted, soon afterwards, for,

24. GEORGE was Abbot previous to 29th July 1472, and held the office till his death, in 1482, during which period he seems to have carried on the restoration of the wood work at the Abbey begun by Abbot Malcolm. A law process betwixt him and William Bishop of Moray was submitted to the mediation of Thomas Bishop of Aberdeen, in whose chapter house, at Old Aberdeen, the parties met, at eleven o'clock forenoon, of 4th August 1478, when the Abbot delivered a paper containing these words :—" My lord, we knaw that owr place, and we has kyrkis within your dioce, for the quhylkis we sal do to your lordeschep as we haff down till ony bischopis in Scotland that we haff kyrkys in thar dioce, except my lord of Sanctandros, our ordinar, and the priuilege of our place beand kepit ; so help me God."

25. DOMINUS WILLIAM BONKYL, a monk of the Abbey, was elected Abbot on 8th August 1482. Thomas Bet, the sub-prior, in his speech proposing him, stated to the monks that he was "a man come of good family, meek, quiet, and zealous for peace, loving God and the church, humble, pious, sweet-tempered, and of good manners, a great counsellor and defender of the church in its affairs, also charitable and good, of age about fifty, a bountiful almsgiver, very discreet in spiritual and temporal matters, born of lawful wedlock, affable, a good friend, and merciful in the communion of the faithful." After the election the monks sung *Te Deum laudamus*, and caused ring the bells of the Abbey church. On 6th February 1483-4, Abbot William granted the church and church lands of Forglen to Alexander Irving of Drum for forty shillings yearly, with service to the King under the *Brechbannach*. This Abbot soon afterwards died, in the summer of 1484.

P

26. SIR DAVID LICHTONE, clerk of the King's Treasury and Archdeacon of Ross, was the next abbot. On 29th July 1484 the Convent assembled for the election of Abbot Bonkyl's successor. They divided in opinion as to the fittest person. William Schevez, Archbishop of St Andrews, was present, and by his advice the Convent agreed to a compromise, by nominating Sir Alexander Masoun, Prior of Fyvie, as "compromissar" for choosing the Abbot. The compromissar immediately postulated Sir David Lichtone, who was received "with great joy," and the bells were rung. The Chapter voted a grant of 3000 gold ducats for the purpose of expediting the bulls of his appointment at Rome. This large sum continued to hang as a burden on the Abbey for a long period afterwards. This Abbot seems to have managed the rents and lands of the monastery with great diligence and attention. The record of leases of lands and teinds, presentations to churches, and other documents issued by the Chapter, are in his time recorded in a manner more full and regular than formerly. It was he who put on record those curious memoranda in relation to the offices of the granitor and cellarer. On 5th April 1486 he and the Chapter engaged "a discret clerk, Master Archibald Lame," (Lamy) for three years after Whitsunday, to teach the novices and younger brethren, for which he was to get ten merks Scots as salary (nearly the ordinary stipend of a parish vicar), besides his daily portion with the monks. On 5th July 1500 the lands of Cairnie and pendicles were let to Janet Brydy and her sons, at the following rents, viz., £11, 6s. 8d. Scots (equal to 18s. 10⅔d. sterling), payable to the monks of the community, for the lands of Cairnie; for the Smiths' lands, near Cairnie, three shillings, to the monks of the *library;* and for the lands under Lamblaw, "beyond our ward," two bolls oats, with other husbandry charges. They were taken bound to grind their corns at the Wardmill; and Janet Brydy was bound not to marry unless with license of the Abbot

and Convent. The last recorded writ granted by Abbot David Lichtone is a lease of the lands of Percie, near Kingoldrum, on 17th December 1502.

27. Previous to Abbot David Lichtone's death the Primate or Archbishop of St Andrews seems to have obtained an interest in the rich benefice of the Abbey. This was JAMES STUART, DUKE OF ROSS, second son of King James III., who became Primate in 1497, and held the Abbeys of Dunfermline and Holyrood *in commendam*. He granted, along with Abbot David, writs of presentation to the churches of Garvock and Nigg on 28th and 31st October 1502. After the death of Lichtone he became also Commendator of Arbroath during the brief period of his survivance, as he died in the year 1503, at the early age of twenty-eight, and was buried in the Cathedral of St Andrews.

This period is marked by the commencement of that *open* declension in the Romish Church of Scotland which rapidly increased during the next half century, till its further progress was stopped by the Reformation. After 1500 the great benefices were grasped by the king and nobles, as livings for their sons, brothers, and nephews, legitimate or illegitimate. The chapters were virtually deprived of their power of election, the duties of discipline and hospitality were equally neglected, and the consequence was general disorder, immorality and ignorance. According to Spottiswood, this tide of corruption reached the religious institutions, especially the monasteries in Fifeshire and the southern parts of the kingdom, about twenty-five years before Lichtone's death, and at the time of the persecution of Archbishop Graham.

28. GEORGE HEPBURN, of the family of Bothwell, and Provost of the Collegiate Church of Lincluden, in Galloway, succeeded James Stuart as Abbot of Arbroath, by the unanimous election of the Chapter, on 3rd February 1503-4 ; and on the 20th of the same month they gave 1500 gold ducats to procurators for expeding the papal

bull in the new Abbot's favour. He held the Abbacy for ten years. He was appointed Bishop of the Isles in 1510, after which the charters relative to Arbroath were granted by him, under the title of "George Bishop of Sodor and Commendator of Arbroath." He also at this period held the Abbey of Iona *in commendam*. In the year 1509 Abbot George appointed James Henrison, clerk of the Justice-General, during his life, to the office of "Advocate" of the Abbey, for a pension of twenty merks. This advocate then held the important office of Clerk of Justiciary, whose official successor is now our modern Lord Justice-Clerk. A lease of the lands of Bogfechil, in the barony of Tarves, bearing the date of 12th January 1511-12, contains the name of the Abbot, of Richard Scot, sub-prior, and the whole other twenty-five monks of the Convent. A writing in the register bears that there existed in the parish church of Inverkeillor, about 1511, an altar or chaplainry dedicated to John Baptist, whose patron was then Magister David Gardyne of Cononsyth, and that Sir John Davidson, chaplain of the chapel of Whitefield, endowed it with certain rents, payable from the baronies of Dysart, Panmure, and Inverkeillor, for the benefit of the souls of King James IV., his Queen Margaret, and others. The last recorded charter granted by this Abbot bears the date of 12th August 1513. He followed King James IV. to Flodden, and fell with him on that disastrous field.

The Abbey register in his time consists almost entirely of leases, without those interesting documents which marked the rule of Abbot Lichtone. But alongside of this and other proofs of the careless and secular administration of the ecclesiastical property, the Chartulary affords evidence of the increase of superstitious notions among the people. We refer to those grants to the altars in St Mary's Chapel and St Vigeans Church, which appear during the government of Abbot George, although the more peculiar and superstitious parts of these deeds do not seem to have been encouraged or confirmed by him. These were afterwards confirmed by his successors, James and David Betoun, who had no scruples on that point.

After Hepburn's death a contest took place for possession of the Abbacy. The competitors were—1st, Gawin Douglas, Provost of the Collegiate Church of St Giles, Edinburgh, well known as the translator of Virgil into lowland Scotch,—under the nomination of Queen Margaret, who was then Regent of Scotland, and was shortly thereafter married to the Earl of Angus, Douglas' nephew: 2nd, John Hepburn, then Prior of St Andrews: and 3rd, Andrew Foreman, Bishop of Moray. They were also competitors for the see of St Andrews, which was vacant by the death of Alexander Stuart at Flodden. Foreman had been declared Archbishop of St Andrews, and Abbot of Dunfermline and Aberbrothock, by the Pope's bull published at Edinburgh in January 1515. The disturbances caused by Hepburn and his friends were so great that the Regent Albany prevailed on Foreman to resign his benefices, and he received again the Archbishopric of St Andrews. Gawin Douglas seems to have retired from the contest for Arbroath, and was next year made Bishop of Dunkeld.

29. JAMES BETOUN, youngest son of John Betoun of Balfour, in the parish of Markinch, Fifeshire, obtained the appointment to the Abbacy from the Duke of Albany on his entry to the regency, amid the scramble for great benefices which followed the battle of Flodden. This ecclesiastic was able to secure many of the greatest appointments in Scotland. The list of his preferments is very long. He was educated at St Andrews from 1491 to 1493, obtained the Chantry of Caithness in 1497, the Provostry of the Collegiate Church of Bothwell and Priory of Whithorn before 1503, the Abbey of Dunfermline in 1504, at which time also he was a Lord of Session. He was made Lord-Treasurer in 1505, and Bishop of Galloway in 1508. He obtained the Archbishopric of

Glasgow in 1509, the office of Lord Chancellor about 1513, the Abbacy of Arbroath in 1515, and the Archbishopric of St Andrews in 1522. He also held the rich Abbey of Kilwinning *in commendam*. He was engaged in almost every political intrigue of his time; and although, during a part of his life, in the enjoyment of great dignity and wealth, yet he experienced considerable reverses. He is described by one writer as "the greatest man, both of lands and experience, within this realme," but "noted to be very subtill and dissymuling." The following character given of him by Knox is, as may be expected, far from favourable, but perhaps not very far from truth :—He was "more careful for the warld than he was to preach Christ, or yet to advance any religion, but for the fashion only ; and, as he sought the warld, it fled him not ; for it was weill known that at once he was Archbischop of Sanctandrose, Abbot of Dumfermeling, Aberbroth, Kylwynnyng, and Chancellare of Scotland ; for, after the unhappy feild of Flowdoun, in which perished King James the Fourt with the greatest part of the nobilitie of the realme, the said Betoun, with the rest of the prelattis, had the haill regiment of the realme ; and by reason thereof held, and travailled to hold, the treuth of God in thraldome and bondage." This statement is made in connection with the trial and death of Patrick Hamilton, whom Betoun brought to the stake on 28th February 1527-8.

When James Betoun succeeded to the Primacy, on the death of Archbishop Foreman, he resigned the Abbacy of Arbroath to David Betoun, reserving, however, the half of its revenues during his life. Shortly after this— his highest elevation—he was obliged to spend some time on a farm among the hills above Leven in Fife, in the disguise of a shepherd, in order to escape the search of his enemies of the house of Douglas, during the feud between that house and the house of Lennox. He erected the buildings of St Mary's College, St Andrews, where the Pedagogium had formerly stood, and got its new constitution as a college confirmed by a Papal bull in 1537. This college is indebted to him and his nephew and successor for the most of its endowments. During part, at least, of the period when James Betoun was Abbot of Arbroath, the Abbey seems to have been practically ruled by Alexander Craill, the sub-prior. In 1539 Betoun, " a man of great age, departed this life, and was buried at St Andrews," before the high altar of the cathedral.

30. DAVID BETOUN was a nephew of his predecessor, and third son of his brother, John Betoun, the proprietor of the estate of Balfour. This Abbot, who figures so prominently in Scottish history, was born in 1494, and was a student of St Andrews in 1509, and of Glasgow in 1511; and he afterwards studied the civil and canon law in France. He became Rector of Campsie in 1519, and about the same time was appointed Resident for Scotland in the Court of France. He obtained, as before stated, the Abbacy of Arbroath, with the half of its income, in 1522 or 1523, and sat as Abbot in the Scottish Parliament of 1525. This beginning of his preferments is alluded to by Sir David Lindesay in the following lines:

> " When I was a young gallant gentle-man,
> Princes to serve I set my whole intent :
> First to ascend to Arbroth I began ;
> An Abbacie of great riches and rent ;
> Of that estate yet was I not content,
> To get more riches, dignitie, and glore,
> Mine heart was set, alas, alas, therefore."

Abbot David Betoun first appears in the Arbroath Chartulary on 18th January 1523-4, as confirming Robert Scot's endowment of the altar of St Dupthacus. On 20th May 1525, he issued a presentation of the parish church of Lunan to Sir David Cristeson, presbyter; so that Walter Miln's entry as priest of Lunan must have been of later date. Betoun, on 23rd May 1525, granted warrant to infeft James Lord Ogilvy in the lands of

"Brekky, as heir to "John Lord Ogylwy, his gudschyr;" and in 1527, he let the croft near the Dern Yett, with the teinds, to John Barbor, for nineteen years, at a rent of £1, 6s. 8d. Scots. This is probably the true origin of the term Barbers Croft, now applied to that piece of ground. On 9th November 1527, he granted a nineteen years lease of the lands of Cairnie and Smiths lands to Alexander Brown Chaplain and others, for the same rents at which they had been let by Abbot Lichtone. The present feu-duty of 18s. $7^{4\cdot12}$d. sterling paid by Sir John Ogilvy for Cairnie, may probably be traced back to these rents. On 5th December of that year, the Abbot granted to Robert Lesly of Inverpeffer a yearly pension of £10 Scots for life, on condition that he should appear "as procurator for the Abbot and Convent in all causes against all persons, except those by whom he has been previously engaged, before the Lords of Council, Session, and Parliament, and give them his counsel in the same as often as required." This lawyer's pension is equal to sixteen shillings and eightpence of our money; but in market value at that time was perhaps nearly equivalent to £10 sterling in our time.

The Chartulary contains various proofs of David Betoun's acts of kindness to his chief female favourite, "Maistres Marion Ogilbye," who is said by Knox to have been seen departing from his castle at St Andrews by the private postern that morning on which he was murdered. She was a daughter of Sir James, afterwards Lord Ogilvy of Airlie, and had several children by Betoun, one of whom was ancestor of the Bethunes of Nether Tarvet; and it was her daughter, Margaret Betoun, whose marriage with the Master of Crawford (afterwards ninth Earl), was celebrated with magnificence at Finhaven castle immediately after the death of George Wishart. One of her sons was styled David Betoun of Melgund. Another son, Alexander Betoun, was Archdeacon of Lothian, and is believed to have become a minister of the Reformed Church. On 22nd May 1528, Abbot David, for a certain sum of money "*and other causes*," granted a liferent lease to Marion or Mariot Ogylwy of the lands of Burnton of Ethie, and other lands near that place. On 20th July 1530 he granted to her a liferent lease of the Kirkton of St Vigeans, with the Muirfauld and the toft of St Vigeans, and a piece of common land lying to the south of the church. These grants were followed, on 17th February 1533-4, by a nineteen years' lease of the eighth part of the lands of Auchmithie, with the brewhouse there and lands belonging to it. The leases are given in liberal terms, and at low rents. The last recorded grant to this lady is dated 10th March 1534, and seems to be a feu of a piece of land in the "Sandypots," for the construction of a *toral* or *ustrina*, lying " beyond and near the Red Wall of the monastery commonly so called." This ground was not far from the site of the present parish church of Arbroath. Marion Ogilvy is styled the " Lady of Melgund" in the record of a plea at her instance before the Bailies of Arbroath, 8th January 1565-6 (Burgh Court-Book); at which time, or shortly before, she was proprietrix of Hospitalfield, near Arbroath. Commissary Maule relates that Thomas Maule, younger of Panmure, had been an attendant on the Cardinal, and was contracted in marriage with his daughter, evidently previous to her marriage with the Master of Crawford. But as he was riding out of Arbroath one day, in company with James V., the jolly monarch called him aside, and bade him " Marry never ane preist's gett ;" " whereupon (adds the Commissary) that marriage did cease." The Cardinal highly resented the slight ; and his resentment ultimately cost Maule 3000 merks. (MS. Account of Panmure Family.)

The leases granted by David Betoun are in much looser and more general terms, and contain fewer restrictions, than those granted by his immediate predecessors ; and often contained power to assign and sublet. This was the intermediate step betwixt the former careful management of the monastic possessions, and the subsequent alienation of them in perpetual feu grants for fixed quantities of grain, or certain amounts of Scotch money, the value of which has now fallen to very insignificant sums.

The monastic register, so far as accessible, ends with a writ granted soon after 5th September 1536; and does not contain transcripts of the writings by which the lands in the more immediate neighbourhood of the Abbey were subfeued. Previous to David Betoun's time the Abbey lands in the shires of Inverness, Banff, Aberdeen, Kincardine, Perth, and Lanark, had been gradually feued away. This was the case also with the lands about Kingoldrum, and the most of those in the parish of Dunnichen. But down to 1536, the Abbey lands in the parishes of St Vigeans, Ethie, and Carmylie, and those of Dumbarrow, were (with the exception perhaps of Letham) retained by the Convent, and were regularly let to tenants in leases of nineteen years. The lands of Ethie were in the hands of the Convent after 1528, as in that year the Abbot let the half of the Mains of Ethie to David Lichton, who had resigned his liferent lease of Burnton of Ethie in favour of Marion Ogilvy; and the "principal place of Athy," with its granary, is incidentally mentioned as being in the Abbot's possession in 1510. It is quite possible that a mansion at Ethie may have been about 1530 the residence of the Cardinal's favourite mistress, who had leases of land on both sides of it. It may be here stated that the last vicar of the Parish Church of Ethie on record was James Ged, who was presented to the perpetual vicarage by David Betoun, on 7th December 1534, after the death of Andrew Chatto, the former vicar.

David Betoun, while in Arbroath, was commencing that career of activity and political influence which has made him the best known if not the worthiest of the Abbots. His general character and his severity toward the Reformers are too familiar to every reader of Scottish history to require any detail in these pages. On 28th February 1527 he formed one of the court at St Andrews which condemned Patrick Hamilton to death. Both previous and subsequent to that event he appears to have been employed on public or state matters in foreign countries. It was probably on that account that he omitted to hold the justice aires of the regality, as alluded to in our notice of the office of bailiery. Sir David Lindesay states that the Cardinal made several voyages to France on public affairs, two of which were regarding the marriages of King James V. with his successive queens, Magdalene, and Mary of Lorraine. He was consecrated Bishop of Mirepoix in Languedoc, France, in December 1537. The following year, through the influence of the King of France, he was made Cardinal, under the title of "Sti Stephani in Monte Cœlio." And about the same time he was nominated Coadjutor of St Andrews, and declared future successor to the primate James Betoun, upon whose death in the beginning of the next year he became Archbishop. On 13th December 1543 he was made Lord Chancellor of Scotland, and in 1544 the Pope nominated him legate *a latere*. By this time he also held the appointment of legate *natus*, as he is said to bear that title in the feu charter of the lands of Colliston, Ruives, Park of Conon, and Guthrie Hill, which he granted on 25th July 1544, to John Guthrie and Isobel Ogilwy his spouse. The deed was subscribed by the Cardinal and twenty monks of the Abbey, whose names were, Robert Durward (sub-prior), Andrew Bardy, David Teyndar, William Crammy, David Craill, Thomas Ruthirfurde, Thomas Scot, Walter Baldowy, William Wedderburne, John Logye, John Peirson, David Scot, Alexander Gov (Gow), Allan Martyn, Alexander Cwby, Richard Craik, John Renny, Christopher Moncur, George Moncrieff, John Anderson. This document has at present fallen aside, a loss the more to be regretted on account of the extraordinary character of some of the illuminations on its margin. It was confirmed by another charter dated 16th November 1544, granted by James Strodaquhyne (Strachan), Provost of the collegiate church of the Blessed Virgin of Guthrie, David Pitcairn, Archdeacon of the cathedral church of Brechin, and John Meldrum, canon of Brechin, and rector of the parish church of Buthergill, as papal commissioners. The numerous dignities acquired by Betoun were not forgotten to be enumerated at the trial of George Wishart, in February 1546, by John Lauder, his accuser, according to Knox's account. " Is not my Lord Cardinall the secund persone within this realme, Chancellar of Scotland, Archbischope of Sanctandross, Bischope of Meropose, Commendatour of Abirbrothok, *Legatus Natus, Legatus a Latere?* And so reciting as many titilles of his unworthy honouris as wold have lodin a schip, much sonare ane asse ; is not he (quod Johne Lauder) ane equall judge apparently to thee ?"

In the year 1541 the Cardinal underwent a temporary disgrace and imprisonment, during the regency of the Earl of Arran, and at this time the Abbacy of Arbroath was given, or attempted to be given, *in commendam*, to John Hamilton the Regent's second son. Mr Innes is of opinion that Betoun did not hold the Abbacy till his death ; and it has been said by others that he resigned that benefice in March 1545-6, with the intention that James Betoun his nephew (afterwards alluded to) should enjoy it ; although his title of Commendator of Aberbrothock was named by John Lauder at Wishart's trial, within three months of his death, which took place at the hands of Norman Leslie's followers on 29th May 1546, as narrated in every history of the period. The Cardinal's bloody and violent death happened in a time of confusion, which it tended to increase ; and immediately after its perpetration a competition took place for the offices which he had held, and among others for the Abbacy, notwithstanding his alleged resignation in favour of his nephew.

31. After the Cardinal's death, Knox states that "Laubour is maid for the Abbacy of Abirbrothok;" and in the midst of some uncertainty, GEORGE DOUGLAS, natural son to Archibald Earl of Angus, may be ranked as the next Abbot, although he enjoyed the benefice only for a short period. Leslie the historian says that the governor (Earl of Arran) "gaif ane gift of the Abbay of Arbroith to George Douglas, bastard sone to the Erle of Angus, notwithstanding that Maister James Beatoun, tender cousing to the Cardinall, was lawfullie provydit thairto of befoir, quhilk maid gret troubill in the countrey eftirwart." Knox, in allusion to this appointment of George Douglas, adds, "in memory whairof he is yet called Postulat." Some have believed the grant to Douglas to have been wholly ineffectual. But Hume of Godscroft, in his history of the house of Douglas, referring to this title of Postulate of Aberbrothock, asserts that Douglas did "not only *postulate* it, but apprehended it also, and used it as his own." The servants and dependents of the Earl of Angus possessed Arbroath in the end of the year 1547, subsequent to the battle of Pinkie. (Tytler, vi. 424.) Long afterwards, in 1570, during the vindictive and bloody war between the King's-men and the Queen's-men, Douglas, who espoused the King's side, took possession of the Abbey, as belonging to him. He was besieged in it by the Earl of Huntly for some time, till the Regent Lennox sent the Earl of Morton with a force to relieve him. Upon this Huntly left the place and went to Brechin, whether Morton followed, and a skirmish took place at the Cathedral; after which Morton hanged forty-four soldiers who had been taken prisoners at the castle. George Douglas became Bishop of Moray in 1571, and retained that see about sixteen years till his death. In the absence of more direct evidence it is supposed that his carrying away the documents of the Abbey and town of Arbroath, as mentioned in King James' charter to the burgh, took

place when he left the Abbey, after his short-lived possession of it in 1570.

32. In the confusion that succeeded the death of David Betoun, and notwithstanding the grant of the Abbacy to George Douglas, it seems to have soon fallen into the hands of JAMES BETOUN, a son of John Betoun of Balfarg, and nephew of the Cardinal. He was educated for the church, and was sometimes styled "Maister James Betoun, Postulat of Aberbrothock." According to Chalmers (Caledonia, iii. 623), he had obtained an appointment to the Abbacy at the time of the resignation of his uncle the Cardinal, in March 1545-6. As postulate of Aberbrothock, he was in November 1549, ordered to find security to "underly the lawis for treasonable intercommuning with Sir John Dudley, Englishman, sometime captain of the fort of Brouchty," and persons were sent to Aberbrothock "to require the place thereof to be given oure to my Lord Governouris Grace, because Maister James Betoune was at the horne." In that year (1549) he is said to have granted a charter of the lands of Guynd, now in Carmylie parish, to John Betoun of Balquharry (Balquharg) for services performed by him, and for "the defence of the monastery against the invaders of the liberties of the church in these times when the Lutherans are endeavouring to invade the same." (Stat. Acc. of Carmylie, 1845.) This grant was probably annulled at the Reformation, as the "Charge of the Temporalitie" describes the "lands of Gund" as set in feu to David Strathauchin of Carmylie.

James Betoun retained the Abbacy, although not without contest, till the year 1551, when he was promoted to the Archbishopric of Glasgow. He enjoyed many eminent stations in the church during the few years which then preceded the downfal of the Romish faith in Scotland. After that event he left this country, and was appointed by Queen Mary ambassador to the Court of France. Her son, James VI., continued him in that office till his death, which took place at Paris on 25th April 1603, in the eighty-sixth year of his age. Betoun is said to have settled his property so as to promote the cause of learning. He bequeathed to the Scottish college at Paris many interesting documents, including the correspondence betwixt Quintin Kennedy, Abbot of Crossragwel, and John Willock, one of the Reformers, in 1559, which has since been printed by bishop Keith and others.

33. LORD JOHN HAMILTON, second son of the Earl of Arran, Governor of Scotland, is believed to have obtained an appointment to the Abbacy so early as 1541, but did not obtain possession till 1551, on James Betoun's preferment to Glasgow. He was at that time only about eighteen years old, and was the last Popish Abbot of Arbroath. But in 1559 he, with his father's family, became attached to the Protestant party: and he afterwards acted conspicuously in most of the political and religious movements of the time, some of which were sufficiently dark. He however gave many proofs of the sincerity of his conversion to the reformed faith. Owing to the lunacy of his elder brother, he was, after his father's death, practically the head of the powerful family of Hamilton during the long period of thirty years. It was during his rule that the remaining lands of the monastery were given away as perpetual feus, till nothing was left except the precinct or site of the monastic buildings, to which the Crown laid claim. Among others it appears that about 1555 he feued the lands and barony of Ethie to Sir Robert Carnegie of Kinnaird, one of the Senators of the College of Justice, and afterwards ambassador to England and France, for £108 Scots yearly. From Sir John these lands descended to John his grandson, who was created Lord Lour in 1639, and Earl of Ethie in 1647. These titles were about 1662 changed to Earl of Northesk and Lord Rosehill.

On 10th May 1560, Abbot John Hamilton subscribed the contract with Queen Elizabeth's lieutenant regarding the siege of Leith. He was one of the assize who, in 1567, pronounced Bothwell not guilty of the murder of Darnley. A letter from him to the General Assembly, excusing his absence on account of the disturbances at the time of Queen Mary's imprisonment at Lochleven, is printed in Keith's History (p. 587). It is dated at Hamilton, 19th July 1567, and concludes, " Zour loving friend at power in all godlines, Arbrothe." He had taken the Queen's part at this period, and afterwards went to France to solicit aid for her deliverance ; but does not appear to have been at the battle of Langside after her escape. He appeared publicly on her behalf toward the close of the civil war which soon afterwards ensued, although he did not personally act much the part of a soldier. He was included in the sentence of forfeiture pronounced against the Queen's adherents in the King's Parliament of August 1571. By the treaty of Perth, 23rd February 1571-2, " Lord Johnne Hamiltoun, Commendator of the Abbay of Arbroithe for himself, and takand the burden upon him for Lord Claud Hamiltoun, his brother, and all utheris, the kin, friends, servants, and partakers now depending properly on the Duke His Grace of Chattelarault, thair father, and the hous of Hamiltoun," with the Earl of Huntly and his dependents, submitted to the authority of the Regent of the infant king, and were restored to their possessions. (Historie of King James the Sext, p. 211.)

Like others of his family, Lord John was suspected of participation in contriving the death of the Regent Moray : he cordially received the assassin at Hamilton after the deed. He was also concerned in the death of Johnston of Westerraw, who had killed one of the Hamiltons, and was in his turn slain by another of the same name. The following scenes, so characteristic of that unsettled period, cannot be better narrated than in the words of the Church historian, Calderwood (iii. 346) : "Upon the seventh of March [1575], the Lord Hammiltoun and Claud, Abbot of Pasley, made public sithement* to the Erle of Angus, in the palace of Halyrudhous; comming the whole bounds of the inner court barefootted and bare-headed; and sitting doun on their knees, delivered him the sword by the point, for the slaughter of Westerraw. This reconciliatioun greeved specially William Douglas of Lochlevin, who desisted not from persute of the slaughter of his brother, the Erle of Murrey. He persued the Lord Hammiltoun comming from Arbrothe, so that he was constrained to retire to Arbrothe. Another tyme, when he was ryding through Fife, he constrained him to flee to Dairsie, and lay about it till the Regent sent and charged them to depart." On the last of these occasions, Douglas was accompanied by the Earl of Buchan, George Douglas (the Postulate), then Bishop of Moray, and about five hundred horsemen. They were determined on the death of Lord John, but he escaped to Dairsie by a stratagem, where he was besieged several days till the Hamiltons, with the Earls of Angus, Rothes, and Errol, had assembled a large force for his relief. Douglas at last was induced to raise the siege, and Lord Hamilton was allowed to proceed on his journey to Arbroath.

Lord John shared in the sudden reverse of his kindred during Morton's regency in the year 1579, on the pretence of accession to Moray's murder, and fled to Flanders in great poverty, having travelled on foot through great part of England disguised as a seaman. He went to Paris, and was very kindly entertained by Archbishop James Betoun, his predecessor in the Abbacy. The powerful house of Guise made great offers to him if he would return to the Romish religion; but his conscientious refusal deprived him of all further favour at the

---

* This was an old Scottish form of making *assythment* or satisfaction for bloodshed.

Court of France. Queen Mary, when under sentence of death, took a ring from her finger, and bade her attendants carry it to him, as the only proof she could give of her sense of the fidelity of his family to her, and of their sufferings on her account, requesting that it might be kept as a lasting token of her gratitude. Although Lord John was thus attached to his royal mistress, he had a large share of the confidence of the Reformed Church; and was generally on the side of those who espoused the cause of civil and religious liberty, so far as understood at the time. The following interview will explain this qualification. The Synod of Fife, in September 1593, had passed sentence of excommunication on the Earls of Huntly, Angus, and Errol, Lord Hume, and two others, for their continued adherence to Popery. King James was much provoked at the measure, and shortly afterwards went to Hamilton and visited Lord John, who was uncle to Huntly. After expressing his esteem for and confidence in Hamilton, the King said: "You see, my Lord, how I am used; and that I have no man in whom I may trust more than in Huntly. If I receive him the ministers will cry out that I am an apostate from the religion; if not, I am left desolate." Hamilton replied, "If he and the rest be not enemies to the religion ye may receive them; otherwise not." "I cannot tell what to make of that," said the King, "but the ministers hold them for enemies: at all events I would think it good that they enjoyed liberty of conscience." Upon this Hamilton cried out, "Then, sir, we are all gone! then we are all gone! If there were no more to withstand, I will withstand." Confounded by the earnestness of Lord John's manner, and seeing his servants approaching, James said, with a smile, "My lord, I did this to try your mind," and immediately changed the subject. (Cald. v. 269, and others.) Notwithstanding the humiliating scene of the assythment, Lord John's character appears in history as one of dignity and consistency, but marked by a certain want of firmness of purpose. Like his father, the Duke of Chatelherault, he was not only respected but loved, and seems to have avoided as far as possible appeals to the sword, in times when it was too often resorted to as the settler of disputes. He often resided at Arbroath, without doubt in the Abbot's house; and frequently visited Maule of Panmure, for whom he had great respect—called him father, and accompanied him in hunting excursions.

During the period of Lord John's adversity Esme Stuart D'Aubigne, the early favourite of King James, procured the revenues of the Abbacy, and in May 1581 confirmed a deed of sale of Newton of Aberbrothock by John Carnegie of that Ilk to Robert Guthrie of Kinblethmont. He was suddenly advanced to great power, and was on 3rd August 1581 proclaimed Duke of Lennox, Lord Darnley, Lord Tarbolton, Dalkeith and Tantallon, Great Chamberlain of Scotland, and Commendator of Arbroath. His fall was as rapid as his rise. The Scottish barons, enraged at his boundless influence over the young King, carried through the revolution called the raid of Ruthven, and compelled D'Aubigne to leave Scotland in December 1582. He died soon afterwards in France, on 26th May 1583. He was a good-natured, gay, accomplished man, with the manners of France, where he had been educated. During the short period of his power there was a running war betwixt him and the ministers of the Scottish Church, who believed, perhaps unjustly, that he continued to be a papist in disguise. Among innumerable charges brought by them against his public proceedings and those of James Stuart, who at that time took the title of Earl of Arran, they complained that, " he procured the title of the Abbacie of Arbrothe, without any provisioun of the ministrie for everie particular kirk of that prelacie, contrarie to the tenor of the late act of Parliament; and also, that " he purchased the gift of the superplus of the thrids of

Arbrothe, as it stood *in anno* 1580, not onlie to stay all farther planting of ministers within the kirks of that Abbacie but also to spoile the whole ministers not planted at these kirks of the part of their stipends taken out of that Abbacie." (Cald. iv., 396.) Another charge, of a more personal nature, was that, "Albeit he promised to procure and mainteane on his expenses a minister, he never had so much as one boy to read one chapter or say grace at the table." The commentary on this curious list of grievances also bears that, "In a French passion he rent his beard, and thinking to strike the boord, strake himself in the thigh, crying, 'The devill for John Durie,' which Montbirneau learned for the first lessoun in the Scotish language."

Lord John Hamilton returned to Scotland in 1585 with his brother Claud and the other exiled lords, and invested Stirling with an army, after which he, as first in rank, and the other nobles were courteously received by the King. He was, by the Parliament of that year, restored to his possessions and honours, made Captain of the Castle of Dumbarton, and appointed Curator to his eldest brother, James Hamilton, Earl of Arran. After this period he enjoyed much of the friendship and confidence of James VI. The act of annexation of the temporality of benefices to the Crown, passed in 1587, provided that "John Lord Hammiltoun, Commendator of the Abbacie of Aberbrothock, sall bruik the fruites of the said Abbacie during his lifetime, in the same manner as he did before, except the profits of the Lands of Craquhy and Milne, the Lands of Tullois and Corstoun, for the whilk he sall be recompensed according to the general ordour to be taken with the remanent ecclesiastical persones quhais rent is paired be the said annexatioun." Lord John took a prominent part in the reception of Queen Anne (of Denmark), and bore the sceptre at her coronation, on 17th May 1590. He was created first Marquis of Hamilton on 17th April 1599, and resigned the Abbey into the King's hands, who conferred the same on his eldest son, James Hamilton, reserving his father's right to the profits during his lifetime. This last Abbot of Arbroath died on 12th April 1604, aged seventy-one.

His son James, thus second Marquis of Hamilton, procured a Charter of the Abbey in 1600; and the King and Parliament, on 6th July 1606, dissolved the lands, patronages, and teinds of the Abbey from the Crown, and erected them into a temporal lordship in his favour, with the dignity and title of a lay lord of Parliament, but divested of the privileges of regality. This statute declares that the Parliament "hes suppressit and extinguischit the memorie of the said Abbacie of Aberbrothok, that thair sall be na successor provydit thairto, *nor na farder mentioun maid of the samin in ony tyme heirefter.*" The Marquis of Hamilton was created Lord Aberbrothock on 5th May 1608. He died on 2nd March 1625, and his son James, third Marquis, was served heir to the lands and barony of Aberbrothock on 5th May thereafter, and retained them at least till 1636. Up to Michaelmas of that year his chamberlain, John Hamilton of Almericcloss, took an active part in the burgh business of Arbroath, and annually nominated one of the bailies.

After that date, according to John Spottiswood (Account of Religious Houses), the lordship, now an ordinary estate, came into possession of William Murray, subsequently created first Earl of Dysart, who retained it but a few years.

Patrick Maule of Panmure seems to have been in terms for a purchase of the estate from the Marquis of Hamilton, and afterwards effected the purchase of it, with the patronage of its churches, from the Earl of Dysart, and obtained a charter in his favour on 26th November 1642. He was Gentleman of the Bed-Chamber to King Charles I., and in 1646 was created first Earl of Panmure. He and the Earl of Dysart did not, down to 1646, nominate any magistrate of Arbroath, but left them to be elected by the council. James, the fourth Earl, lost Arbroath with his other great possessions through his forfeiture after 1715, but they were purchased from the York Buildings Company in 1764 for £49,157, 18s. 4d., by William Maule, Earl of Panmure of Forth, and have since remained in the possession of that eminent family.

IV.—CAUSES OF DISSOLUTION.

The Abbey of Arbroath may be said to have enjoyed about three hundred and twenty years of vitality and usefulness in a greater or less degree, namely, from 1178 till about 1500. During the earlier portion of this period we believe that the institution of monasteries (not of monachism) was a benefit to the population of Europe. However much the system may have become liable to ridicule and censure, as observed during its more recent, and consequently better known history, which was a time of comparative superannuation and gross abuses, it is to be recollected that at an early period it contributed largely to help forward that improvement in manners, literature, and civil and religious liberty which at last rose up to, and far beyond, its own level. But the system was too artificial, and in some respects too unnatural to enable it to keep pace with the progress of civilisation and enlightenment, so that monasteries instead of being, as they once were, ahead of the age, were found to have stood still, while society around them continued to advance so as to leave them far behind.

The remaining sixty years of the Romish history of this great monastery was, in respect more especially to its higher functionaries, a period of corruption and very visible decay ; for about the close of the fifteenth century universal disorder seems to have rushed in like a flood, not only on this, but on almost every monastic establishment in Scotland. This religious house consequently did not fail to share the fate of these other establishments, in regard to which it has been well remarked by an erudite writer (Chalmers' Caledonia, ii. 508), that "when their usefulness was gone their oblivion began." The more apparent, because physical ruin and desolation, which at last overtook this once noble institution, about 1560, may therefore be looked on as the natural and inevitable consequence of the prior moral and mental degradation to which it had been subjected by the grandees of the period, who overlooked every object which it had been intended to subserve, in their desire for possession of its revenues.

The inordinate ambition and incompetency of the men who at that period became ecclesiastics, not in order to serve the church but their own cupidity, are well described by Gawin Douglas, to whom we have already alluded, and who being himself a dignitary of the Romish Church, cannot be suspected of Protestant prejudice. In the strange alliterative prologue to the eighth book of his translation of Virgil's great poem, written in 1513, not long previous to the battle of Flodden, he says:

> "Priests [who] suld be patterers,[1] and for the people pray,
> To be papes of patrimony and prelatis pretendis;
> Ten teinds are ane trump, bot gif he tak may
> Ane kinrik of parish kirks, coupled with commendis.[2]
> Wha are workers of this war, wha wakeneis of wae,
> Bot incompetable clergy that Christendom offendis?
> Wha rieves, wha are riotous, wha reckless bot thay?
> Wha quells the poor commons bot kirkmen weel kend is.
> There is nae state of their style that standis content;
>   Knight, clerk, nor common,
>   Burgess nor baron,
>   All would have up that is down;
>   Welterit the went."[3]

[1] Repeaters of the *Pater noster*.

[2] That is, the tithes of ten churches are accounted trumpery unless he may take a whole country of parish churches coupled with *commendams* or Abbey rents.

[3] The state of affairs is overturned.

Douglas' description of the corruptions of the Romish church is substantially the same with that given by Sir David Lindesay a few years afterwards. In his Complaint to the King's Grace, this poet of the Scottish Reformation writes thus:

> Thae lordis tuke na mair regaird,
> Bot quha micht purches best rewaird.
> Sum to thair freindis gat beneficeis,
> And uther sum gat bischopreis,
> For every lord, as he thocht best,
> Brocht in ane bird to fill the nest,
> To be ane wacheman to his marrow,
> Thay gan to draw at the cat harrow :[1]
> The proudest prelatis of the kirk
> Was fane to hyde thame in the mirk,
> That tyme, so failzeit was thair sicht.
> Sen syne thay may nocht thole the licht
> Of Christis trew Gospell to be sene,
> So blyndit is thair corporall ene,
> With warldlie lustis sensuall,
> Taking in realmes the governall,
> Baith gyding court and sessioun,[2]
> Contrar to thair professioun ;
> Quhareof I think they sulde have schame,
> Of spirituall preistis to tak the name ;
> For, Esayas into his wark,
> Callis thame like doggis that can nocht bark,
> That callit are preistis and can nocht preche,
> Nor Christis law to the pepill teche.

Before Knox was born the glory had departed from the great school of religion and letters which once existed at Arbroath, so far as purity of doctrine and morals, literature or common decency were concerned. Even the Chartulary shows that after Abbot David Lichtone's death, little remained except fast increasing idolatry and saint worship, with unblushing prostitution of the endowments for the gratification of sensual pleasure and ambition. Knox and his coadjutors the Reformers appeared just in time to inter those now dead and corrupting institutions which had become too offensive to be allowed to remain longer unburied. And

[1] Every one helped or countenanced another.   [2] The Court of Session.

while no lover of the grand or beautiful can survey the ruins of Arbroath Abbey without lamenting the gradual destruction of the great church during the last three hundred years, it should be also recollected that desolation did not overtake it until it had for sixty years at least outlived its usefulness and the whole original purposes of its erection.

The most affecting circumstance connected with its downfal was probably the condition of some of the poor monks, who were too destitute of influence to share in the spoliation of the period; and yet in whom alone was to be found any sincere attachment to religion, whether under the outward form of remaining adherence to Rome, or the adoption of the reformed faith. There can be little doubt that at Arbroath, as well as at Newbottle and other monasteries, there were, after the Reformation, "aged, decrepit, and recanted monks," whose *portions* were, or ought to have been, reserved to them amid the appropriation of the rents to others. We find a reservation of "monks portions," without any indication of their number, inserted in legislative acts relating to the Abbey of Arbroath thirty years subsequent to the downfal of the Romish religion.

We have not been able to identify any of the monks in David Betoun's time as afterwards holding the offices of ministers or readers in the reformed church, although it is quite probable that some of them may have lived till 1560, and have been so employed. In the General Assembly of 1562, a complaint against John Erskine of Dun, the Superintendent of Angus, related to "*many popish priests* admitted to be readers of kirks within his diocese." One of these was Thomas Lyndsay, a monk of Arbroath, and reader at the churches of Arbroath and St Vigeans in 1570–4, whom Lord John Hamilton appointed Almoner of the Abbey in June 1570. (Burgh Records.) From the reservation of their "portions," and other indications, it is clear that some of the older monks continued to linger out their days within the Abbey precinct or its vicinity. The Burgh Records of Arbroath allude to another monk, entitled "*Den* Thomas Fethy," who lived in the town a year or two after the Reformation, and was styled "Maister of Comoun," apparently from his having had the charge of the common pasture of the town. After his death other two monks, named Den Alexander Gib and Den John Quhit (White), appeared at the burgh court in 1566 as administrators of his affairs, and collectors of debts due to him. The entry in the court book regarding them is in the following terms: (7 December 1566), "The quhilk day thir parsonis fowlowand comperit with Den Alexr. Gib and Den John Quhit, anent the dettis awand to Den Thomas Fethy, wmqll maister of Comon: that is to say, Mathow Morison restis awand xx sh; Johne Ramsay, cordiner, xvj sh viij d; James Boyis, xl sh; Copyn Guthre, iij sh iiij d; James Pekyman, vij sh: and the bailyeis commandit the officers to pund for the samin."

These are the latest notices of the ordinary members of this great monastic establishment which we have found. Some remarks on the general condition and employment of recanted Romish priests in Scotland about the same period will be found in Appendix, No. II.

CHAPTER XIII.

DESCRIPTION OF THE CONVENTUAL BUILDINGS.—FORM OF THE CHURCH, TOWERS, DIVISIONS, COLUMNS, GALLERIES, ROOFS, DOORS, WINDOWS. DIMENSIONS OF BUILDINGS: EXTERNAL AND INTERNAL APPEARANCE OF CHURCH: REMAINING STATUES: CONVENTUAL SEALS: BELL ROCK.

LIKE many cathedral churches erected at the same period, the Abbey Church of Arbroath was reared in the usual form of a Latin cross, that is, with the head of the cross towards the east. The main body of the Church, forming the stalk of the cross, consisted of a high centre aisle, with an aisle on each side of less than half its height. These side aisles stopped at the west end of the chancel, leaving the centre aisle to extend two divisions further to the eastward. About two-fifths of the distance from the east end these long aisles were intersected by the transept forming the arms of the cross. It consisted of a high aisle running from north to south of equal dimensions in height and breadth with the long central aisle; and it had toward the east a side aisle of equal dimensions with the other side aisles. The great central tower was erected on the four pillars where the high aisles crossed each other. The north and south side aisles were each terminated on the west by a square tower which projected several feet beyond them on either side, and beyond the high aisle in the centre. These towers were of three storeys, and reached in their square form to a height of ninety feet or thereby, and overlooked the roof of the centre aisle. The north tower bears marks of having been raised to a greater height than the south tower. They had double buttresses at each corner diminishing toward the top in a very graceful manner. The lowest storeys of the towers were adorned with two rows of blind arches, and the upper storeys were lighted by pairs of tall lancet windows on every side, except where they joined the church. These elegant towers, with the intervening deeply recessed door, surmounted by the rich work of its porch, and the great circular window of the middle aisle gave to the west front of the church a most superb and beautiful aspect.

The internal portions of this extensive building were known by various terms. The nave consisted of the middle and side aisles from the west front to the great tower in the centre. The north and south transepts included the high and side aisles on both sides of the tower. The great choir (termed in the Abbey writs the *meikle queer*) included the high aisle betwixt the tower and chancel, with the aisles on either side. And lastly the chancel was an extension of this high aisle without any side aisles. It contained the high altar or stone table raised on a platform, reached by four very broad steps or degrees. The floor of the church, or at least a part of it, was paved with square glazed tiles of various colours. Beside the four great pillars which supported the central tower, there were twenty-four pillars betwixt the middle and side aisles. All these pillars measured seventeen and a-half feet in height from the floor to the top of the capitals; while the four centre pillars mounted upwards to a height of at least forty-five feet from the floor. The diameter of these pillars was eight feet, and the diameter of the lesser pillars was five feet, measured across their stalks. They were all formed externally of slender columns nearly round set on one base; there being ten such columns in each of the four great pillars, and eight in each of the others; and each pillar appeared like a cluster of tall columns joined together. Their capitals were adorned by carving, principally in the stiff-leaf or early English style. Richly moulded arches, in the pointed style, sprung from the capitals, and supported the upper walls of the high aisles. Next above these arches was the blind storey, containing thirty *triforium* windows, running along the sides of the high aisles. These windows were not seen from without, as they looked into the dark galleries betwixt the vaulting and roof of the said aisles. Each window was adorned with triple columns at the sides, and a centre column and double arches within. One of these windows remains to shew the elegance of the other twenty-nine. They were again surmounted by the *clere* storey windows which gave light to the upper part of the high aisles. There were thus three storeys or ranges of windows round the church; the upper and lower ranges of which were also adorned by double columns and arches.

The side aisles were covered by ribbed and groined vaults of stone reaching to thirty feet in height. But the internal roofs of the high aisles, or their inner vaulting, if they were finished in that manner, must have been of wood, and probably reached to a height of eighty-three feet above the floor. An open gallery of light and elegant stone work still remains above the west door; and another open gallery still exists running along the inside of the south transept gable, which, together with two lower ranges of clustered columns and blind arches, gave to this part of the church a very rich appearance. The interior of the chancel was also surrounded by columns and arches which shew much taste. The walls of the west towers, the four great gables, and west walls of the high transept aisles were perforated with galleries or arched passages on a level with the blind storey, so that persons could go round the whole building at this height.

The church possessed at least four doors. The great western door bears marks of having been the last formed. Its top is a deep semicircular arch of the latest Norman style, with peculiar mouldings, rising from six columns on each side, flanked by small blind arches in the pointed style. The doorway as now existing is ten feet wide and fourteen feet high; the ornamented stone work by which the passage was contracted having been removed several years ago. The other doors, namely one on the north and two on the south side of the nave have elegant pointed arches: and the eastmost one is flanked by columns and a blind arch on each side. The walls contain the holes from which wooden beams were stretched behind these doors when wished to be secured. The western door was surmounted by three pointed windows in the ornamental work of the porch, and by a very magnificent circular window covering nearly the whole breadth of the centre aisle, and the frame of which is about twenty-eight feet in diameter. Each of the west towers was lighted by ten lancet windows; and the body of the church had thirty-nine pointed windows of various heights on the north, and as many on the south side, including those in the transept gables, beside a circular window at the top of each of these gables. The east or chancel gable contained nine pointed windows, with one of a different form, probably round or triangular, at the top. There is little doubt that the central tower was lighted by twelve windows at least, or three on each side, above the roof of the church; so that the whole number of windows or lights (not including the triforium) was one hundred and twenty-six. None of the pointed windows were divided by stone mullions, whatever was the interior form of the circular windows; such mullions not having been generally adopted at the time of erection. The roof of the church was covered with lead, from which the rain fell into leaden gutters, protected by parapets of stone. These parapets were reached by circular stone staircases, one of which remains in the gable of the south transept; and the frame of another may be seen in the south-west tower.

The following measurements will give an idea of the actual size of this edifice and some neighbouring buildings. The total length of the church over walls is 284 feet, thus —nave and west wall 153 feet, centre tower 40 feet, great choir 51 feet, chancel and east wall 40 feet. Total width of nave and choir over walls 71 feet; the centre aisle being 37 feet and each side aisle being 17 feet wide. Length of transept from north to south over walls including centre tower 140 feet. Width of transept over walls including high and side aisles 54 feet. The central tower was about 40 feet square, and each of the west towers measure about 30 feet square. The walls of the side aisles are 30 feet in height. The height of the side walls of the middle aisles was about 67 feet. The rigging of the upper roofs was about 89 feet high; and it may be assumed that the great central tower, without any spire, rose at least to a height of 140 feet from the ground. The vestry built by Abbot Panter, and containing his arms, measures about 19 feet square within walls. The lower apartment is vaulted with stone, upwards of 30 feet in height, and adorned on three sides with columns and blind arches. It is lighted by two elegant windows (one of which is a twin window); and a small turret, still existing, overtops its south-west corner.

The cloister court measured about 100 feet square within the boundary walls, and occupied the site of the modern garden south from the nave. The dimensions of the Abbot's house are 78 feet in length from east to west, and 40 feet in width over walls. This dwelling was wainscotted internally with dark oak, bearing many figures in relief; but the whole has been ruthlessly destroyed, except two doors which yet remain to shew what has been lost.

A range of building two storeys in height, and about sixty feet in length, extends due westward from the south-west tower of the church to the great gateway. The basement storey is formed into vaults, covered with groined arches, in a state of good preservation. The great gatehouse of the Abbey precinct, looking towards the north, at the west end of this building, measures 64 feet in length from north to south, and 30 feet in breadth over walls. The outer or north clear gateway, formed of clustered columns, and a moulded arch, obtusely pointed, is $16\frac{1}{2}$ feet in width, and about 17 feet high. It was formerly contracted by masonry for greater security; and it still exhibits the groove for letting down the great iron portcullis, which with its chains now forms the modern heraldic representative of the town of Arbroath. The arch at the south end of the gatehouse and those in the middle where the hinged doors were hung are of a plainer character. The ribbed and groined roof which covered the passage way was surmounted by a large apartment, the walls of which yet remain. It is lighted on the north by a square-headed window divided by a mullion, and a small round window above, all enclosed in a pointed arch of the decorated style; and is adorned by blind arches, and large deep corbels on either side. The south end of this apartment is also lighted by a plainer pointed window in the same style, and there are several pointed windows on each side. West of the gatehouse there stood a vaulted apartment 28 feet long and about 18 feet wide within. This was succeeded by the hall called the Regality Court-house, covered with groined arches, and measuring 40 feet long and about 18 feet wide within. This hall was surmounted by other apartments, the roof of which is marked on the east wall of the tower. The donjon tower, supported by double buttresses at the corners, measures 24 feet from north to south, and 21 feet from east to west over walls, and is about 70 feet in height to the bottom of the bartizan. The walls are five or six feet in thickness. This tower commanded the three approaches to the Abbey, and it still has a formidable look.

The conventual buildings which had formerly stood on the south side of the church have been referred to in a previous chapter. The plot enclosed by the convent walls (which were from 20 to 24 feet in height), and called the precinct, extended to about 1150 feet in length from north to south. It was 706 feet broad at the north end, including the length of the great church, and 484 feet broad at the south end. Its form was exactly that of a wooden *stoup*, with the bottom or broad end looking to the north; excepting that the east wall had a curve outwards for some distance about midway from each end.

The church was externally destitute of those numerous small turrets and pinnacles which superficial admirers of Gothic architecture now prize so highly; and of which a florid specimen is given in the new Houses of Parliament. The builders being sagacious men saw that such external ornaments were neither fitted for the climate nor the material of the fabric. Its external beauty consisted in its great altitude and fine proportions, with the well-balanced adjustment of all its parts, which at first was fitted to give a limited idea of its great bulk till it was compared with the neighbouring buildings.

But the principal glory of the church was internal. A view of the vistas of its lofty vaulted aisles,—separated by its twenty-eight massive clustered pillars, and illumined by the light which streamed through its hundred and twenty-six windows, and adorned with innumerable columns, capitals, and arches, with tombs, statues, crosses, screens, and altars, which met the eye in every direction—can only be understood by those who have visited the large cathedral churches of England or the Continent; as there is not any existing Gothic building in Scotland equal to Arbroath Abbey Church in size, altitude, or continuous grandeur and unity of design.

All these tombs, altars, screens, and crosses, except a few insignificant fragments, have vanished. The remains

R

of the statues consist of three mutilated, headless trunks, now placed in the vestry. One of these has been formed out of a block of very hard and dark coloured shell marble; and has been supposed to be a statue of the founder William the Lion, because the feet rest on the body of a lion. The robe is large and flowing, knit by a girdle, from which a purse hangs on the left side, and the figure was originally recumbent. It exhibits remains of three or four pigmy figures which, on a close inspection, appear to be knights in armour, engaged as if they were arranging the drapery. This statue, without the head, measures four feet three inches in length. Another truncated statue is three inches longer, and is evidently formed to stand upright. It consists of very fine freestone, and clearly represented a high church dignitary, most probably one of the abbots. The hands, which had held a crosier, or may have been clasped, are broken off. But mutilated as it is, this figure displays a very great degree of beauty and grace in the arrangement of the drapery and disposition of the limbs. The robes from the neck to the feet are adorned with finely-carved lace ornaments, which bear traces of having been richly gilt. The other statue is of a size fully greater than the two above noticed, but so mutilated and wasted, owing to the softness of the sandstone of which it is composed, that it is difficult to say more respecting it than that it also appears to have been the figure of an abbot.

The graves within the area of the church had been ransacked long ago, most probably at the Reformation. Three of these are before the high altar, where it is said the founder was interred; but it is impossible to determine whether any of the bones now shewn to visitors really belonged to the material frame of this Scottish monarch.

The Conventual Seal of the Abbey was round, and measured $3\frac{1}{2}$ inches in diameter. It was well executed, considering its age; and it represents on the obverse side Thomas á Becket at the altar with four assassins approaching to murder him, while a figure kneeling on the steps below is believed to represent the penance of King Henry II. The inscription is:—" SIGILLVM : ABBATIS : ET : CONVENTVS : SCI : THOME : MARTVRIS : DE ABERBROTHOT." The counter seal represents a shrine with open folding-doors, displaying the Virgin and child seated and crowned, and surrounded by a legend, which has been found to read as follows:—" PORTA SALUTIS AVE : PER TE PATET EXITVS A VE : VENIT AB EVA VE : VE QVIA TOLLIS AVE."

The impression of a beautiful seal, used by Abbot John Gedy, and appended to the Act of Parliament settling the successor to the Crown in 1371, contains in its upper compartment the Virgin and child, with an angel worshipping on either side. The middle compartment represents the murder of Becket and the King's penance at the altar; while a figure seated and fully draped occupies the lower compartment. This seal is oblong, and measures about $2\frac{1}{4}$ inches in length. The outer inscription is:—" SIGILL : ABBATIS : SCI : THOME : DE : ABERBROTHOC;" but another inscription, in much smaller letters, cannot be given with certainty.

We have met with no reference in the records of the Abbey or burgh of Arbroath to that outlying reef known as the *Bell Rock*, which is associated with the memory of the Abbots of Aberbrothock. During the times of the Papacy the shipping which belonged to this part of Scotland was very limited; and those who have noticed the wear of rocks within flood-mark in the neighbourhood of Arbroath can easily conceive that, at the period referred to, this rock may have stood above the line of high-water, so as to be less dangerous to mariners, except at night and during fogs than it latterly became. As stated by Mr R. Stevenson, civil engineer, in his article " Bell Rock " (Edinburgh Encyclopædia), the earliest name of the rock was "Inch-scape." It was afterwards called "Inch-cape," and latterly, the "Bell Rock.' What might appear at one time in the form of a *scape*—the Scottish name of a straw bee-hive—would at other states of the tide bear the common form of a bell, and this circumstance very probably gave rise to the more generally understood term *Bell Rock*. This supposition is a more natural way of accounting for the origin of the term than the unsupported tradition that the Convent of Arbroath had affixed a bell to the rock, to give warning to mariners. "It would be difficult to conceive any machine of this kind, which in such a situation could have been useful;" and we do not believe that such an unusual signal could have been in operation in former times without allusion to it being found in the pages of some contemporary record or annalist. The existence of the name and nonappearance of the bell might readily lead to the idea that a bell had once been there, and that the erecter was John Gedy or some other Abbot of the monastery. This idea, however, as well as the story of its removal by a Dutch or Danish shipmaster, who afterwards perished at the rock in consequence of his own act, although sufficiently romantic, and stereotyped by Southey's beautiful ballad, is met by so many sound objections as to lead to the conclusion that it must be classed among the fables. But the signal-tower securely placed on this hitherto treacherous rock, by the Commissioners of Northern Lights, in the years 1808-9-10, is no myth. Its graceful form rising from the waters during the day, its well-known red and white flames gleaming afar under the sky of starry nights, and its bells sounding along the waves in misty weather, is now hailed by the mariner in gladness as a friendly guide on which he may safely depend while steering his course in the vicinity of the dangerous coast of St. Thomas.

APPENDIX.

No. I.

NOTE ON THE DECAY OF FEUDAL POWER, AND EMANCIPATION OF THE RURAL INHABITANTS OF SCOTLAND.

THE three great events in Scottish history after referred to have been often treated in their political and religious aspects. But they also marked the commencement, advancement, and completion of the deliverance of the inhabitants from baronial and feudal bondage. A notice of them in this respect may help to enable us to understand how Scotland in the nineteenth comes to be so superior to the same country in the twelfth century; while in some other lands the cause of liberty has been stationary, or rather retrogressed.

The first of these events was the War of Independence into which the nation was plunged during the days of Wallace and Bruce, by the unprincipled attempt of Edward the First of England to subjugate our country under the sceptre of England, as his predecessor Henry the Second had previously done with the kingdom of Ireland. When the barons, clergy, and burgesses of Scotland, the only freemen then within its limits, found *themselves* in danger of being reduced to real if not professed slavery, and had the prospect of seeing the fruits of their labours and the fairest portions of their grounds, with their political privileges, seized or controlled by strangers, they then learned to sympathise with and respect the poor hinds and "thralls" whom, in the days of their prosperity, during the long and peaceable reigns of William and the Alexanders, they had neglected, despised, and oppressed, and without the help of whose sinewy arms they found that they could neither man their armies nor save themselves from being ultimately reduced to a like state of servitude. In short, they seemed to have discovered that which Poland and some other nations have not found out at this day—namely, that in order to save their country from a foreign yoke, they must give the body of the population an interest in that national freedom which is to be fought for; and that it would be vain to expect a people to exercise the valour and virtues of patriots in a war the only stake in which, to them, is merely a change of taskmasters.

Scotland's barons and burgesses, with the help of their hinds and labourers—who, it may be observed, are now no longer described as thralls and bondmen—did nobly achieve their independence, although at the cost of much blood and treasure, and at a loss to the kingdom of population, wealth, and prosperity, which the next four centuries were unable to repair. But this disastrous period, pregnant as it was with daring deeds, implanted in the breasts of Scotsmen a love of freedom, and a determination to secure it at all hazards, which has not been and will never be eradicated.

We may be excused from introducing this interesting period of our history when it is recollected that Arbroath is celebrated as the scene of the noblest declaration in behalf of national freedom which was ever made by the senators of this or any other country. In the very midst of Scotland's contest with all the power of England, the nobility, barons, and freeholders of the kingdom met at the Abbey of Arbroath on the 6th day of April 1320, and drew up the famed letter to the Roman Pontiff, in which they asserted the ancient independence of the country, and declared their resolution to maintain that independence to the last man, in spite of all the prowess of England's King, and whether his Holiness should be induced to recognise their rights or not.

Some of the passages in this document are exceedingly remarkable, as proceeding from the supreme council of a poor and half-ruined country so far back as five hundred and forty years ago. The penman is believed to have been the bold and public-spirited Abbot and Chancellor Bernard, already referred to. After describing the miseries which the invasions of Edward the First had brought upon the kingdom, they alluded to their monarch and deliverer, Bruce, in the following terms: —" At length it pleased God, who alone can heal the wounded, to restore us to freedom from these innumerable calamities by our Most Serene Prince, King, and Lord, Robert, who, for the delivering of his people and his own rightful inheritance from the hand of the enemy, did, like another Macabeus, or Joshua, most cheerfully undergo all manner of toil, fatigue, hardship, and hazard. Divine providence, through the right of succession by the laws and customs of the kingdom, which we will defend till death, and with the due and lawful assent and consent of all the people, made him our king and prince. To him we are obliged and resolved to adhere in all things, both on account of his right, and also from his merit, as being the person who has restored security to the people in the possession of their liberties. But after all, if he shall leave the principles he has so nobly pursued, and consent that we or our kingdom be subjected to the King of England or the English, we will immediately endeavour to expel him as our enemy, and as the subverter both of his own and of our rights, and will make a king who will defend our liberties; because so long as a hundred of us shall remain alive, we will never subject ourselves to the dominion of the English; for it is not glory, riches, nor honour, but liberty alone that we fight and contend for, and with which no upright man will part except with life itself." The writer of a manuscript "Accompt of the Familie of Hamilton," in Panmure House, concludes, very justly however, that this celebrated letter was never delivered to the Pope, seeing that the principal writing, duly sealed, has been found among the Scottish records. He thinks it probable that Bruce, dissatisfied because his *hereditary* right to the kingdom was not sufficiently recognised in it, had forbidden the transmission of the document.

It was sometime after the close of his struggle that Barbour, in his "Bruce" (written in 1375), gives the following powerful description of freedom and slavery:—

> "A! fredome is a nobill thing!
> Fredome mayse man to haiff liking;
> Fredome all solace to man giffis:
> He levys at ese that frely levys!
>
> "A noble hart may haiff nane ese,
> Na ellys nocht[1] that may him plese,
> Gyff fredome failyhe: for free liking[2]
> Is yharnyt[3] our all othir thing.
>
> "Na he that ay base levyt fre
> May nocht knaw weill the propyrte,[4]
> The angyr,[5] na the wrechyt dome,
> That is cowplyt to foule thyrldome.
>
> "Bot gyff he had assayit it.[6]
> Than all perquer he suld it wyt;[7]
> And suld think fredome mar to pryse,[8]
> Than all the gold in warld that is."

The second great event which advanced the cause of emancipation was the Reformation from Popery in the sixteenth century. The effects of this event are well

---

[1] Nor nothing else. [2] Free will. [3] Desired or longed for. [4] Nature.
[5] Old Scotch for sorrow. [6] Tried it. [7] Then he should know it perfectly.
[8] More to prize.

described by the writer of a book entitled, "Historical Remarks on Government," who, after alluding to the slavery in which the common people were previously held, adds: "To complete their unhappy situation—to the exercise of this aristocratical power over their bodies—we must add the tyranny of the Church of Rome over their consciences. It was not till after a vigorous exertion of their minds in detecting the errors of the Church of Rome at the Reformation that the same excitement shewed the abject state in which they had always been kept by their kings and the barons. They then began to have some idea of their natural rights, and to perceive the illegality of those oppressive measures that had been constantly used to continue their slavish dependence on these two powers." Killigrew, Queen Elizabeth's envoy, observed this change so early as 1572, when he wrote as follows: "Methinks I see the noblemen's great credit decay in this country; and the barons, burrows, and such like take more upon them." (Letter, Killigrew to Burghley, 11th Nov. 1572, State Paper Office.) But the political freedom, as well as the amelioration of manners, which certainly sprung from the Reformation, were not very apparent in the history of Scotland till some thirty years after that event. It is not so much about the year 1560 as between 1590 and 1600 that our statutes, chronicles, and courts of law records, shew the greatest steps toward improvement of manners—departure from the old physical force barbarism—and introduction of the common people into a place in society higher than they had previously been permitted to occupy, or had probably ever believed they would enjoy. This is just, however, what was to be expected. During these thirty or forty years the old generation, who had been bred up in the midst of papal ignorance and mental apathy and slavery, had died out, like the generation that came out of Egypt; and during the same space the younger generation, who had been educated with a knowledge of the Scriptures, and had their minds excited to activity and intelligence under the ministrations of the Reformed preachers, were now grown up, and were taking the management and control of the political and social relations throughout the country. A striking instance of this change is found in the erection of many villages into burghs of barony at that period, and of the conversion of their ward-holdings into feu-holdings; that is, they were relieved from the obligation to follow the barons in war, and bound to make a small annual return of money or poultry instead.

The third and last period of deliverance was during the sixty years which elapsed from the Revolution in 1688 to the abolition of heritable jurisdictions in 1748. The Revolution was rather the *occasion* of this deliverance than the immediate cause of it; for we are speaking of baronial rather than of monarchical bondage. It is also remarkable that the efforts made to undo that great event, which fixed and established British freedom in the highest departments of State, were made the immediate causes of emancipating the lowest classes in the country from the domination of the classes next above them in rank. Down to this period, many feuars and vassals were bound to follow their feudal superior in his wars against all to whom he might be opposed, the king only excepted. But when the cause of quarrel was, as in 1715 and 1745, Who was the rightful king? the superior, of course, held the exception to apply only to the king whom *he* acknowledged, and not to the *usurper*, against whom he mustered his dependents; and these dependents were bound to adopt their lord's side of the disputed question upon pain of forfeiture of their possessions. This rendered it necessary for the Legislature to curtail such powers after the rising of the Scottish clans in 1715, and to abolish them entirely in 1748, soon after the Rebellion of 1745. Such a tenure of property was a remnant of a barbarous age, and of times of little or no central government; and was not less dangerous to a civilised State than oppressive towards the victims of its operation, who were often obliged, contrary to their inclinations, to leave their homes at the bidding of a restless superior, and engage in conflicts which might cost them liberty or life, and, at the least, involve themselves and others in hardships and losses. To complete this abolition of feudal dominion, the whole judicial powers which had formerly been annexed to property were swept away at the same time, leaving only a remnant so limited and hampered by restrictions that these have scarcely ever since been thought worth the exercising.

The unmitigated bondage of a section of the people of Scotland continued however to survive all the events alluded to, as if in order to show the depth from which the inhabitants in general had been raised by successive steps. These were the workmen at coal-mines and salt-pans, formerly referred to, who continued bound by law to perpetual service, merely by their entering to work, and who were transferable, along with the works, to a purchaser as part of the property. Even the statute of 1748 excluded them, by name, from that emancipation which it granted to others, excepting that it *very considerately* declared that the powers of their proprietors over their persons should not extend to *life or demembration*. Twenty-seven years afterwards a special act of parliament, declaring them free from 1st July 1755, was in great measure evaded; and their bondage continued to subsist till the closing year of the last century, when another statute declared that they should be thenceforward absolutely "free from their servitude:" and thus perished the last remnant of legal slavery in Scotland.

One short sentence in the statute of 1748 refers to the miserable prisons into which, for ages and centuries, the barons had thrust their victims during pleasure, and with or without trial. That law enacted that "every prison shall have *windows or grates open to inspection from without,*" clearly evincing the existence at that time of dens having neither light nor air except when the door was opened; or of still more dismal abodes of misery, such as those of the regality prison of Arbroath, in the tower which still frowns over the High Street, the pits in the castle of St Andrews, and many other old baronial seats. Into such a "pit" the magistrates of Arbroath thrust a poor "witch" in the year 1568. Such loathsome cells seem to have been well-known to the sacred writers, from their allusions to "the pit," the "horrible pit," sitting in "*darkness* and the *shadow of death*, bound in affliction and iron." Indeed prisons generally were, till within a recent period, in every sense of the word, *blackholes;* and this, the original nucleus, formed till lately an indispensable part of even modern prisons, scarcely modified by the glimmer of day-light admitted by the window or grate prescribed by the Act of 1748; and which only served to make darkness visible. The walls of the Town-house of Arbroath exhibited till within these few weeks the frame of the slit which "lighted" the blackhole, sixteen inches high and six inches wide, but almost closed by an iron bar. Let any one visit modern prisons, regularly examined by Her Majesty's inspector, and their state published, and then let him visit the ancient prison of Arbroath in the tower—keeping in view the condition in which it was during the days of baronial power—and he will have little reason to regret the loss of what are occasionally termed the good old times of our fathers.

APPENDIX, No. II.

SKETCH OF THE LIFE AND TIMES OF JAMES MELVILLE, MINISTER OF ST. VIGEANS DURING THE PERIOD FROM 1560 TO 1600, BEING A SUPPLEMENT TO THE SKETCH OF THE ABBOTS OF ARBROATH.

As this minister was for many years the only ecclesiastic of note in the district of Arbroath, after the fall of the monastery and the dispersion of its inmates, and as he was contemporary with, and took a prominent part in, the greatest moral and religious revolution which this country has witnessed, a sketch of his life, and of his connection with the ecclesiastical occurrences of that stirring period, forms substantially a continuation of the religious history of Arbroath during the forty years which elapsed from the Reformation till the end of the sixteenth century. The following remarks on the transition from Romish priests to ministers, readers and teachers in the reformed church, will illustrate an obscure point in the history of the time, and explain some circumstances alluded to in these pages.

The question must have occurred to attentive readers of the history of Scotland in the sixteenth century:—What became of all the Popish priests after the Reformation? It has been calculated, upon what appear to be fair data, that at that period the whole number of parish priests, monks, nuns, and preaching friars would amount at least to about two thousand; and, with the exception of the bishops and greater abbots, this body of ecclesiastics falls at the era in question as completely into oblivion, so far as our ordinary histories are concerned, as if they had then ceased to exist. A few of them, such as Walter Miln of Lunan, Dean Forrest of Dollar, and Knox, became famed as martyrs for the Protestant faith, or as successful reformers; and a small number of monks and nuns were allowed to remain during their declining years in some of the monasteries, upon their conforming to the reformed religion. Thus, in 1562, £240 Scots of the rental of the Abbey of Newbottle in Mid-Lothian were set apart for the maintenance of six *recanted* monks. But the united numbers of both these classes were but a small proportion of the Scottish ecclesiastics of the time; and the state of the country was not such as to admit of their being readily absorbed into other professions, for which, indeed, from age and habit they would be generally unfitted.

Our church histories, however, contain certain allusions which afford an answer to the question not less creditable to many of the popish priests of Scotland than pleasing to the members of the reformed church, in which they found employment and bread, and to the edification of which they, though in a humble manner, helped to contribute. It is well known that from the scarcity of ministers able to preach the doctrines of the reformed faith, one minister had to take charge of various churches, while at each of these churches a reader was stationed, whose duty it was to read the Scriptures, conduct the psalmody, and, if qualified, to lead in prayer and join some observations with the passages read by him. The occasional unfitness or irregularities of this class of men when noticed in the judicatories of the stern reformers of the time bring to light the fact that to a large extent they had been Romish priests, and that from this cause the new wine was sometimes too strong for the old bottles. The number of priests who became readers in Angus and Mearns has been already alluded to as the occasion of a complaint against Erskine of Dun. The complaint is not founded on the fact that they had once been priests, but that they were then "unqualified and of vicious life." From the low state of literature in Scotland at that time it is probable that Erskine might find no one in the parish or vicinity, except a priest, able to read, and that he had little or no room for choice in the matter. On a subsequent occasion, in 1584, when the ministers and readers of the Synod of Merse and other districts of the south of Scotland were ordered by King James to subscribe a writing promising their obedience to Archbishop Adamson and to the statutes of that year, commonly called "the black acts," they all declined except a few ministers "with diverse readers, *who were all preests before.*" (Cald. iv. 210.) The reformers were sometimes annoyed by the readers presuming to "minister the holie sacrament without having the word of exhortation in their mouths"—a fault very characteristic of Romish priests, especially such as were in Scotland at that period, and into which they would more readily fall from the extreme scarcity of ministers. Many of these readers, who exhibited the requisite qualifications, were, sooner or later, raised a step higher, to the office of "exhorter," and others were appointed to the full office of the ministry; and even those who never rose above the subordinate rank of readers of Scripture were allowed, for many years after the Reformation, to reside in the parish manse, which, together with a small money salary—the possession of the glebe or kirk lands and the vicarage or small tithes—enabled them with frugality to live in circumstances of perhaps as much comfort and respectability as parochial teachers do in our time.

We believe that many of these half-reformed priests were also employed as teachers, either in conjunction with their office as readers, or separately. In the Assembly of December 1562, Knox states that it was a subject of complaint "that wicked men war permitted to be schoolmaisteris, and so to infect the youth; amongis whom one Maister Robert Cumyn, schoolmaister in Aberbrothock, was compleaned upoun by the Laird of Dun, and sentence was pronounced against him." Calderwood, in allusion to the same matter, says that Cumyn was accused "for infecting the youth committed to his charge with idolatric." The nature of the accusation and the title "Maister," as then used, clearly shew that this Arbroath teacher had been a Romish priest. It is not stated whether this school was at St Vigeans church or in the town of Arbroath. The latter view is most probable, as the magistrates of Arbroath had a school, of which, on 10th November 1564, they appointed David Black "maister," with £10 of the Lady Chaplainry, and four shillings for "ilk freeman's bairn within the town," as salary. Numerous burgh schools were set up at this period, many years previous to the first state provision for parochial schools. Most probably, owing to its vicinity to Arbroath, St Vigeans possessed no parochial school during the next fifty years, till at least 1613, while the neighbouring parishes of Inverkeillor and Panbride then possessed such seminaries. In October 1573, about the time that Melville became minister of Arbroath, and very probably under his influence, the bailies and "haill neighbours" of the town resolved to establish a *grammar* school, and to pay the master eight shillings for "ilk bairn in the town," and £20 out of "Our Lady's benefice, or dirigie dues, with his chalmer maill free," that is, a free house. David Mychell was engaged as first teacher. (Burgh Court Book.) This grammar school was for a long period taught in a house still remaining on the east side of the High Street, a little distance north of the Parish Church, and now to be found in a narrow lane, called, in memory of the school-house, the School Wynd. The house retains a Latin inscription, built into the wall, but concealed from view by a coat of plaster. A quaint specimen of the Latin language and of the style of English poetry and prose possessed by one of its teachers, who describes himself as "John Carnegy, Doctor to the

Gramer School of Aberbrothock," may be seen on a grave-stone erected by him in 1679, within the Arbroath burial-ground, to the memory of his wife, whom he compared to three eminent females, in the following manner:

> "Uxor casta, parens felix, matrona pudiæ,
> Sara viro, mundo Martha, Maria Deo.
> Here lyes wife was chast, a Mother Blest,
> A modest woman, all these in on chest;
> Sarah unto her mate, Mary to God,
> Martha to men, whilst here she had abode.
> As we be——so shall ye."

Mr or *Magister* James Melville was fifth son of Richard Melville of Baldovy in the parish of Craig, a family of eminence in the sixteenth century. Richard Melville was brother of John Melville, proprietor of the neighbouring estate of Dysart; and both were cadets of the house of the Melvilles of Glenbervie, who long held the office of hereditary sheriffs of Kincardineshire. He had nine sons, four of whom became ministers of the Reformed Church of Scotland, viz., Richard, the eldest (father of James the author of the well-known diary), who became minister of Inchbryock or Craig and Maryton; James, the subject of this sketch; John, the sixth son, who was minister of Craill; and Andrew, the youngest, the learned Professor of Theology at St Andrews, who became famed for his opposition to Prelacy. James Melville of St Vigeans was educated at St Andrews, of which university he was a graduate. At the first General Assembly of the Church, held in December 1560, where only *six* ministers were present, the names of James and Richard Melville, and John Erskine of Dun, were included in a list, along with other eight, of those who were "thought apt and able to minister;" and from the necessities of the time, it is evident that they were all without delay employed as preachers. James Melville continued to exercise the office of the ministry for at least thirty-six years after this date, during one of the brightest periods of our

Church's history, between its emergency from the darkness of Popery, till its partial subjection to the arbitrary measures of King James. He, during a long period, held a prominent part in the Reformed Church, and possessed much of the confidence of his ministerial brethren. He does not bulk so largely to the eye as Knox, or his younger brother Andrew, or even his nephew James; but though he "attained not to the first three, he was honourable among the thirty." His name frequently occurs in commissions and remits under circumstances where only ministers of high respectability, learning, and tried faithfulness could be employed.

Melville was a parish minister in 1565; and like many others at that time, was destitute of stipend, in consequence of Queen Mary's courtiers having squandered the thirds of the Popish benefices, which had been promised to the Reformed preachers. James Melville, his nephew, when a child, remembered "the order of the fast, keipit in anno 1565—the evil handling of the ministerie be taking away of their stipends; for Mr James Melville, my uncle, and Mr James Balfour, his cusing-german, [were] bathe ministers and stipendles, with gude, godlie and kynd Patrick Forbes of Cors." At that time Knox wrote "a comfortable letter, in name of the assemblie [which met December 1565], to encourage ministers, exhorters, and readers to continue in their vocation, which, in all likelihood, they were to leave off for laike of payment of their stipends; and to exhort the professors within this realme to supplie their necessities." About this period Melville appears to have been minister at Tannadice, a parish of which St Mary's College held the patronage. He was a Member of Assembly in December 1565, and signed along with other nine,—including Craig, Pont, Lindsay, Winram, Christison, Row, and Erskine of Dun, all men of eminence and learning,—an excellent letter written by Knox, and sent by the Assembly "to the Bishops of Ingland, that they wald be content gentlie to handle the brethren preachers, touching the habits, surpcloathes, and other abuilziements, whilk appearantlie tend more to superstitioun nor to edificatioun." At the fourteenth General Assembly, held in June 1567, where the learned Buchanan was moderator, he, along with six of the most erudite ministers of the Church, were appointed to decide questions of a difficult and delicate kind, regarding marriage and similar points, and reported their answers to the Assembly, who recorded them as satisfactory solutions.

It is to Melville that the Church is indebted as the instrument of procuring the education of his nephew James Melville, as a minister, after which the boy had been anxiously, but hopelessly, aspiring in the face of his stern father's resolution to make him a farmer or tradesman. After narrating in the most artless style how, when his father had sent him to the smithy for "dressing of hewkes" (sickles), and some iron instruments, "he begoude to weirie soar of his lyff," and prayed God "that it wald please his guidnes to offer occasion to continow me at the schollcs, and inclyne my father's hart till use the saming," he adds, "Within a few dayes thairafter, Mr James Melvill, my uncle, comes to Baldowy, and brings with him a godlie lernit man named Mr Wilycam Collace, wha was that sam yeir to tak up the class as first Regent of St Leonards Collage within the Universitie of St Andros; after conference with whome that night, God moves my fathers hart to resolve to send me that sam yeir to the Collage." Thus, at the critical moment, his fortunes were decided by the well-directed influence of his uncle, who had discerned those rudiments of natural talent and worth to which his father, the minister of Maryton, with much better opportunity, had been blind. This family transaction took place about the year 1571. At the Assembly, which met at Stirling in August this year, we find Mr Melville assisting in the business, especially in the more learned departments, and acting in a committee for examining the commissioners' or superintendents' "bookes of visitations." While Melville was minister at Tannadice (1567 to 1571) another James Melville was minister at Menmuir and Fearn. Some suppose that the latter, and not the former, as we believe, was afterwards the minister of St Vigeans.

In or before the year 1574 James Melville was translated from Tannadice and settled as minister of St Vigeans. It is probable that he was a member of the Assembly which met at Edinburgh on 7th August of that year; and we are unable to account for the Assembly's intimate knowledge of the state of matters about Arbroath. except on the supposition of Melville's presence and active representations. Among other articles "proponed to my Lord Regent's grace" (Regent Morton), the Assembly craved "that his grace will tak a generall order with the poore, and especially in the abbeyes, suche as Aberbrothe and others, conforme to the act made at Leith, and in speciall, to discharge tithe-sybboes, leekes, kaill, unzeons [onions], by an act of secret counsell, whill [till] a parliament be convened, where they may be simply discharged." The minister of St Vigeans may be held entitled to much of the credit of this excellent overture in behalf of the poor, and for relief from the absurd tithing of leeks and other garden vegetables, which had been continued down to this time. In the register of minister and readers, made up in this year according to Morton's plan, the churches of "Aberbrothok, or Sanct Vigians, Athie, Kynnell," are placed under the charge of "Maister James Mailvile, minister," with a stipend of £160 Scots, besides the vicar's manse and glebe. This was considerably beyond the average stipends of the time, and formed a respectable income, although it now appears very small when converted into sterling money. From the collectors' books we can ascertain that about 1562 a small boll of meal could be purchased for £1 Scots, or twenty pence sterling, and in 1574 the average price of meal in Angus was twenty merks per chalder, or sixteen shillings and eightpence Scots per boll, thus showing that money was about twelve times scarcer, and of twelve times more value in the market than it is now. Melville had a reader stationed under his directions at each of these three churches. His "residare at Aberbrothok or Sanct Vigians," was Thomas Lindsay (a member of the Convent of Arbroath, and almoner of the Abbey), who had a salary of £17, 15s. 6⅔d. Scots (equal to about £1, 9s. 7d. ⁵⁻⁹ᵗʰˢ sterling), and eight bolls of bear. David Miln was his reader at Ethie, with a salary of £16 Scots, and the kirk-lands; and David Fyff was his reader at Kinnell, with a salary of £12 Scots.

At this time the other churches in the district of Arbroath were clustered together in the following manner:—Dunnichen, Idvies (Kirkden), Guthrie, and Rescobie were served by Mr James Balfour as minister, with a stipend of £133, 6s. 8d. Scots, and the kirk lands; and readers officiated at each church. The churches of Maryton, Inchbriock, Lunan, and St Skay, were served by Richard Melville, already alluded to, as minister; whose stipend was £100. He had one reader for Maryton and Inchbriock, and another for Lunan. But the register bears that "Sanct Skaa or Dunnynaid neidis na reidare." Inverkeillor, by itself, had one minister, Mr Andrew Strathauchin, whose stipend was two chalders of meal and eight bolls of bear, and it also possessed a reader. The churches of Arbirlot, Panbride, and Monikie were under the care of three readers, and under Charles Michelson as minister, who had a stipend of £100. The churches of Barry, Monifieth, and Murroes were under Andro Auchenleck as minister, with the ordinary stipend of £100 Scots; and readers officiated at each of the churches.

In further illustration of the ecclesiastical state of Scotland at this date, fourteen years after the Reformation, it may be stated that Edinburgh, including the

Canongate and Duddingston, possessed only four ministers in 1574, while no other town in the kingdom (including New Aberdeen, Dundee, St Andrews, Perth, Leith, and Glasgow) possessed more than one each. In the large districts of Annandale, Eskdale, Ewesdale, and Wachopedale, containing thirty-eight parishes, there was only one settled minister, viz., at Lochmaben, and a reader at Ruthwell. The whole number of parishes in Scotland named in the register amounted to 988,—not including those in the Shetland and Western Isles and Argyleshire, of which no notice is taken. About 715 readers were employed in these parishes, which were arranged in 303 clusters ; and the total number of ordained ministers was only 289, while there were then probably few or none waiting for churches. To these 289 ministers, eleven may be added for Argyle and the Isles, and we thus find the whole regularly ordained Protestant clergy of the kingdom nearly three centuries ago not to exceed 300, or little more than one-tenth of the Protestant clergy of Scotland at the present day ; as the printed lists shew that, in 1859, assuming temporary vacancies as supplied, the establishment employs about 1216, and other Protestant denominations employ about 1623 ordained clergymen, making a total of 2839.

Soon after this period the minister of Arbroath is found attending at the death-bed of his elder brother Richard, the minister of Maryton, who " died the 53rd year of his age, in the moneth of June, *anno* 1575, in a icterik [bilious] fever ; maist godlie, for, after manie most comfortable exhortations maid to the noble and gentler men of the county, who all resorted to visit him during his disease, and to his breither, and frinds who remeaned about him ; about the verie hour of his death, he caused reid to him the 8 chapter of the Epistle to the Romans ; and immediatlie after, his brother, Mr James, minister of Arbrothe, asking him what he was doing ? Lifting upe eyes and handis toward heavin, with reasonable might of voice, he answerit, 'I am glorifeing God for the light of his gospell,' and na mae intelligible words thairefter." (Melville's Diary.)

At the Assembly which met at Glasgow in April 1581, Melville, along with Erskine of Dun, William Christison of Dundee, and James Anderson of Bendochy and Kettins (both ministers of note), were appointed commissioners to adjust and fix the bounds of the presbyteries in Angus and Mearns, which till that period were styled the presbyteries of Dundee, Kirriemuir, Kettins, Bervie, and Fordoun.

Melville possessed a considerable share of that courage which was a special characteristic of the family to which he belonged. Although James Melville, his nephew, went to Perth on the occasion to which we are to refer, in order to strengthen the hands of his "uncle Andro," to whom he was so greatly attached, it was not he, but the minister of St Vigeans, who, along with Andrew Melville, Erskine of Dun, and about fifteen other commissioners from the General Assembly, presented to the young king at Perth, in July 1582, the "Grievances of the Kirk," caused chiefly by the measures of the Duke of Lennox and the profligate Earl of Arran, who were oppressing both the church and the nation. After the grievances were read, Arran exclaimed "with thrawn brow and boasting language, who dare subscribe these treasonable articles?" "We dare and will subscribe them, and will render our lives in the cause," replied Andrew Melville; and taking the pen from the clerk he and the other Commissioners adhibited their names to the document. They were dismissed with courtesy and respect, as Arran was confounded at their boldness; and the English strangers then present were unable to account for it, except on the supposition that they had an armed force in readiness to back their demands.

Nothing is fitted to give a higher idea of the character and attainments of the minister of Arbroath than the circumstance of his being a regular member of the learned, select, and pleasant company, who at the time of the Assemblies in Edinburgh, before King James quarrelled with the church, usually met at the house of John Durie, then one of the Edinburgh ministers, father-in-law of James Melville the younger, who writes that he (Durie) " was of small literature, but haid seen and marked the great warks of God in the first Reformation, and was a doer therein, baith with tongue and hand. He was a verie guid fallow, and tuk delyt, as his speciall comfort, to haiff his table and houss filled with the best men. Ther ludgit in his house at all these assemblies in Edinbruche, for comoun, Mr Andro Melvill, Mr Thomas Smeton, Mr Alexander Arbuthnot (three of the lernedst in Europe), Mr James Melvill [of Arbroath] my uncle, Mr James Balfour, David Fergusone, David Home, ministers, with sum zelus and godlie barrones, and gentilmen." Durie himself was, like Andrew Melvill, of undaunted courage, and altogether a stranger to fear. It is his name which is now attached to the fine air to which the old version of the CXXIV. Psalm was formerly sung. This, as many are aware, arose from the following incident. After a temporary banishment from Edinburgh, through Lennox's influence, Durie, on his return, was escorted up the High Street by two thousand citizens, bareheaded, singing this Psalm in four parts " well known to the people." Lennox was more astonished at this scene than at anything which he had seen in Scotland.

The three first named ordinary guests of John Durie were the learned Principals of the Colleges of St Mary, Glasgow, and Old Aberdeen. Arbuthnott the Principal at Aberdeen was of the house of that name in the Mearns. He is well known as an elegant Latin poet. He was versed in mathematics, philosophy, theology, law, and medicine; and was much loved by all who knew him. Smeaton the Principal of Glasgow College was also a man of great learning and many acquirements.

James Balfour, a relation of the Melvilles, and brother-in-law to James, the nephew, was the active, bold, and public-spirited minister of Guthrie and Idvies (Kirkden.) He was for many years afterwards one of the ministers of Edinburgh, along with Bruce, Pont, Balcanqual, and others, of whom King James' courtiers, and some of the Judges of the Court of Session, stood more in dread than of any other body in Britain. Balfour hesitated at first to preach his belief in the court version of the Gowrie conspiracy; and for this crime the Privy Council on 11th September 1600, appointed him to make public confession in the towns of Dundee, Arbroath, Montrose, and Brechin. When advanced in years, and "sore troubled with gout and deafness," he was one of the eight ministers whom King James compelled to travel to London, and kept there for nine months, in the most cowardly manner, principally on their own charges, till matters were fully put in train for the erection of Episcopacy in Scotland. When first ushered into the royal presence King James chatted familiarly with Balfour, and rallied him on the length of his beard. At the close of their residence in London, when Andrew Melville was imprisoned in the Tower, and James Melville confined at Newcastle, the king confined Balfour first at Cockburnspath, and then shortly afterwards commanded him to confine himself at Alford, in Aberdeenshire. "He was conveyed out of Edinburgh the 11th of August [1607] by the magistrates and some of the council. Being diseased, he stayed at Inverkeithing, and went not to Aufurd. Thus the ministers sent for to Court were used without any process, and against all law and order." Such is Calderwood's remark on the miserable usage which this old and deaf minister received at the hands of a monarch of three kingdoms, to whom he had been personally well known, for no other reason than his refusal to give public acquiescence to that new form of Church government which both he and the king had repeatedly sworn to repudiate.

David Ferguson was the old minister of Dunfermline, one of the first Reformers, who " spak verie plesandlie and comfortablie of the beginning and success of the ministrie ; how that a few number,—viz., only sax, wharof he was ane—sae mightilie went fordwart in the wark, but [without] fear or cair of the warld, and prevalit, when ther was nae name of stipend heard tell of ; when the authoritie, baith ecclesiastik and civill oponnit themselves, and skarslie a man of name and estimatioun to tak the cause in hand." Ferguson was a collector of Scottish proverbs, and had so much humour that he could not resist giving expression to a caustic joke, whether in the presence of the king, at an Assembly or Presbytery, or in reference to the inauguration of a tulchan bishop at St Andrew, where the hoarse notes of a " corbie, crouping on the roof of the kirk," was explained by him to mean, Corrupt ! corrupt ! corrupt ! It was he who, in the palace of Dunfermline, administered to King James the reproof, " Sir, ban not," when the king had lost his temper, and swore by the devil, because Ferguson worsted him in a conversation about bishops. During another conversation the king gave to Ferguson as a poser, if with all his learning, he could explain why the house of the Master of Gray (an unprincipled but favourite courtier) had lately shaken during the night, to which Ferguson instantly replied, " Why should not the devil rock his ain bairns ?" He and the three Principals were all *old moderators* of Assembly, each of them having at least presided twice in that venerable court, and Andrew Melville ultimately no less than six times. The Principals exercised their wit and learning in the composition of Latin verses and epigrams, and quoted Ovid and Horace in the original as readily as some can now quote Shakspeare or Burns ; and although Ferguson could both joke and reason in Latin, he and Durie preferred to express their strong common sense, and intimate acquaintance with their Bibles, in quaint and good old doric Scotch.

It is not surprising that James Melville the younger should delight in his admission to such a society, and love to dwell on the recollection of the piety, learning, and wit which it contained.

During a trying period, when civil and religious liberty was at a low ebb, under the baleful administration of Stuart Earl of Arran, and in consequence of the Acts of Parliament, 1584, passed by his influence, Erskine of Dun, in his old age, bent to the storm, and prevailed on most of the ministers of Angus to subscribe their approval of these obnoxious Acts. The compliance of many excited no remarks, but it was considered matter of surprise when James Melville of Arbroath, and James Balfour, the most uncompromising clergymen in the district, went to Edinburgh and subscribed the deed of approbation in the year 1583.

Melville soon afterwards acted a prominent part in one of the most singular and picturesque scenes that ever took place during the long and varied contest between the Prelatists and Presbyterians of Scotland. St Vigeans parish being within the diocese of St Andrews, its minister was a member of what was then termed the Synodical Assembly of Fife, although it included many parishes in Angus and Perthshire. At a meeting of that body held at St Andrews in April 1586, James Melville the younger, as last moderator, "made the exhortation," the bishop (Patrick Adamson, Archbishop of St Andrews), "placing himself hard besyde me, with a grait pontificalitie and big countenance; as he braggit he was in his awin citie, and haid the king his maisters favour, he neidit to fear no man." After discoursing on the duty of every man not to think of himself more highly than he ought to think, but to think soberly, Melville turned to the bishop, sitting at his elbow, and directing his speech to him personally, he "recompted to him schortlie his lyff, actiones, and procedings against the Kirk, taking the Assemblie there to witnes and his awin conscience before

God, if he was not an evident proof and example of that doctrine, whom, being a minister of the Kirk, the dragon had sae stangit with the poison and venom of averice and ambition, that, swalling exhorbitantlie out of measure, he threatened the wrack and destruction of the haill bodie in case he were nocht tymouslie, and with courage, cut off." The bishop tried to reply to this extraordinary application of the discourse, but was "so dashed and stricken with terror and trembling that he could scarce sit, let be to stand on his feet," and ultimately left the synod. After repeatedly requesting his attendance to answer other charges, the synod, in a manner too summary, resolved to excommunicate the bishop for contumacy. But, in the meantime, they appointed "Mr James Melvill, minister at Arbrothe, Mr James Balfour, minister at Edvie," and other two members, "to passe again to the said Mr Patrick, earnestly to travell with him, according to the effect of the former admonitiouns, and to intimat that he was judged worthy of excommunication, and decerned to be excommunicated instantlie in case he continued still disobedient." Upon their returning and reporting their interview with the bishop, the minister of Arbroath and other two were sent back to confer with him at his request, and to repeat the former message; after which the bishop personally came to the synod, where much procedure of a very unpleasant nature took place, which was ultimately concluded by the synod formally excommunicating the archbishop "as an ethnick [a heathen] or publican." The bishop retaliated the sentence in his own way, as Melville writes : " A day or twa after, he penned an excommunication, and, in a bishoplie manner, sent out a boy with ane or twa of his jackmen, and red the sam in the kirk, wherby, be his archiepiscopall authoritie, he excommunicated Mr Andro Melvill, me, and a certain mae of the brethren." As the bishop looked on the Melvilles as the main leaders of the opposition to him, it is more than probable that James Melville of Arbroath was one of the *certain mae of the brethren* included in the decree of excommunication, and was delivered over to satan along with his brother and nephew. The synod's excommunication of the bishop was removed at the next General Assembly, where no notice was taken of his retaliatory sentence.

At the General Assembly, which was held in Edinburgh on 10th May 1586 (referred to in our last article), James Melville of Arbroath was one of seven members appointed for Angus and Mearns to try and take probation of bishops and commissioners if they found occasion of slander to arise by them in life, doctrine, or conversation. At the same time, reports as to the bounds of Presbyteries (formerly adverted to) were given and disposed of; and the Presbytery seats of Angus and Mearns were appointed by this Assembly to be at Dundee, Brechin, Montrose, and Bervie. Arbroath was not a Presbytery seat at this period. It is about this time, or between 1576 and 1586, that we have the first indication of a separate ministerial charge in the town of Arbroath. In a general list of churches made up at this Assembly, we find "Athe, Aberbrothe, and St Vigeans," all named separately and apart from one another. There is no reason to believe that Ethie ever possessed a separate minister since the Reformation; but the town church of Arbroath was provided with a minister at this period or soon afterwards; and as James Melville of St Vigeans evidently possessed much of the spirit of James his nephew (who most disinterestedly laboured for and effected the separation of the charges of Anstruther and Kilrenny), we may safely give to him much of the credit of getting the new charge established in the town of Arbroath, where, by that time, it would be greatly needed. A new arrangement as to Presbyteries was made at the Assembly of April 1593, when those of Angus and Mearns were named the Presbyteries of Dundee, Arbroath, Brechin, Meigle, and Cowie. Mr Melville was the first of eight ministers within the Sheriffdom of Forfar, who were appointed by the Privy Council on 5th March 1589, to take active measures "for suppressing the traffic of Jesuits and seminary priests," in consequence of the alarm occasioned by the discovery of the letters called the Spanish blanks. A few years afterwards at the General Assembly, held in Montrose in June 1595, his name appears in the history of the councils of the Church, so far as we can trace, for the last time. He and John Durie, who was now minister at Montrose (having been forced by the king to leave Edinburgh), were appointed commissioners for Angus to examine and report as to dilapidation of benefices by tacks or otherwise. After this period he did not appear prominently in the public transactions of the times. King James was now commencing those schemes for the exaltation of arbitrary power, which were ended fifty years later by his son being brought to the block; and James Melville seems to have left the maintenance of the struggle for the liberties of the Church to the exertions of younger men, such as his brother Andrew, and his nephew James, both of whom that struggle has immortalised. And the king, on the other hand, did not lack young ministers, especially in Forfarshire, willing to abet and forward his plans.

The latest notices of this worthy minister are given by Dr M'Crie in his Life of Andrew Melville. He quotes from the Commissary Records of St Andrews that, on 27th April 1591, Thomas Ramsay in Kirkton (East Kirkton of St Vigeans) bound himself "to pay to the richt worchipful Mr James Melvill, minister of Aberbrothock, four bolls beir, with one pek to the boll, and twa bolls aitmaill, with the cheritie, guid and sufficient stuff—the mail to be for the said Mr James awin aeting, all guid and fyne, as ony gentill man sall eat in the countrie adjacent about him; or, failzeing deliverie, to pay for every boll 4 lib. money." The increased money value of the meal at this time, when compared with the prices of 1562, affords a striking view of the increase of national wealth and prosperity during the first thirty years after the Reformation. About five years later (March 1596) he obtained decree against John Richardson " for the feu farme of the kirk-lands of Aberbrothock, assigned to him by the Lords of Counsel—viz., 2 bolls wheat, 28 bolls bear, and 20 bolls ait meal."

The bright rays of Reformation light which, at an early period had emanated from the towns of Dundee and Montrose, and spread over a large part of Angus and Mearns, were at this time becoming gradually obscured, and were succeeded by a night of comparative ignorance and subserviency. This change of matters in Angus did not escape the notice of King James, who, in order to obtain the full benefit of it for the advancement of his plans, and in the exercise of his boasted *kingcraft*, forthwith removed the General Assemblies of the Church to Dundee and Montrose, where they were held in the years 1593, 1595, 1597, 1598, and 1600; and in these Assemblies he at last succeeded after much opposition in getting the church to consent to certain measures which ushered in the establishment of Prelacy. That opposition, however, did not arise from the ministers of Forfarshire, at least after the death of Erskine of Dun, Melville of Arbroath, Durie of Montrose, and Christison of Dundee; for, as the readers of our church histories are aware, the Synod of Angus and Mearns was the only Synod within Scotland which in 1607 tamely submitted to the imposition of a *constant moderator*, in obedience to a clause inserted by King James into an Act of the Convention of ministers, who had met at his command at Linlithgow during the previous year. Whether this state of matters originated from the number of partially reformed priests, who may have obtained ministerial charges in Forfarshire, as complained of in 1562, and who, according to the usual course of things, would beget a succession of professional sons in their own likeness—or whether it arose from other causes—it is not now easy to decide, but it is certain that during a long period after these assemblies the ecclesiastics of Forfarshire in general held an obscure position, and did not exercise that influence in the church which they had previously done, and which the natural situation, size, and wealth of the district would have warranted one to expect.

We have been unable to ascertain the exact date or the circumstances of James Melville's death, and there is no inscription to his memory about the Church of St Vigeans. It is evident that this event took place at the close of the sixteenth or the beginning of the seventeenth century. The end of the sixteenth century was a critical period in the history of the church, which had at the same time to mourn the loss of several other reformers of eminence, such as David Ferguson, John Dury, Thomas Buchanan, Principal Rollock, Adam Johnston, David Black, and John Lindsay, some of whom were, like Melville of Arbroath, thereby saved from soon afterwards appearing on the stage of persecution, by being convicted as traitors for *prorogating a General Assembly*, and declining the authority of the Privy Council as incompetent judges in the matter; or by undergoing the ungenerous treatment to which King James at the same period subjected a number of their brethren in England.

The clergyman of whose life we have given a rapid sketch deserves the grateful remembrance of the inhabitants of Arbroath and St Vigeans. He was one of the band of early reformers who, amid much privation and opposition, during the forty years between 1560 and 1600 sowed broadcast those precious seeds of civil and religious liberty of which we are now reaping the fruit. This period of our history is by far too little studied. That at its commencement they achieved our freedom from ignorance and superstition no sound Protestant will doubt. Their actings and sufferings, during the latter portion of the period referred to, in behalf of civil liberty (which they clearly saw must stand or fall with religious freedom) were neither sufficiently appreciated in their own day nor are even now properly understood. But if they had not boldly maintained the liberty of the pulpit in its reference to state affairs—few or none of which are, perhaps, altogether neutral toward Christianity and civilization—it is probable that our singular and much-valued liberty of "*the press*" (which then had no existence) would have been yet to contend for. The reformed ministers were sometimes banished or imprisoned for the liberties which they used ; but if some of our modern periodicals had then existed in Scotland, and had used such freedoms as they now do with the acts and characters of statesmen, their publishers would, under the exercise of similar powers, have been speedily consigned to the dungeons of Blackness Castle, or confined in the remotest of the Shetland Islands. No doubt the old Scottish pulpit liberty was, like other kinds of liberty, occasionally liable to run into licentiousness, but not at least on the wrong side of morality, and this is more than can be said for some portions of what has been considered its antitype—the modern press. It was Melville and his compeers in Scotland who laid the foundation of that free expression of opinion under the British Constitution which is so justly prized at the present day.

APPENDIX, No. III.

SELECTIONS FROM THE RECORDS OF THE MAGISTRATES AND COUNCIL OF ARBROATH, ILLUSTRATIVE OF THE MANNERS AND CUSTOMS OF THE INHABITANTS ABOUT THE TIME OF THE REFORMATION.

THESE selections are in the first place burgh, made from a court-book in the town-house of Arbroath, very carefully written in the old character, and extending from Michaelmas 1563 to 1575. The entries here given are only specimens of many others of a similar kind.

12 November 1563.—The quhilk day Magy Thornton, of her awin fre will, oblist her to pay vj sh to the bailyeis and town, gyf shoe tuk in ony brandy to sell in tym to cum, without leif of the bailyeis.

26 Nov. 1563.—The qlk day it is found be the bailyeis and court that Richart Brown sall pass to the chapell the morne, and ask Jonat Cary and Jhon Ramsay her son forgyffness for calling her ane shoe witch, and him ane he witch; and the said Jhon Ramsay sall ask the said Richart forgyffanes for calling him theif carll.

2 Jan. 1563-4.—The qlk day it is fund be the assys aboue writyn that Jonat Carynton the spous of Robert Spynk, Jhon Spynk her son, and Agnes Spynk her douchter, his down wrang in the trubling of Tybbe Boury and Jhon Stewart her servand; and lykweyes the said parsons ar fund in the wrang for the trubling of Mage Henderson; and the said Jonat, Jhon her son, and Agnes her dowchter, ilk ane of them, ar amerciat for the trubling of the said Tybbe, Jhon, and Margreit,

and dowm gyffin thairvpon.—Decernit be James Pekyman, chancler.

The qlk day Nyniane Hales is cum lawbroich for David Guthre that Jhon Spynk sall be skaithles of bodily harm of the said David, ondyr the payn of law.

The qlk day it is decernit be the assis aboue writtyn that yf ony of the foirsaids parsonis molest or trubill udders in tym to cum, and be complainet, they sall pay xxi sh to be disponit as the bailyeis thynks expedient for the tym ; to the qlk the saids parteis consentit.

25 February 1563-4.—The qlk day Jhon Cargyll and George Garden ar chosyn punders to keip the comown griss and corn, and sall have for ilk aker of the falds and burrow rudis of quheit, ry, banis, peis, and aits, iiij d; and the saids punders sall mak the griss and corns haill at the end of the bair seid, or fynd ane punder thairfor, quhairthrow the man that hes sustend the skaith may be recompensit and satisfeit.

It is statute be the bailyeis and counsell gyf ony man mispersone ane of the townis flesh prissers and ony uder officers in the exsecution of the office thairof, thay, be burges or his wyf, sal pay viij sh for the first tym, and xvi sh the nyxt tym, and say oft as thay mak falt to be dowblit; and gyf thay be onfre, the man sal be put [in] the stokis and the woman in the gowis for the first tym, and gyf they comit sick lyk again they sal be banist the town for yeir and day.

Item, that na maner of personis have middenis upon the hyegait langer nor viii dayis, nor stanes nor clay langer nor yeir and day, onder the payn of viij sh.

It is stated and ordainit that thair be nae mercats upon the Sabouith day befoir aucht hours, noder flesh nor uder merchandeis, on the pain of viii sh.

2 June 1564.—Nyniane Clement, minister, is made fre and burgess, and hes maid the aith to the town, as use is, and sall pay the spyce and wyne to the bailyeis and counsall.

26 June.—David Ferror is amerciat for falt of presens to ansuer for braking of the common statute in halding of tuitherds, and down gyffyn thairupon.

27 July.—Anent the day assignit to Jhon Hales to enter Alexr. Paterson, burges in Dundee, for the wrangous braking of the mercat cors of this broich, and waytaking of ane part of the wark of the samin, comperit the said Jhon Hales and aleggit the said Alexr. Paterson to be passet to his merchandeis fourth of this realm, and desyret the bailyeis to assign him ane competent term to present the said Alexr.; at quhais request the bailyeis assignit the sext day of October nyxt to cum to the said Jhon to enter the said Alexr. onder the payn of xl lib., conform to the act maid thairupon befoir; and gyf the said Alexr. comperis not the said day the said Jhon Hales obleist him as afoir, gyf the said Alexr. be within the realm to enter him within the tolbuith of this broich, he beand warnit fourty dayis of this be the bailyeis and officers, and day assignit thair to, how soon or quhat tym he be requirit. [This entry is deleted in the original record.]

28 July.—The qlk day comperit George Halis and said in jugment gyf ther wes ony sik thing as ane witch Jonat Lam wes ane, and James Davis affirmet the samin; and the bailyeis descernit the said mater to pass to ane assize this day xv dayis. [The trial did not take place.]

2 September per David Peirson and William Scott.—Willyam Crysty is amerciat for braking the comon statute, sellyng his aill derrer na iii d the pynt, and dowm gyffyn thairupon.

The qlk day Willyeam Crysty maid the aith in jugment that he dreids bodelye harm of Willyeam Scott, bailyie, and desyrit law bowrowis of hym; and David Peirson, bailyie, stud gude for his coleig, that the said Willyeam Crysty suld sustan na harm be the said Willyeam Scott.

Curia capitulis burgi de Arbroithok tenta in pretorio ejusdem per David Peirson et Wm. Scott, secundo die mense Octobris Anno Domini M. quadmo sexagesimo qto. [1564.]

The qlk day David Peirson is chosyng bailye for the plaice [the Abbey], and Wlm. Scott for the town ; George Garden and Jhon Cargyll, officers; and John Dunlop, clerk.

6 Oct.—James Davis hes tayn the comon firlots, custom, and ladyll, for aucht merks vij sh ; and James Ramsay is cum caution to the bailyeis for the said viij merks.

Nyniane Clament hes tayn the sowth buith, onder the tolbuith, for xiiij sh vi d ; and David Peirson the northmost buith, for x sh iiij d ; and Sant Nycholas thre buttis of feld land set to David Ferror for three yeirs, for three punds vi sh in the yeir.

The names of the Counsall : Adam Peirson, Jhon Aikman, Willyeam Bardy, Patre Ramsay, Jhon Lyne, Alex. Lyell, Jhon Halis, James Ramsay, Copyne Guthre, Nyniane Halis.

Lynars : Alexr. Lyell, Jhon Lyne, Jhon Akman, Jhon Halis, Jhon Dunlop.

Dyikprissers : Thom. Gardyne, Wlm. Ochterlony, Jhon Peirsone, Wat. Jak, Nyniane Yowng.

Jhon Henderson said in jugment that David Bran is ane comoun theif ; upon the qlk the said David askit act.

Wilm. Ochterlony is cum sourtie and lawbroich for Jhon Henderson that David Bran sal be skaithles of hym of bodely harm, onder the payn contenit in the law.

Kepars of the keyes of the kyst : Jhon Hales, Patre Ramsay, Wilm. Ochterlony.

10 Nov.—David Blak is electit and chosyng maister of schuill, and sall have ten pundis of our lady chaiplanry ilk yeir to his fe, and iiij sh for ilk fremans barn within the town, and his wantaig of the barns without the town, sa lang as the said David maks gude service thairfoir.

19 January 1564–5.—Comperit Andro Fethy in Gund, and persewit Thomas Garden, burges in Arbrot, for xx sh

mony for rest of certain bair, and referit the samin to the said Thomas aith; comperit the said Thomas, and maid the aith in jugment, and deponyt that he wes not awand to the said Andro ane peny mony nor silver; and the said Andro said in jugment, Be all the wordis of this buyk he is mensworne; upon the qlk the said Thomas askit act of court.

Comperit Alexr. Wat, and aleggit that Jonat Paterson his wyf did mony divers thyngs by [without] his comand and counsall; and thairfoir protestit quhatever show dyd to his hurt in tym to cum, suld not be hurt nor skaith to him; and askit act of court thairupon.

3 February.—The bailye Wilm. Scot, at the comand of the comoun counsall, delivert the akir qlk was Wat Nycholl's in the ald fald to David Segat; the said David payand thairfor to the town aucht merks, and the said David oblist hym to cum and duell within this broich, and scott, lott, walk, and ward with them.

The bailyeis comandyt Jhon Dunlop to gyf Andro Gib his twa potts again qlk was tayn for Sant Nycholas anwell, the said Andro payand to James Ramsay, depositer, xl sh, qlk fourty schelenis Jhon Hales payit to the said James.

2 March.—Anent the complaint of Nyniane Clament, mynister, upon Jonat Boyis for myssaying hym, alegand that he cawsit her to part with twa barnis; the bailye and court takand cognission in the said mater, fyndis the said Jonat's complant of nan effect nor avayll, and the said Jonat is maid be the bailye and court to cum to the chapell upon Sonday nyxt to cum, or gyf show may not that day, to cum ony uder day or tym befoir the bailyeis and nybors quhow sown schow may be haill of body, and ask the said mynister forgiffanis; and gyf schow duis siklik in tym to cum, to be put in the gowis, and set thair fra the son riysing qll [till] the ganging to thairof, and forder indurand the bailyeis will; and dowm gyffyn thairupon.

17 March.—It is decretit be the bailyeis and court that David Lychtoune in Newtown sall deliver to Jonat Brown in Crowdy all the corns and sheip qlk ar contenit in ane decreit, gyffyn be Nynian Hales, Jhon Akman, Wlm Ochterlony, Jhon Ochterlony, and Jhon Ledall, qlk parsonis sall conven upon sonday, and decern upon certain claims debatabill betwixt the said David Lychtoune and Jonat Brown ; and baith the saids parteis ar sworn in jugment to stand at the deliverans ; and thairupon the saids David and Jonat requirit act.

In the action and caus mwfit be Nyniane Ywong agains Rob. Croftis anent the warrandys of twa schelenis anuell rent, clamyt be Den Thomas Fethy, master of comon, of the tenement of land quher the said Nyniane dwellis, upon the west syd of Coipgait, qlk tenement the said Robert sald and analeit to Thomas Young, fader to the said Nyniane, fre of all anuellis excep the kyngis mark, as his charter producit befoir the bailyeis, maid thairupon, at mair lynth proports, &c.

4 April 1565.—The sam day James Schabart protestit that he mycht haue tym and place to call Wlm Yowng and his spous for twa pair of schetis, ane welwet parclaith, sewyne powder weschell, ane bucrowm apron, 16 wder dudis, gair worth twenty punds, qlk the said James allegges by the gair that wes prisit.

11 May 1565.—Thom. Grant is maid fre man of the broich, and hes maid the aith to the town, as us is, and sall pay to my lord of Regy vj sh viij d.

It is statut and ordanit be the bailyeis and comunite that quhatsomever person within this broich byis flesh fra ony fleshar and payis not the samin within aucht dayis the fleshar sall shaw to the officers, and than incontenent the officers sall pas with the said fleshar and pund the avail of the flesh without ony calling or jugment ; and gyf the said fleshar causes pund wrangusly, he sall restoir the pund agane, with viij sh to the bailyeis.

It is fund by interloquiter and ward of court that George Bowar hes doun wrang in the myssaying of Wlm Crysty, and is ordained that the said George sall pass to the mercat cross and ask the said Wlm forgyfanis for amendis; and gif he duis siklyk in tym to cum to the said Wlm or ony uder honest man, he sal be banist the town.

20 June 1565, (Statut of myddynis).—It is statut and ordanit be the bailyeis and comunite that thair be na mwk, turves, clay, nor stanis laid upon the he cawsay within four fut to the rigging-stane upon every syde; and every man to have the cawsay clen ilk fyften dayis anent his heyd rowm, under the payn of viij sh, excep clay or stanis to ane bigand, to be our seyn at the sycht of the bailyeis and counsal.

The bailyeis and nychtbours hes commandit James Ramsay, depositur, to gif Jhon Farar, litstar, ten punds mony of the comon gud to supple and help hym, quhill [till] God releve the said Jhon that he be abill to pay the samin againe.

The xxvij day of July anno 1565, the bailyeis counsal and comunite of this broich, patrons of our lady chaiplanry at the brig-end of Arbrot, now wacand in thair hands, for just and gud causis and yeirly augmentation of the rentell and uphald of the bigging qlk is now rouynws, with ane consent and assent grantit and gef in few and heretaig to Thomas Lyndsay [reader] twa ruids of land with the hous and pertnands, pertenand to the said chaiplanry, lyand within the said broich, upon the est syd of Newmercatgait, efter the tenor of ane charter to be maid thairupon onder the comon seale of the town.

9 September.—The qlk day Andro Benet said in jugment to David Saddlar, Be Goddis wounds, theif smaik, I sall have thee stikkit; upon the qlk wordis the said David Saddlar twk aith, and requirit the bailyeis to gyf him lawbroich of the said Andro and

Robert his broder. [Caution is found, and an assize of fifteen jurymen impannelled.]

The qlk day it is fund be the assiss abwn wrltyn and deliverit be Thomas Gardyn, chansler, that David Saddlar hes down wrang in the trublyng and hurtyng of Andro Benet and Robert Benet his broder, and trublyng of the town; and for the trublan of the town the said David sall pass to the mercat cross and ask the bailyeis and nyetbours forgyffnes, and gyf he dwis sik lik in tym ta cum he sal be banist the town for yeir and day; and anent the hurt and skaith down be the said David to the said Andro and Robert Benets, the pronunciation thairof is continuyt to this day fyfteen dayis with consent of the bailyeis that the hurt of tham may be the better cognossit be the assis.

7 January 1565-6.—The bailyeis, with awis of court, hes gyffyn the baxters ane act that the twa penny laif be vij once, guid and sufficiant stuff; and the brosters sell na derer aill nor thre pennies the pynt, onder the payn of dalyng the braid and aill to the puyr, and viij sh to the bailyeis wha that beis convict for brekyn the samin.

18 January.—The qlk day in actioun and caus mwfit be Marion Ogilvy of Melgund aganis David Lyell and David Ferror, allegit sourteis and cawtioners for the sowm of four skoir merks mony for David Bell anent the by rown malis of the lands of Spittelfeld, comperit the said David Bell with David Lyell and David Ferror his alleggit cautioners, and denyit that he auch or suld pay the saids sowm of four skoir merks, quhill just compt and rekning be maid betwix him and the saids honorabyll lady, &c.

1 February.—Comperit Alex. Gardyne of Brax, and desyret the bailye that he mycht have ane officer creat in his court to execut the office of stuardry within his lands of Brax, and presentit Alex. Hantown to be creat: at quhais request the bailye gef the aith in jugment to the said Alex. Hantown, qa maid the aith of fydelytie

that he svld leillelie and trewlye execut the office of stuardry within the said lands, but faid or favor, hatrent or luf of ony manner of parson; and the bailye deliverit ane wand in jugment to the said Alex. Hantown to the effect forsaid.

25 February.—The qlk day be the awiss and consent of the bailyeis and haill counsel, George Garden and Jhone Cargill are chosyng punders to keep the comon gyrss and corn and sall have for ilk aker of banis, peis, quhit, ry, or aits within the comon fald, burrow rudis ——— and Disland, iiij d. with thair pwnlands and tedder panies us and wont, and viij sh to the bayleis of thair gudes that breks order.

8 March.—The haill counsall hes consentit that Mr Thomas Mekyson collect and tak up the anuellis and malis pertenand to Sant Nycholas chaiplanry that restis ontayn up be James Ramsay, depositer of twa yeirs bypast, and forder indurand the will of the bailyeis and counsall. The said Mr Thomas makyn thankfull pament of three pundis usuall mony yeirly to the depositer of the town: And lykwis Thomas Lyndsay is chosing and electit to garder and tak up our lady anuellis and malis that ar ontayn up be the said James Ramsay, and forder indurand the will of bayleis and counsall; and sall have four punds yeirly down of the rentall, and mak his compt to the town of the rest.

1 April 1566.—It is statut and ordaint be the bailyeis and nyctboris that na manner of comoun meill sellars hald within thair house mair maill nor ane firlot, and will not sell to the nyctbours, the kepars of the said meill sal pay viij sh the first tyme, and the secund tym to tyne thair fredom; and gyf he be comandit be the bailyeis or officers to sell his meill and disobey, thay sall be banist the town for yeir and day.

4 May.—It is thought expedient be the bailyeis and haill counsell that every on fremans boit that ridis in the havyn sall pay ancorag, iiij d ilk tyme.

31 May.—It is statut and ordanit be the bailyeis and nychtbors that gyf ony bestis be fund within comon upon the nycht, fra the evening sky gayn tue tyll the day sky ryis, that ilk best sall pay ij sh to the takar of the best, and viij sh to the baylcis for thar contention.

26 July.—The qlk day the bailyeis and counsall hes comandit Thomas Lyndsay to gyf Jhone Paramor xl sh of our Lady anuellis becaus he is ane puyr man ; and als hes ordanit to gyf David Blak xl sh of the saids anuellis to pass to Edynbro to seek relief of the queins thrids of the said chaiplanry.

26 August.—Anent the ordour tayn for eschewyng the pest, it is statut and ordanit that na maner of parson within this broich resauve ane stranger or out man within thair hous day nor nycht without lecens askit and optenit of the bailyeis, onder the payn of tynsall of his fredom and comon landis ; and the brekeris heirof to be haldyn as suspect ; and the quarter maisters to pass nychtly and wesy thairefter gyf ony beis strykyn with infirmitie or rasaue strangers, and schaw the samin to the bailyeis. Follows the names of the quarter maisters : David Lyell, Jon Ledall, Jhon Lyell, Jhon Akman, Ja. Pekyman, Wm. Bardy, Jhon Hales, James Ramsay, Copyn Guthre, Patro Ramsay, Jhon Lyne, Wm. Ochterlony, Nyniane Yowng, David Ferror, Henry Craik.

20 Sept.—It is fund be the bailyeis and court that Alex. Akman rasauit his gudbroder within his hous, quha cam fourth of Montross contrar the actis of this broich, and is amerciat thairfor ; and gif he dwis siklik in tym to cum he sall tyne his fredom, and be banist this towne for yeir and day.

The qlk day Jhon Akman, in presens of the bailyeis and court, oblish hym onder the payn of his lyf, lands, and guidis, that thair sall cum na danger nor skaith to this town throw his rasaiuing of George Brown or his wyf ; and gyf he dwis siklik in tym to cum he sall tyne his fredom and his comon landis.

23 Sept.—It is fund be the bailyeis and court that Jhon Hynd hes brokyn the statut of the town maid anent the pest, passyng to Breichin mercat without leif of the bailyeis, and thairfor his fredom is dischargit, and hys comon lands wacand, conform to the act maid thairupon: and siklik Archibald Mathau for gyffyng meit and drynk to his [sic] without leif of the bailyeis.

4 Oct.—It is statut be the bailyeis and counsall that thair be na derrar aill sauld nor iij d the pynt, and that the twa penny laif be ten once fra this day fourth, onder the payn of daling of the aill and braid, and viij sh to the bailyeis.

11 Oct.—It is statut be the nychtboris that bailyeis sall haue xl sh of ilk parson that breks the actis anent the statute of the pest, and the rest to pass to the comon weill.

21 Oct.—Alex. Gardyn of Brax is ordanit to be wardit within the tolbwith qll he aske the bailyeis forgiffanis for missaying tham; and David Ferror is sourtie to enter the said Alex. on Fryday nyxt to cum to fulfill the samin, and to pay his onlawis.

13 Dec.—The bailyeis and counsall hes decernit and ordanit that all the anuellis quhilk pertenyit to the Derigeis be tayn vp and disponit be the awiss of the bailyeis and counsall, conform to the ordour of Dunde and Sanctandross; and na manner of man that suld pay the saids derige anuellis hald ony part thairof in his awin hands.

5 Feb. 1566-7.—Anent the complaynt maid be Nyniane Clement mynister, apon James Baxter for the wrangus uptaking of the rudis of his yard in the Abay called Denichin yard,—the bailyeis ordained the officers to pass with the said Nyniane and mak opyne the yettis and durris of the said yard to hym, and red and woid the samin to the said Nyniane.

28 Feb.—The qlk day the officers ar chosyn punders, and sall have of ilk akar of peis, banes, quhit, and ry, oatis, iiij d, and thairpunlay use and wont.

7 April 1567.—Wlm Storok apellit frà the jugment of the elderis and decanis anent the wordis of injurie gyffyn to hym be Jhon Lyne and Bessie Hunter his spous: the said Jhon Lyne offeret hym rady to fulfill thair decreit in all punctis.

18 April.—It is decernit be the bailyeis, minister, elderis, and decanis that gyf Jhon Ramsay, webster, missay Jonat Lam his moder with wordis of injurie, he sall tyne his fredome and comon lands the first tym, and the secund tym to be banist the town.

16 March.—It is statut be the bailyeis and nyctboris that thair be na twitherdis fra this furth, conforme to the actis maid thairupon, onder the payn of viij sh onforgyffyn.

12 Jan. 1567-8.—It is statut and ordanit be Jhon Hales bailyie and the counsell that na out man be maid fre nor burges of this broich for sewyn yeirs to cum, and for divers causes concernyng the comon weill.

May 1568.—The xxvij day of Maij the counsall decernit that Agnes Fergusson, witch, suld be put in the pit, and have bott v d ilk day.

4 June.—The haill nyctboris hes consentit and grantit that Nyniane Clement, mynister, have the thirdis of our Lady chaiplanry and Sant Nycholas chaiplanry, gif thair be no releif gottyn thairfor within forty days.

11 Oct. 1568.—The bailies hes grantit that George Gardener sall have vj d of ilk fyer hous for rynging the bell to the prayeris, and making service in the kirk.

4 March 1568-9.—The qlk day for divers causes concerning the comon weill and releif of the taxation fra the rayd of Breichin, it is concludit and decernit be the bayleis and counsall that the haill comon gress be devydit and partit, and set to every man puir and rich that plesses to tak part of it.

7 Oct. 1569.—Patre Ramsay, Nyniane Hales, George Halis, and Slewyn Mckysoun hes tayn the comon myll and motor for four skoir four punds for ane yeir, and hes

resauit the said myll with all gangand gair, and sall deliver her siklyk at the yeir's end.

2 June 1570.—The qlk day, in presens of my lord comendator of Arbrot, anentis the election of ane elimosiner for dew admynistration and distribution of the anuellis and yeirlic apportionment of ald to the puyr, convenit the maist part of the indwellarrs of the said elimosinarie, qlk ar dettit in pament of the said yeirly duetye and acceppit Thomas Lyndsay, redar, ane of the Convent of Arbrot, appointit thairto be my lord for elimosinor in tymes cuming, durying my lord's plesur, togedder with Jhone Akman, Decane, to be coadjutor and helper for inbringing thairof; the said elemosinar's entres thairto sal be at whitsonday last by past in the yeir of God ane thowsand fyf hundreith seventy yeirs, to vptak, rais, intromit and vplift the said ycirly rents and discharge the samin, and yeirly to gyf thairwpon as sall be neidfull.

2 Oct.—Thir persons ar chosen taxtars to stent the town for furnishing aucht men to ryd with my lord to the Regent. [Eight names follow.]

27 June 1572.—Thir persons are chosyng to ride with my lord to the raid of Breichin,—John Akman, James Pekyman, Wm. Bardy, Andro Dunlop, James Ramsay, Nyniane Halis; and all the rest of the honest men of the town oblist tham to ryid thair tym about when requirit, or ony of the said personis war chargit thairto in tym to cum.

9 Oct. 1573.—The qlk day it is concludit be the counsal anent the order of the kyrk that quhatsumevir be decernit be the mynister, elders, and deconis for observing of gud ordour sal be put to execution be the bailyeis and counsal with diligens.

27 Oct.—The qlk day the bailyeis and haill nyctboris concludit that thair be ane maister of grammer schuill providit, and to mak hym yeirly viij sh of ilk barn within the town, and twenty punds to be maid to hym of our Lady benefeice or derygeis anuellis, with his

chalmer maill fre; and Dauid Mychell is rasauit thairto for this yeir; quha hes promist to enter thairto at new yeir day nyxt to cum.

3 Nov.—It is fund be the bailyeis and court that Jhon Watson hes down wrang in the trubling of Jhon Lam, and gyf it beis fundyn that the said Jhon Watson molest or trubill the said Jhon Lam or ony uders within this broich in tym to cum he sal be put in the irins indurand the bailyeis willis.

The qlk day the bailyeis sittand in jugment comperit Jhon Lam and maid the aith that he dreds bodily harm of Jhon Watson, and that he farit that the said Watson suld fyir and burn his dwellyng hous apon the nycht in his fury; and protestit gyf he sustenit ony skaith be hym that he micht opten the samin apon the jugis because he culd get na law brouch of the said Jhon Watson.

19 March 1573-4.—The bailyeis comandit Besse Thomsone not to molest nor truble Elspet [illegible] vnder the payn of x sh; and gif the said Elspet missayis the said Besse sche shall be banist the toun.

8 Oct. 1574.—The qlk day James Sthathart hes tayn the firlott, custum ladyll, and ancarage for xvij li, iiij d; and David Person sourtay for payment.

That the fischeris put thair fische to the schoir, then to the mercat, for the space of thre houris, vnder the pain of aucht sh.

Item, that all personis heifand erd of thair housses vpon the comon calsay cary away the sam within aucht dayis vnder the pain of aucht sh.

Item, that na man lay muk or middens vpon the calsay ony langer nor aucht dayis vnder the pain of aucht sh.

15 Nov.—The qlk day it is fund be the bailyeis and court that Willm Guthre, for imprecation, that is to say, for wissing to heif hymself thre deyis in hel, or to heif the pest in Arbrot,—for the qlk he is decernit to be

bundin to the cross qll the preching be done, and incontinent thairefter to be caryit to the see, and thair to be dippit thris, and pay aucht schillings; and gif he dois siclik to be banist ffor evir.

The volume of records from which the following entries have been selected is in the library at Panmure House. It extends generally over the period from 1605 to 1647; and bears the following title:—"M. A. P. *Aspiret ceptis Jesus*, 1605. *Composita burgi de Aberbrothok, per me mag'rum Alexandri Peirsone clericus ejusdem, scripta teste meis signe et subscriptione manualibus* A. Piersone N.P." Then follows a list of small feu-duties payable from properties in the original burgh, with "the rental of the akars of the comon lands of Aberbrothok," specifying their situation, the names of their possessors, and the quantity held by each; and bearing that they had been let in "feu ferme" at the rates of 10 shillings, 8s. 4d., and 6s. 8d. Scots for "ilk akar." "Sum of the hail burow is iij^{xx} xv lib. vj sh viij d." [£75, 6s. 8d. Scots.]

The second portion of the volume is a series of accounts kept by the burgh treasurers, from 1606 to 1614; and exhibits the sources of revenue and the items of expenditure during that period. A few of these are here given in addition to those which were quoted in reference to the old harbour. (1605-6.)—To Andro Chrystie for nailles and mending of the auld kirk dor v sh. [This *old* church was very probably the Lady Chapel.] Item—To Alex. Rynd for pudder qlk was usit at the kingis deliverie [*i.e.*, from the gunpowder plot.] Item, for mending of the brig port xl sh. (1606-7.)—To Andro Chrystie for upputting of the sluices at the myll in tyme of pest xviij d. (1607-8.)—Delyverit to the menstrallis at St Thomas day xxx sh. For vij deillis to mend the ports in time of pest vi lb. [This was a general pestilence mentioned by Sir James Balfour and other annalists.] To Wm. Ramsay for

mending the yett at the north port iiij sh. (1608-9.)—
Delyverit to the conventione of burrowis v lib xvi d.
For candell to the kirk 1 sh. (1609-10.)—Summa of the
haill charge of the said thesauror of his intromission
above written of the comone guid of the said burgh
during the space forsaid [year to Michaelmas 1610]
is the soume of iiij c iij ˣˣj lib xvij sh [£461, 17s. Scots.]
For buistis of comfettis when the bischop and Erle of
Crawfurd was here, xviii sh. (1610-11—Charge.)—David
Chrystie convict in xl sh unlaw for not puting his maill
to the mercat, refusing to sell the samyne to the nyctboris,
and forstalling the said mercat. Wm. Schabart convict
in 3 lib unlaw for drawing his knyff and striking Jone
Young thairwith, and in x lib unlaw for the effusion
of his bluid. David Chrystie convict in xxxii sh unlaw
for striking David Gray elder. Annane Spynk youngar
convict in xvi sh unlaw for abusing his father in braking
his bucket and stoup at the wall. Summa of the haill
charge, iiii c xxxvii lib xvij sh iiij d [£437, 17s. 4d. Scots.]
Discharge: For the communion bread xviii sh. To
William Allane to gang to Aberdeine xl sh. For candill
to the kirk lv sh iiij d. For ane desk to the schuill
iij lib. For mending of the wey house dore vi sh. For
mending the water mett ii sh. For mending the colmettis
vi sh vi d. Summa of the haill discharge is v c iiij lib
xii sh iiij d [£504, 12s. 4d. Scots.] (1211-12—Charge.)—
Andro Dall for his fredome and burges bankit xiiij lib.
The grass of Boullishill bank, Seyait, Madiegramis croce,
and Newgait gevine to James Carnegie for iiij merks.
The grass of Paromers dykis betwix the mylne and
chappell vi sh viij d. *Vnlauis.*—Item, Alex. Spynk
convict in xxxii sh for abusing and minassing Thomas
Rennie at the bar; and the said Thomas in xvi sh for
upbraiding him also. Jhone Haillis, mariner, convict in
Ten lib unlaw for the effusione of the blood of ane poore
man. Thomas Lyell, James, Alex., Thomas Synpsone,
ilk ane of theme convict in v lib unlaw for drawing

U

thair swerdis, and in x lib unlaw for the effusing thairwith of the blood of Thomas Gray and Margaret Gardyne; and in xvi sh for trubling the toune. Andro Chrystie convict in v lib unlaw for abusing William Myles his wyff in thair awin hous under silence of nycht, drawing ane durk to have strukin theme thairwith. Summa of the haill charge iiij c v lib. ii sh vi d. Discharge: To the post that brocht the billis for keeping of the conventione of burrowis haldin in this burgh xiij sh iiij d. For wyne and sugar to my Lord of Burlie xlvi sh. To David Lyel at comand of the bailyie to the provest of Abird[een] for wyne and sugar vi lib. To David Lyel at command of the bailyie for the provest of Kynneillis denner and uthers with him, quhen he first repairit the knok lii sh. To the comoun post to carie the billis for keeping of the said generall conventione of burrowis halden heir xx lib. To Alex. Rynd for towis to the bell l sh. To him for towis to the pace of the knok xij sh. To the officiar that sumond the bailie to the checker vi sh viij d. To Kathren Haillis at comand of the auld bailyie iij lib x sh. To her at comand of the bailyie for wyne to my Lord Marques xxxij sh. To Alex. Peter for twa buistis of scortchettis and confettis xxvi sh viij d. To David Lyel for wyne that the commissioners of burrowis drank quhen they sat heir vj lib. To Alex. Crostie for aill to the said conventione iiij lib. And to Jhone Rennie, baxter, for ane peck floure of bread, and baiking thairof to the said conventione xiiij sh. To Thomas Cuming for ane pund of butter to the bread v sh. To the collector of Edr. for oure pairt of the taxatione grantit be the burrowis to the comissioners ryding to court xx lib. To James Low for fyve grait aik trees to mend Mylnegait brig vi lib xiii sh iiij d. To hym for carieing theme to the brig iij sh. To Alex. Rynd for iiij aik treis to cover the brig xl sh. To the provest of Kynneill for mending of the knok xxiiij lib. For wyne to him xxxviii sh. To the officiar that sumount the bailyie to the Parliament xi sh viij d. To Alex. Rynd for ij dellis and j tree to the tolbuith xxx sh. For j c plenshon naillis to naill the dellis with xvi sh. For mending of ij loftis of the wey-hous and poynd-hous vi sh viij d. For ane bar to the kirk dor and ij bar naillis iiij d. For xx unce of pouder to wapon schawing xxiij sh iiij d. For my fee x lib. To Kath. Haillis for iij pynts wyne the 5 of August [commemoration of the Gowrie conspiracy.] For a pynt of wyne and a buist of comfittis to Sir Johne Carnegie xxii sh iiij d. To Johne Ogiluie for ane band to hing the suasche [drum] to xv sh. To the menstrellers for thair fee xiij lib vi sh viij d. Summa iiij c xvij lib ix sh vi d.

(1612-3) Discharge for tua faldome towis to the bell iiij sh. For x lib and vij vnces gad iron to be ane tong to the bell, and warkmanschipe thairupon xlviij sh vi d For clenging of the bodie of the harbour x sh. To Mr Henric Philp, minister xxx lib. For doune casting of the dyik at the kirk dor to mak passage to my Lord Marques viij sh. The 5 of August, for wyne iiij lib xviij sh. The 5 of Novr., for wyne xxiiij sh. To the menstrellaris xxxviij sh.

The third portion of this volume bears the title : " Heir beginneth the secund court buik of the actis of the burgh of Aberbrothok wryttine be me Mr Alexr. Peirsone, comoun clerk thairof." It extends from 3rd September 1617 to 22nd April 1647 ; and contains entries of the elections of magistrates, councillors, and other officials, admissions of burgesses, services of heirs, extracts of law writs, leases of grass and town's dues, and convictions and fines for assaults and other breaches of law. The following are a few abbreviated samples of these :—

6 October 1617.—Per Thomas Peirsone of Lochlandis, and Mr John Granger, bailies. The quhilk day, the saidis baillies demitting their offices, be laying doune the wand of iustice, removeing furth of iudgement, Mr Patrik

Carnegy is electit and chosin baillie for my Lord Marques of Hamilton, Lord of Arbroith, be vertew of my Lord Carnegyes letter iudiciallie producit haiffing comissione to that effect of my Lord Marques : David Ramsay is electit baillie for this burgh for this yeir incomming be pluralitie of voittis of the nyctbouris theirof ; wha sittand doune in iudgement gaiff thair aythis *de fideli admistra°ne* to exercise iustice and iudgement without fead or favour: And theirvpone requirit actis.

Counsall—Geroge Piersone, Mr Jhone Granger, Thomas Piersone, Jhone Aikmane, elder, Mr George Aikmane, Alexr. Rynd, Alexr. Peter, Robert Lyne, Andro Eliot, James Wood, Jhone Ochterlony, Robert Ochterlony.

Lynneris—George Piersone, Jhone Aikmane, elder, Alexr. Rynd, Robert Lyne, Andro Eliot, Jhone Ochterlony.

Dyikpryssris—Andro Haillis, Thomas Mudie, Charles Dalgatie, Jhone Bardie.

Flesche and Skin Pryssris—Alexr. Rynd, Alexr. Peter, Thomas Mudie, David Tueddell.

Meill-mercat Oversieris—David Wood, Jhone Renny, elder, David Sethe, Thomas Wood.

Fische-mercat Oversieris—Alexr. Rynd, Alexr. Peter, Charles Dalgetie, Jhone Bardie.

Constabulis—David Wood, Jhone Allane Skinner.

Officearis—Williame Mudie, W'am. Mekisoune, Adame Grant.

Qlk haill persones forsaids gaiff their aythes faythfullie and trewlie to exerce the saids offices durang the yeir incuming: Whervpon they requirit actis.

9 November 1619.—Alexr. Lord of Spynnie is maid and creat burges and freeman of the said burgh.

4 June 1620.—Alexr. Straquhan in South Tarrie, is maid and creat burges and freeman.

31 October 1620.—Mr Alexr. Hay, clerk to the Privie Seill, and Peter Hay, his substitut, are maid and creat burgeses and freemen.

31 March 1621.—Mr James Futhie, sone lawfull to umquhil Hendrie Futhie of Bysack, is maid and creat burges and freeman.

9 April.—Mr John Lyndsay, Admiral Deput, and my Lord Lyon to his Majestie [with others], are made burgesses.

11 September 1624.—Sir John Carnegy of Athy, Knicht, [with others] are made burgesses.

5 May 1625.—The salmon fishing within the haill bounds of the liberties of this burgh, togidder with all other fishing within the haill bounds of the said burgh liberties of the watter of Brothok, given to Andro Wood for thretteine yeires, for yeirlie payment of fourty schillings.

26 February 1630.—Mr Simeon Durie, minister of this burgh, maid burgess.

24 June 1631.—Alexr. Lord of Spynny [and others] created burgesses.

3 March 1633.—The baillies and counsel, for the sklaitts and other stones of the chappell and for the timber thereof, disponed be Johne Ochterlony, youngar, to the towns vse, set in tak to the said Johne, the gras of the Lady Lon for the space of seven yeirs from April 1637.

13 April 1636.—Walter Bischop of Brechin [his servants and others] created burgesses.

3 October.—The saids ballies having demitted their saids offices of baillierie be laying down the wand of justice, they remoueing themselffs out of the iudgement seat, Mr John Granger and William Peirsone ar elected and chosen Baillies of this burgh for this yeir incuming, Be the auld and new Counsel, and be the persons nominat and chosin of the crafts to have voit in the said election.

23 Nov. 1637.—The customes and anchorage set to Alexr. Meikesone for ane hundred and thretteine merks.

19 Sept. 1639.—Mr David Durie, sone lawfull to Mr Simeon Durie, minister, and Mr George Granger, scoolemaister, maid burgesses.

28 August 1643.—Patrick Maule of Panmure, and his eldest sone George, maid burgesses.

2 May 1649.—The gras efter specified is set [as follows]:—The gras betwix the Mylnegate Port and the Pethfit to James Anderson for 20 sh. The gras of Hurklesden and the gate betwix the meikill dub and the head of Henrie Fullartoune's land on the est syd therof, to Johne Meikeson for Lochlands, for 14 lib. 3s. 4d.

THE END.

LIST OF SUBSCRIBERS.

LIST OF SUBSCRIBERS.

Viscount Arbuthnott, 2 copies.
A. Airth, Primrosehill, Laurencekirk.
G. Allan, Barngreen, Arbroath.
Rev. William Allan, ,,
Alex. A. Anderson, writer, Forfar.
James Anderson, writer, Arbroath.
James Anderson, writer, Duke Street, Edinburgh.
John A. Anderson, writer, Arbroath.
John C. Anderson, writer, Duke St., Edinburgh.
Miss Margaret Anderson, High Street, Arbroath.
Robert W. Anderson, writer, Forfar.
W. Anderson, Royal Hotel, Arbroath.
John Andson, Tow Law, Darlington.
W. Andson, Springfield Terrace, Arb.
William Arrott, M.D., ,,
David Arrott, M.D., ,,

Alex. Balfour, manufacturer, ,,
James Barclay, writer, Forfar.
T. Barclay, Sheriff-Clerk, Cupar-Fife.
William Barry, druggist, Arbroath.
Rev. D. A. Beattie, Towie, Aberdeenshire.
Rev. James Beattie, Cupar-Fife.
R. Beattie, Panmure Street, Arbroath.
George A. Bell, teacher, Kinnell.
A. Binny, banker, Arbroath, 2 copies.
Charles Black, banker, Carnoustie.
David D. Black, town-clerk, Brechin.
Rev. William Blair, M.A., Dunblane.
S. Bowden, Colliston Mill, Arbroath.
J. Boyle, Grange of Conon, ,,
John Borrie, merchant, Carnoustie.
Alex. Brown, East Abbey St, Arbroath, 2 copies.
Alex. Brown, Town-Clerk's office, ,,

Andrew Brown, High St., Arbroath.
T. Buncle, Arbroath, 2 copies.

Patrick Cables, shipbroker, Arbroath.
Alex. Campbell, manufacturer, Dundee, 2 copies.
James Campbell, merchant, Liverpool, 2 copies.
William Cargill, Leysmill.
W. F. L. Carnegie of Spynie and Boysack, 2 copies.
C. Chalmers of Monkshill, Aberdeenshire.
John I. Chalmers of Aldbar, 4 copies.
David Chapel, writer, Arbroath.
George R. Chaplin of Colliston.
John Chisholm, merchant, Arbroath.
Rev. Andrew Clark, ,,
David Clarke, writer, Forfar.
Wm. Clark, manufacturer, Arbroath, 2 copies.
Jas. Cloudsley, White Hart Hotel, ,,
Rev. Alexander Comrie, Carnoustie.
G. Cooper, Superintendent of Police, Forfar.
C. W. Corsar, flaxspinner, Arbroath.
Wm. H. Corsar, flaxspinner, ,,
Rev. David Crichton, ,,
David Crighton, writer, Forfar.
George P. Cromar, wine-merchant, Arbroath.

David Dewar, George Inn, Arbroath.
Jas. A. Dickson, Provost of Arbroath, 6 copies.
William Dove, blacksmith, Arbroath.
Charles Dowell, bleacher, Kellyfield.
W. Ducat, baker, Arbroath, 2 copies.
Rev. William Duke, St Vigeans.

LIST OF SUBSCRIBERS.

C. Duncan, cabinetmaker, Arbroath.
David Duncan, manufacturer, ,,

Lowson Fettes, High Street, Arbroath.
David Fleming, merchant, ,,
Thomas Forbes, merchant, ,,
Robert Forbes, Hatton Mill, Kinnell, 2 copies.
Gilbert Fraser, teacher, Arbroath.
Douglas Fraser, manufacturer, ,,
Patrick A. Fraser of Hospitalfield, 10 copies.

A. Gardyne, 3 Elm Villas, Hackney, London.
D. Gardyne, baker, Arbroath, 2 copies.
Peter Gardyne, ,,
S. Gellatly, bookseller, ,,
W. Gibson of Maulesbank, ,,
Rev. John Gillies, ,,
Alex. Gordon, Springfield Terrace, Arbroath, 4 copies.
James Gordon, builder, Arbroath.
John Gordon, West Keptie Street, Arbroath.
John Govan, W.S., Edinburgh.
Grant & Cuthbertson, W.S., ,,
James Grant, writer, Forfar.
Geo. Grant, manufacturer, Arbroath, 2 copies.

Duke of Hamilton & Brandon, 2 copies.
Peter Haggart, Crieff, Kirriemuir.
John Hay of Letham, 2 copies.
Rev. Joseph Hay, A.M., Arbroath.
Robert Henderson, Tarrybank, ,,
Michael Hinchy, Supt. County Police, Forfar.
Rev. Alexander Hislop, Arbroath.
James F. Hood, Bookseller, ,,

Cosmo Innes, advocate, Edinburgh, 2 copies.
R. Ireland, High Street, Arbroath.
R. Irvine, teacher, ,,

Miss Jack, High Street, Arbroath.
Andrew Jervise, Inspector of Registrars, Brechin, 2 copies.
Dick Johnston, shipowner, Arbroath, 2 copies.

William Johnston of Annesley.

James Keay, writer, Arbroath.
Ben. M. Kennedy, ,,
Andrew Key, M.D., ,,
John Kidd, shipowner, ,,

A. R. Laing, Glasterlaw Works.
Wm. Lawrence, druggist, Arbroath.
James W. Legge, A.M. Grammar School, Aberdeen.
William Leitch, West George Street, Glasgow.
Rev. Alex. Leslie, M.A., Arbroath.
Peter Leslie, Millgate, ,, 2 copies.
Thomas Leslie, shipowner, ,,
John Lindsay of Almeriecloss.
George Livingston, writer, Arbroath.
A. S. Logan, Sheriff of Forfarshire, 2 copies.
Mrs Logan, Glover Street, Arbroath.
Walter Low, Tottenham, Middlesex.
Aw. Lowson of Elm Bank, Arbroath.
William Lowson, writer, Forfar.
D. M. Luckie, Arbroath.
John Lumgair, jr., manufacturer, Arbroath, 2 copies.
R. Lumgair, manufacturer, Arbroath.
Andrew Lyall, ,,
George S. Lyon, tanner, ,,

J. M. M'Bain, accountant, Arbroath.
J. Macdonald, Town Clerk, ,, 4 copies.
Patrick Macdonald, painter, ,,
William Macdonald, writer, Elgin.
Alex. M'Millan, currier, Arbroath.
Robert M'Omie, grocer, ,,
Jas. M'Taggart, bookseller, ,,
William Marwick, writer, ,,
Rev. Wm. Masterton, Inverkeillor, 2 copies.
Patrick Meffan, banker, Forfar.
Rev. Chas. Merson, M.A., Colombo, Ceylon.
Rev. Peter Merson, Elgin.
William Mill, founder, Arbroath.
James S. Miller, Surveyor, Montrose.
Alex. Milne, F. C. College, Glasgow.
John Mitchell, Forth Street, Alloa.
T. R. Moncrieff, printer, Arbroath.

LIST OF SUBSCRIBERS.

"Monkbarns," Edinburgh.
Rev. John Montgomery, M.A., Inverleithen, 2 copies.
James Morgan, S.S.C., Edinburgh.
Jas. Mudie, manufacturer, Montrose, 2 copies.
John Mudie of Pitmuies, 4 copies.
J. Muir, banker, Arbroath, 5 copies.
Rev. John Muir, St Vigeans, 4 copies.

Earl of Northesk, 10 copies.
James Neish, The Laws, Dundee.
A. Nicol, manufacturer, Arbroath.

Sir John Ogilvy of Inverquharity, Bart., M.P.
D. B. Ogg, Catherine Bank, Arbroath.
W. A. Ogg, King Street, Cheapside, London, 3 copies.
J. Ogilvy, Lawton Mill, Inverkeillor.
W. G. Oliver, saddler, Friockheim.

Lord Panmure, K.T., 4 copies.
J. S. Paterson, East Seaton, Arbroath.
John Paton, F.S.A., Scot., Meadow Place, Edinburgh, 2 copies.
Jos. N. Paton, Dunfermline.
David Peacock, merchant, Arbroath, 2 copies.
Robert Peat, writer, Forres.
Rev. Andw. Peebles, M.A., Colliston, 2 copies.
James W. Peters, South John Street, Liverpool.
Alexander Petrie, grocer, Arbroath.
William Petrie, manufacturer, ,,
Richard W. Phillip, writer, ,,
J. A. Pierson of The Guynd, 4 copies.
David Pithie, merchant, Arbroath.

James Rait of Anniston, 4 copies.
Lieut. Lewis Rees, Auchmithie.
John Rees, ,,
Jas. Renny, jr., Picardy Place, Edinburgh.
William Renny, Crescent, Camden Town, London, 2 copies.
A. Ritchie, writer, Arbroath, 2 copies.
P. Ritchie, manufacturer, Arbroath.
G. Robertson, confectioner, ,,
Jas. Roberts, High Street, ,,

John F. Rodger, writer, Edinburgh, 2 copies.
William Rollo, banker, Arbroath.
James Rorie, merchant, ,,
Adam Roy, painter, ,,
William Roy, mason, ,,
Alex. Ruxton, Bonhard, Arbirlot.

Mrs Ann Salmond, Cairnie, Arbroath.
D. Salmond, farmer, Arbikie, Lunan.
David Salmond, surgeon, Arbroath.
Joseph Salmond, shipowner, ,,
Wm. Salmond, manufacturer, ,,
Wm. Salmond, jun., draper, ,,
Rev. John Sandison, ,,
Captain Samuel Scoltock, Long Ditton, Kingston-on-Thames.
Alex. Scott, Hatton Mill, Kinnell.
Thomas Scott of Viewfield, Arbroath, 4 copies.
William Scott, merchant, ,, 2 copies.
Dr Sharpey, Woburn Place, London, 2 copies.
William Shiress, writer, Brechin.
W. Sivewright, merchant, Arbroath.
William Sim of Lunanbank, 2 copies.
Alexander Simpson, Carnoustie.
John W. Simpson, manufacturer, Arbroath.
Alexander Smith, teacher, Arbroath.
David Smith, sen., writer, ,,
David Smith, writer, ,,
Jas. Smith, merchant, Seaforth, ,,
James Smith, shipowner, ,,
J. Smith, manufacturer, Carnoustie.
William Smith, writer, Arbroath.
Rev. Alexander Sorley, ,,
D. R. Soutar of Lawhead, 2 copies.
Thomas Soutar, farmer, Leys.
William Stiven, accountant, Dundee.
Walter Stuart, Pall Mall E., London.
John Suttie, merchant, Arbroath.

Thos. R. Tailyour of Newmanswalls, Montrose.
James Taylor, Sheriff-Clerk Depute, Forfar.
Patrick H. Thoms, banker, Dundee.
J. Thomson, ironmonger, Arbroath, 2 copies.
Rev. R. Thomson, Mollinburn, Moffat.

LIST OF SUBSCRIBERS.

Rev. Alex Thomson, Constantinople.
Thos. Thomson, teacher, Chapelton.
Robert Thornton, writer, Forfar.
Geo. S. Todd, M.D., Friockheim.
John Traill, F.R.C.S., Arbroath.

Rev. Geo. Walker, Kinnell, 2 copies.
John Walker, Town-Clerk's office, Arbroath.
J. Walker, manufacturer, Arbroath.
Robert Walker, teacher, ,,
James Wallace, wright, ,,
Geo. Webster, Sheriff-Clerk, Forfar.
Geo. Webster, M.D., F.R.G.S., Dulwich, London, 2 copies.
William C. Webster, accountant, Arbroath.

James Weir, merchant, Arbroath.
Miss Margaret Weir, St Mary Street, Arbroath.
Robert Whyte, writer, Forfar.
Alexander Will, mechanic, Arbroath.
Mrs Williams of Abbeybank, ,,
Charles Wilson, merchant, ,,
Patrick Wilson, Arbroath, 2 copies.
James Winton, merchant, Arbroath.
James D. Winton, writer, ,,
James Wright, Rosely, ,,
Wm. Wright, East Abbey St., ,,
Wm. Wrongham, merchant, Dundee.

Thomas Yarrow, engineer, Arbroath, 4 copies.
James Young, writer, Forfar.

www.ingramcontent.com/pod-product-compliance
Lightning Source LLC
Chambersburg PA
CBHW030746250426
43672CB00028B/1098